MENTORING RELIGIOUS EDUCATION TEACHERS IN THE SECONDARY SCHOOL

This book helps mentors working with beginning teachers of religious education to develop their own mentoring skills and provides the essential guidance their mentee needs as they navigate the roller coaster of their first years in the classroom. Offering tried-and-tested strategies, it covers the knowledge, skills and understanding every mentor needs. Practical tools offered include approaches for developing subject knowledge and lesson planning, as well as guidance for the effective use of pre- and post-lesson discussion, observations and target setting to support beginning religious education teachers.

Together with analytical tools for self-evaluation, this book is a vital source of support and inspiration for all those involved in developing the next generation of outstanding religious education teachers. Key topics covered include the following:

- Models of mentoring
- Your knowledge, skills and understanding as a mentor
- Developing mentees' religious literacy through classroom practice
- Supporting the planning of effective and creative RE lessons
- Developing mentees' knowledge and skills in the RE curriculum
- Supporting the delivery and evaluation of lessons
- Observations and pre- and post-lesson discussions and regular mentoring meetings
- Helping new religious education teachers develop their professional practice.

Filled with the key tools needed for the mentor's individual development, this book offers an accessible guide to mentoring religious education teachers with ready-to-use strategies that support, inspire and elevate both mentors and beginning teachers alike.

Helen Sheehan is Course Leader for the Post-Graduate Certificate in Education (PGCE) in Religious Education, and responsible for all humanities PGCE provision (RE, History, Geography, Citizenship & PSHE and Social Sciences) at Sheffield Hallam University, UK.

MENTORING TRAINEE AND EARLY CAREER TEACHERS

Series edited by: Susan Capel, Trevor Wright, Julia Lawrence and Sarah Younie

The **Mentoring Trainee and Early Career Teachers** Series are subject-specific, practical books designed to reinforce and develop mentors' understanding of the different aspects of their role, as well as exploring issues that mentees encounter in the course of learning to teach. The books have two main foci: first, challenging mentors to reflect critically on theory, research and evidence, on their own knowledge, their approaches to mentoring and how they work with beginning teachers in order to move their practice forward; and second, supporting mentors to effectively facilitate the development of beginning teachers. Although the basic structure of all the subject books is similar, each book is different to reflect the needs of mentors in relation to the unique nature of each subject or age phase. Elements of appropriate theory introduce each topic or issue, with emphasis placed on the practical application of material. The chapter authors in each book have been engaged with mentoring over a long period of time and share research, evidence and their experience.

We hope that this series of books supports you in developing into an effective, reflective mentor as you support the development of the next generation of teachers.

For more information about this series, please visit: https://www.routledge.com/Mentoring-Trainee-and-Early-Career-Teachers/book-series/MTNQT

Titles in the series

Mentoring Teachers in the Primary School: A Practical Guide
Edited by Kristy Howells and Julia Lawrence, with Judith Roden

Mentoring Geography Teachers in the Secondary School: A Practical Guide
Edited by Grace Healy, Lauren Hammond, Steve Puttick and Nicola Walshe

Mentoring Teachers in Scotland: A Practical Guide
Edited by Sandra Eady, Jane Essex, Margaret McColl and Kay Livingston

Mentoring Religious Education Teachers in the Secondary School: A Practical Guide
Edited by Helen Sheehan

MENTORING RELIGIOUS EDUCATION TEACHERS IN THE SECONDARY SCHOOL

A Practical Guide

Edited by Helen Sheehan

Routledge
Taylor & Francis Group

LONDON AND NEW YORK

Designed cover image: © Caia Image / Getty Images

First published 2023
by Routledge
4 Park Square, Milton Park, Abingdon, Oxon OX14 4RN

and by Routledge
605 Third Avenue, New York, NY 10158

Routledge is an imprint of the Taylor & Francis Group, an informa business

British Library Cataloguing-in-Publication Data
A catalogue record for this book is available from the British Library

ISBN: 978-1-032-04243-5 (hbk)
ISBN: 978-1-032-04244-2 (pbk)
ISBN: 978-1-003-19108-7 (ebk)

DOI: 10.4324/9781003191087

Typeset in Interstate
by SPi Technologies India Pvt Ltd (Straive)

MIX
Paper | Supporting
responsible forestry
FSC
www.fsc.org   FSC™ C013985

Printed in the United Kingdom
by Henry Ling Limited

CONTENTS

FIGURES

TABLES

TASKS

CONTRIBUTORS

Helen Bromley taught religious education (RE) in secondary schools in Hertfordshire and London, where she was head of RE before joining the team at York St John to work on the PGCE RE. She then joined Leeds Trinity University where she leads the RE provision for secondary ITT. She continues to teach RE and sociology in a secondary school alongside her role at the university.

Dr Kate Christopher teaches secondary religious education (RE) in East London and is an RE adviser. Her work focuses on the curriculum and teachers' professional development. She works with teachers in developing the curriculum, designing teaching resources and supporting their understanding and confidence.

Rebecca Davidge gained her BA (Hons) in religious studies and sociology at Cardiff University, which she followed with postgraduate teacher education at Birmingham University, she later gained her MA in education (Religion and Values) from the University of Worcester. She has more than 20 years of teaching experience across a range of secondary schools in the West Midlands. Rebecca joined the University of Worcester as PGCE secondary subject lead for religious education, where she also teaches undergraduate courses in the Department for Education and Inclusion, specialising in religion, values, interfaith and education contexts.

Sally Elton-Chalcraft is Professor of Social Justice in Education and Director of the Learning Education and Development research centre, University of Cumbria. She co-convenes the Religions, Values and Education special interest group for the British Education Research Association and publishes in the areas of religious education, anti-racism, special educational needs, school leadership and education in India. She is the editor of two teacher education textbooks, *Teaching RE Creatively* and *Professional Studies in the Primary School*.

Gill Golder is Professor of Teacher Education at the University of St Mark and St John, Plymouth. She works supporting multi-academy trusts carrying out impact evaluation projects and the University Teaching Excellence Framework and Knowledge Exchange Framework submissions. For details, please visit https://www.marjon.ac.uk/about-marjon/staff-list-and-profiles/golder-gillian.html.

Lara Harris is a former PGCE student at Chester University and trained as a teacher of religious education (RE) in 2016. She started her career at Upton Hall Girls Grammar school on the Wirral and, in September 2022, became the head of RE at Neston High School.

She has worked as a subject mentor for Liverpool Hope University and Chester University for the past two years. She holds an MA in Christian theology and a BA (hons) in theology and religion from the University of Durham.

Dr James Holt is Associate Professor of Religious Education at the University of Chester. He leads on the RE provision in all aspects of teacher education. Prior to his role at Chester, he was a secondary school teacher for 13 years.

Dr Rachael Jackson-Royal is Head of Religious Education (RE) and a local NATRE group leader. She undertook her BA in religious studies at Kings College, University of London, and a master's in religious studies at SOAS, University of London, and in 2012, she completed a doctorate. She has been part of the Religious Education Council qualifications committee, liaises with exam boards (serving on teacher's consultation groups) and Ofqual over the GCSE and A level in RE, has written textbooks, and writes a research update for each issue of *Professional Reflection of RE Today* magazine. She is particularly interested in helping teachers to engage more with research and looking at how theories of learning could be embedded in RE lessons.

Alison Keyworth was previously the Director of the Institute of Education and led the Masters in Coaching and Mentoring at the University of St Mark and St John, Plymouth. She now runs her own coaching business and acts as a guest lecturer sharing her expertise in coaching and mentoring across the South West.

Dr Abigail Maguire is Head of Undergraduate Studies at Moorlands College, Dorset. She has worked in education in a variety of contexts, initially as a secondary school religious education (RE) teacher and then moving into higher education. Abigail's PhD research explores the experiences of teachers tackling controversial issues in secondary RE the classroom. Follow her on Twitter @AbiMaguire5.

Dr Sjay Patterson-Craven is currently Associate Head of Department for Secondary and Further Education at Edge Hill University with specific responsibility for initial teacher education (ITE). She has worked in higher education for the past six years; prior to this, she taught for 11 years in secondary education. Her EdD explored the teacher agency of beginner religious education teachers' post-ITE.

Mark Plater has spent a lifetime in religious education (RE), teaching at all levels, from elementary to higher education, and in a range of contexts: faith, secular, British and overseas, state and private contexts. He has been training secondary school RE teachers for nearly two decades. His research work is also within the field of RE, with a special interest in teaching about mysterious phenomena.

Summan Rasib graduated from the University of Huddersfield where she obtained a bachelor's degree in religion and education. She later went on to complete the PGCE programme at the Leeds Trinity University. With seven years of teaching experience, she is now Associate Assistant Headteacher & Head of Department of a Church of England School located in West Yorkshire.

Lucy Rushforth is a religious education teacher, mentor and Head of Year at St Thomas More RC High School. Lucy holds a BA from Leeds Trinity University and a PGCE from the University of Chester.

Jane Savill is a tutor at University College London, Institute of Education. Her background is in secondary education with a focus on religious education. Her main interests are supporting teachers as leaders of learning in creating an accessible curriculum. Jane has worked on a number of teacher education projects alongside practicing teachers and teacher-educators in different countries around the world, including Dubai, Ghana, India, Jordan and Myanmar. Follow her on Twitter @jsavill9.

Clare Shaw was a senior lecturer in primary initial teacher education leading on mentor development at the University of St Mark and St John, Plymouth. She now acts as a University tutor supporting mentors and trainees in school placements.

Dr Helen Sheehan taught religious education (RE) in secondary schools in Nottinghamshire and Lincolnshire before joining the secondary education team at Sheffield Hallam University, where she leads the RE provision on all initial teacher education (ITE) routes (undergraduate and postgraduate) across both primary and secondary. She is also the vice-chair of Sheffield SACRE. Her doctoral research focused on the importance of subject specialist provision within secondary postgraduate ITE.

Paul Smalley is Programme Lead for Edge Hill University's three-year Secondary Undergraduate QTS programme. Prior to this he was a middle leader in three high schools in three different counties. He is the executive assistant of NASACRE (The National Association of Standing Advisory Councils on RE), a trustee of the IFN (The Inter Faith Network for the UK) and an REC (Religious Education Council of England and Wales) board member, as well as sitting on the Liverpool Diocesan Board of Education and the Board of a Multi-Academy Trust. His research has been in the fields of RE policy and practice, collective worship and spirituality, and he has also published work on teacher development. Follow him on Twitter @PabloPedantic.

Alexis Stones, BA, PGCE, MA, is subject lead and tutor for the PGCE in Religious Education at University College London (UCL), Institute of Education. She has worked for many years as an RE teacher and has research interests in knowledge and subject specialisms and the relationships between religion and science in the RE classroom. She co-leads the Peace Education Subject Interest Group at UCL and is lectures in initial teacher education at the National Gallery, London. Follow her on Twitter @alexisstones.

Dr Lisa Vickerage-Goddard began her career as a secondary school religious education (RE) teacher in South Yorkshire before becoming Senior Lecturer in RE (Secondary ITE) at Newman University, Birmingham. She completed a doctorate in education at the University of Sheffield, where she looked at policy enactment of the Prevent Duty Strategy and the implementation of Fundamental British Values in UK Secondary Schools. Lisa has vast experience across different sectors of the RE world, including schools, school governance, SACRE, Diocesan Synod and Academia, and aims to use this knowledge to raise the profile and quality of RE.

Dr Kathryn Wright is Chief Executive of Culham St Gabriel's Trust and on the board of the Religious Education Council of England and Wales. She has been a secondary teacher of religious education (RE) and an independent consultant working with universities, local authorities, diocese and multi-academy trusts over the last 20 years. She completed her doctorate in 2018, 'A Pedagogy of Embrace' researching the teaching of RE in Church of England Schools. Follow her on twitter @kathrynfenlodge.

AN INTRODUCTION TO THE SERIES

Mentoring trainee and early career teachers

Mentoring is a very important and exciting role. What could be better than supporting the development of the next generation of subject teachers? A mentor is almost certainly an effective teacher, but this doesn't automatically guarantee that he or she will be a good mentor, despite similarities in the two roles. This series of practical workbooks books covers mentoring teachers in most subjects in the secondary curriculum, in primary schools and in Scotland. The books are designed specifically to reinforce mentors' understanding of different aspects of their role, for mentors to learn about and reflect on their role, to provide support for mentors in aspects of their development and enable them to analyse their success in supporting the development of beginning teachers (defined as trainee, newly qualified and early career teachers).

This book has two main foci: first, the focus is on challenging mentors to reflect critically on theory/research/evidence, their own knowledge and practice, how they work with beginning teachers, how they work with more experienced teachers and their approaches to mentoring in order to move their practice forward. Second, the focus is on supporting mentors to effectively facilitate the development of beginning teachers. Thus, some of the practical activities in the books are designed to encourage reflection, whilst others ask mentors to undertake activities with beginning teachers.

The book can be used alongside generic and subject books designed for student and newly qualified teachers. These books include *Learning to Teach in the Secondary School: A Companion to School Experience*, 9th edition (Capel, Leask and Younie, with Hidson and Lawrence 2022) which deals with aspects of teaching and learning applicable to all subjects. The generic book is complemented by two series: Learning to Teach [subject] in the Secondary School: A Companion to School Experience; and A Practical Guide to Teaching [subject] in the Secondary School. These books are designed for student teachers on different types of initial teacher education programmes (and indeed a beginning teacher you are working with may have used/currently be using them). These books are proving useful to tutors and mentors in their work with student teachers, both in relation to the knowledge, skills and understanding the student teacher is developing and some tasks which mentors might find it useful to support a beginning teacher to do.

It is also supported by a book designed for newly qualified teachers, *Surviving and Thriving in the Secondary School: The NQT's Essential Companion* (Capel, Lawrence, Leask and Younie, 2019). This book covers material not generally needed by student teachers on an initial teacher education course, but which is needed by newly qualified and early career teachers in their school work.

The information in this mentoring book should link with the information in the generic texts and relevant books in the two series in a number of ways. For example, mentors might want to refer a beginning teacher to read about specific knowledge, understanding and skills they are focusing on developing, or to undertake tasks in the book, either alone or with their support, then discuss the tasks. It is recommended that you have copies of these books available so that you can cross-reference when needed.

In turn, the books complement a range of resources on which mentors can draw (including other mentors of beginning teachers in the same or other subjects or age phase, other teachers and a range of other resources including books, research articles and websites).

The positive feedback on *Learning to Teach* and the related books above, particularly the way they have supported the learning of student teachers in their development into effective, reflective teachers, encouraged us to retain the main features of that book in this series. Like teaching, mentoring should be research and evidence-informed. Thus, this series of books introduce theoretical, research and professional evidence-based advice and guidance to support mentors as they develop their mentoring to support beginning teachers' development. The main focus is the practical application of material. Elements of appropriate theory introduce each topic or issue, and recent research into mentoring and/or teaching and learning is integral to the presentation. Tasks are provided to help mentors identify key features of the topic or issue and reflect on and/or apply them to their own practice of mentoring beginning teachers. Although the basic structure of all the books is similar, each book is different to reflect the needs of mentors in relation to the unique nature of each subject.

The chapter authors in the books have been engaged with mentoring over a long period of time and are aiming to share research/evidence and their experience. We, as series editors, are pleased to extend the work in initial teacher education to the work of mentors of beginning teachers. We hope that this series of books supports you in developing further into an effective, reflective mentor as you support the development of the next generation of teachers.

Susan Capel, Julia Lawrence, and Sarah Younie
October 2022

ACKNOWLEDGEMENTS

First, I would like to acknowledge the contribution of Jo McShane to this project. She helped to bring the book together in its early stages; without her there would be no book!

I would also like to thank all the chapter authors for sharing your expertise. It has been a privilege to work with you all. Thanks also to Georgia Prescott (University of Cumbria) for her input on the early drafts of chapter eleven.

Particular thanks to Susan Capel, our series editor. I could not have coped without her willingness to share her knowledge and expertise with me as a first-time book editor. Her generous approach to working with me has been much appreciated.

Finally, I would like to extend a personal thank-you to my husband, David, and children, Grace and Joel, for their patience and support as I took on another huge project.

GLOSSARY

Advanced Level (A level)   An academic qualification in England, Wales and Northern Ireland in a specific subject that can lead to university, further training, or work. Pupils usually sit examinations at the end of Year 13.

Locally Agreed Syllabus (AS)   Each local authority in England must write its own syllabus for religious education which outlines the scope and sequence of teaching. Some schools, such as voluntary aided schools, academies and independent schools, are free to write their own syllabus.

Assessment for Learning (AfL)   Assessment in a school context where outcomes are used to modify teaching with the intention of promoting pupils' learning.

Continuing Professional Development (CPD)   The term used to describe ongoing learning activities engaged in by teachers to further develop their professional knowledge and skills.

Core Content Framework for Initial Teacher Training (CCF)   The statutory framework that defines the minimum entitlement of all trainee teachers in England in relation to the content of initial teacher training programmes.

Department for Education (DfE)   The government department responsible for children's services and education.

Early Career Framework (ECF)   A framework that builds on the Core Content Framework to provide a research-based programme of training and support for teachers in the first two years of their career.

General Certificate of Secondary Education (GCSE)   An academic qualification in England, Wales and Northern Ireland in a specific subject. Pupils usually sit examinations at the end of Year 11.

Higher Education (HE)   Tertiary education leading to the award of an academic degree.

Higher Education Institution (HEI)   A tertiary education provider.

Host Teacher   The teacher of a class being taught by a trainee teacher. This is usually a subject specialist, but not the colleague designated as the trainee's mentor.

Initial Teacher Education (ITE)   A term used to describe courses that lead to qualified teacher status. Some prefer it to the term initial teacher training, or ITT, as it places emphasis on education rather than competency focused training.

Initial Teacher Training (ITT)   A course that leads to the award of qualified teacher status. This is the term preferred in policy documentation (as an alternative to ITE).

Multi-Academy Trust (MAT) A group of state funded academies that work together under a shared funding agreement.

National Association of Teachers of Religious Education (NATRE) NATRE is the subject teacher association for religious education professionals across the UK.

Office for Standards in Education, Children's Services and Skills (Ofsted) The government body with responsibility for inspecting services providing education and skills for learning of all ages, and for inspecting and regulating services that care for children and young people.

Pedagogical Content Knowledge (PCK) A concept introduced by Shulman to describe knowledge developed by teachers about how to teach content in appropriate ways to enhance student understanding.

Postgraduate Certificate in Education (PGCE) A one-year postgraduate course that combines academic study with training in schools leading to an academic qualification and qualified teacher status.

Qualified Teacher Status (QTS) The qualification required to work as a teacher in state schools in England and Wales (although academies are permitted to recruit teachers without QTS).

Religious Education (RE) A compulsory subject in the English curriculum that seeks to develop pupils' understanding of religion and worldviews.

Religious Studies (RS) This the title of General Certificate of Secondary Education and A level qualifications; the title Religious Studies indicates that it is an academic study rather than part of broad-based, compulsory religious *education*.

Scheme of work This is an overview that outlines the work to be done in the classroom over a specific period (e.g., a term or an academic year). It indicates the content that must be covered, key terminology and may outline suggested activities or resources. It may be referred to by different terms in other contexts (e.g. unit of work or programme of study).

Standing Advisory Council on Religious Education (SACRE) An independent body, formed by the local authority, to advise them on religious education for schools within that authority. They are responsible for monitoring provision in religious education (RE) and collective worship, and for reviewing the agreed syllabus for RE every five years.

INTRODUCTION

The importance of mentoring

In recent years, there has been much focus on the importance of mentoring for beginning teachers. In relation to initial teacher education, in England Ofsted has highlighted that "mentoring is critical for developing trainees' knowledge, understanding and practical application" (2020, p. 20) and research done for the Department for Education (2018) concluded that quality, subject-specific mentoring could be key to reducing the attrition rate among teachers in the early years of their career. Therefore, it is important that beginning teachers are mentored by subject specialists who have good knowledge of subject-specific pedagogy (Carter, 2015). The role you have taken on, that of a mentor to beginning RE teachers, is crucial for supporting a teacher through their initial teacher education, first and early years of their career and ensures that they become effective and reflective teachers of RE.

The purpose of this book

As a mentor you will find that, over time, you work with beginning teachers with different needs and at different stages in their professional development. Whatever the circumstances, you are in a position to have a significant impact on how beginning teachers perceive themselves as teachers of RE at the start of their careers. This book is designed to give you practical support in your mentoring role. It seeks to develop your knowledge and understanding of approaches to mentoring and explore what the effective mentoring of beginning RE teachers might look like. It also aims to support you as you apply these ideas in your own setting.

The authors who have contributed to this book bring with them a broad range of expertise in relation to RE and mentoring. All have been secondary RE teachers at some point in their career and are currently teachers, mentors and tutors in initial teacher education or have a role that focuses on the development of practice in the teaching of RE. They have drawn not only on their experience but also on a range of wider research and evidence. It is intended that, through the further resources and references included at the end of each chapter, you will be able to pursue some of the ideas explored in the book in greater detail.

The book explores the nature of mentoring in the context of RE specific challenges and debates. As RE departments are often small, some readers may have picked up this book because, although they are not themselves an RE specialist, they are mentoring a beginning

RE teacher as there is no one else who can take on the role. It is therefore intended that, for them, this book will help develop an understanding of some of the issues that can emerge when teaching RE so that they can effectively support a beginning teacher. However, it is anticipated that the majority of readers will be RE specialists; it is intended that the book helps them think about how to conceptualise their knowledge and expertise so that this can be shared with a beginning teacher. This seems particularly important as the book was being written at an interesting time in the development of RE in England. The publication of the Commission on RE report in 2018 and the Ofsted *Research review series: religious education* in 2021 have stimulated debates about the RE curriculum that are shaping teachers' thinking and impacting classroom practice. In particular, the discussion surrounding whether RE should become known as religion and worldviews (R&W) is engaging many teachers, and debates about the nature of knowledge, in particular how RE might draw on disciplinary knowledge, is impacting curriculum choices. It is important that beginning teachers understand the impact of these developments on their classroom practice and will need knowledgeable mentors to help them with this. These debates have also impacted this book; some authors have referred to the subject as R&W due to the content of their chapter, whilst others talk about RE (as it is still referred to in legislation and guidance). It is, of course, the case that, although the subject is called RE in Northern Ireland, it is referred to in different ways in the other home countries. Although sometimes called RE in Scotland, depending on the context it may also be referred to as *Religious and Moral Education* or *Religious, Moral and Philosophical Studies*, and in Wales, since 2021, the subject has been called *Religion, Values and Ethics*. Nevertheless, it is hoped that the points made, and principles outlined, can be transferred to any of these situations (and perhaps some international contexts too).

The structure of the book

The book is organised into three sections: the big picture, the complex picture and the practical picture.

The first section, the big picture, focuses on you as a mentor. It explores models of mentoring and how the mentoring relationship might change and develop over time. It also introduces RE-specific considerations as you seek to develop your thinking about what subject-specific mentoring might look like in practice and how your own positionality, worldview, and experience of teaching RE might impact on you as a mentor. Whatever your level of prior experience, you are invited to consider how you might develop your skills further and reflect on what you will gain from your mentoring experience.

The second section, the complex picture, explores the complexity involved in mentoring beginning RE teachers in the current climate. This section explores some of the key questions and debates to support you in developing your own thinking so that you can articulate this clearly for beginning teachers. It also supports you in considering the implications of recent developments in RE for beginning teachers. Although these chapters focus on some big questions, the tasks included throughout suggest ways in which you might work within this complexity with your beginning teacher.

The final section, the practical picture, focuses on important elements of your day-to-day work with your beginning teacher. It explores some teaching and mentoring activities – planning, teaching lessons, conducting lesson observations and engaging in post-observation discussion – to consider how to make the most of the opportunities presented in a RE-specific context. This section also addresses some specific challenges; teaching GCSE and A level, teaching controversial issues, engagement with the wider subject community and continuing professional development. In each case, it explores how you can effectively support beginning teachers as they develop their skills as specialist teachers of RE.

I hope that you find each section of the book helpful and supportive as you seek develop your knowledge and skills in relation to mentoring a new generation of RE teachers.

References

Carter, A. (2015). *Carter review of initial teacher training*. https://www.gov.uk/government/publications/carter-review-of-initial-teacher-training

Department for Education. (2018). *Factors affecting teacher retention: Qualitative investigation. Research report*. Available at: https://assets.publishing.service.gov.uk/government/uploads/system/uploads/attachment_data/file/686947/Factors_affecting_teacher_retention_-_qualitative_investigation.pdf

Ofsted. (2020). *Building great teachers? Initial teacher education curriculum research: Phase 2*. https://www.gov.uk/government/publications/initial-teacher-education-curriculum-research/building-great-teachers

SECTION 1
The big picture
Mentoring beginning religious education teachers

1 Models of Mentoring

Gill Golder, Alison Keyworth and Clare Shaw

Introduction

Your job as a mentor is to develop a positive working relationship with a beginning teacher to enable them to grow and develop both professionally and personally. How you go about this will be influenced by a number of factors, such as your own experience of being mentored in the past and your common-sense opinions of the role. These are important starting points, but you are likely to grow as an effective mentor when you also base your approaches on evidence. This chapter (and this book) is designed to support you in considering the evidence to underpin your practice.

The chapter starts by looking at different definitions of mentoring. It then looks at the importance of the context in which you are working as a mentor, highlighting a number of documents from England and other countries, which impact your mentoring practice. The chapter then considers three mentoring models which a mentor could adopt to inform their practice. These models underpin various roles you undertake and hence the other chapters in this book.

At the end of this chapter, you should be able to:

- Have a greater understanding of what is meant by the term *mentoring* for a beginning teacher.
- Have an appreciation of the key context in which you work that may influence the manner in which you act as a mentor in school.
- Have an awareness of the plethora of mentoring models that exist.
- Compare and contrast three developmental mentoring models and how these could be used to support your role as a mentor.

DOI: 10.4324/9781003191087-2

Before reading further, undertake task 1.1.

Task 1.1 Mentor reflection: Reflecting on your understanding of mentoring

Reflect on what you understand by mentoring by considering the following questions:
How would you define mentoring?
How does your definition inform your practice as a mentor?
How do the various policy and guidance documents relevant to your context influence your mentoring practice?
Do you base your mentoring practice on personal experience or on a model (s) of mentoring? If a model, which one (s)? Why?

Definitions of Mentoring

Mentoring is widely used in many contexts for the purpose of helping people to learn and develop, both professionally and personally. There are numerous and frequently contradictory definitions of mentoring, with accompanying models of how mentoring is best approached (Haggard, Dougherty, Turban and Wilbanks 2011). Whilst different models might utilise different terminology and vary in emphasis regarding the role of a mentor, what remains consistent is the view that mentoring is a supportive, learning relationship. The mentor, with their more extensive experience, is there to support the learner's development. The quality of the relationship between mentor and mentee is extremely important.

The terms *mentoring* and *coaching* are at times used interchangeably. Both aim to develop the professional or professional competencies of the client or colleague. Although mentoring and coaching have much in common, an important difference between the two is the focus of developmental activities. In mentoring, the focus is on development at significant career transitions whereas in coaching, the focus is on the development of a specific aspect of a professional learner's practice (CUREE 2005).

Montgomery (2017) suggested that definitions of mentoring often involve the concept that advice and guidance to a novice, or person with limited experience, is given by an experienced person. In this way, mentoring can be seen to be hierarchical, a top-down approach largely based on a one-way flow of information. Mentoring describes

> a relationship in which a more experienced colleague shares their greater knowledge to support the development of an inexperienced member of staff. It calls on the skills of questioning, listening, clarifying and reframing that are also associated with coaching.
>
> (Chartered Institute of Personnel and Development [CIPD] 2021, p. 2)

In contrast, other definitions of *mentoring* follow a less hierarchal structure. These include peer mentoring (Driscoll, Parkes, Tilley-Lubbs, Brill and Pitts Bannister 2009) and group mentoring (Kroll 2016). In these approaches to mentoring, the flow of information is more bidirectional. Montgomery (2017) suggested that they are more personalised as mentoring is adapted to an individual mentee's goals and needs more effectively. Higgins and Thomas (2001) suggested that top-down mentoring had greater impact on short-term career outcomes and individually driven mentoring supported long-term career development more effectively. Whether the focus is on short- or long-term tailored development of a mentee, there are common aspects to all forms of mentoring. These include providing a supportive environment in which to help mentees achieve goals and improve their skills, whilst also offering space to discuss personal issues.

In education, school-based mentors play a vital role in the development of student teachers and the induction of newly qualified teachers. They also support other staff at points of career development. As with mentoring in other contexts, there is a focus on learning, development and the provision of appropriate support and encouragement. The definition of a mentor outlined in the *National Standards for School-based Initial Teacher Training (ITT) Mentors* in England (Department for Education [DfE] 2016b, p. 11) is someone who 'is a suitably experienced teacher who has formal responsibility to work collaboratively within the ITT partnership to help ensure the trainee receives the highest quality training'. However, in initial teacher education in many countries, including England, assessment of the beginning teacher is integral to the mentor's role. This is supported by Pollard (2014), who suggested that the role of the mentor in initial teacher training (ITT) has developed because of three aspects, the complexity of the capabilities teachers need to meet, the focus on high professional standards in school and the transfer of knowledge from one generation to another. Before reading any further, undertake task 1.2.

Task 1.2 Mentor reflection: Understanding the term *mentoring*

1. Research the terms *mentoring* and *coaching*.
2. List a variety of terms that you associate with coaching and mentoring
3. Make a list of common and unique characteristics for both.

The Context in which You Are Working which Underpins your Mentoring Practice

Mentoring is increasingly important in a range of fields, both in the UK and internationally, as a tool to support recruitment into a profession, retention in that profession, professional learning, networking and career development. In teaching, it is widely recognised that there is a strong relationship between professional learning, teaching knowledge and practices, educational leadership and pupil results (Cordingly et al. 2015). As such, there has been an increase in the development of policy and guidance documents, as well as frameworks, toolkits and factsheets, produced over the past few years to support educators and others in fulfilling their roles as mentors.

As a mentor, it is important to recognise and embed current policy and statutory guidance into your mentoring practice. There are a number of key documents that underpin the mentoring process in initial teacher education and beyond in England and elsewhere. These constitute the key external drivers in shaping mentoring practice in school. Being aware of these is important, but knowing how to use them to support your work with a beginning teacher can add purpose and validity to what you do (there are examples of how to do this in other chapters in this book). They also enable you to recognise the value of being a mentor in school, as 'effective professional development for teachers is a core part of securing effective teaching' (DfE 2016c, p. 3).

Table 1.1 not only highlights policy and guidance documents that influence the work you do in school with a beginning teacher in England but also signposts you to examples of international equivalence documents to enable you to make comparisons internationally.

Now complete Task 1.3.

Task 1.3 The context in which you carry out your mentoring duties

Reflect on the context in which you carry out your mentoring duties. Ensure you are familiar with the relevant documents mentioned earlier (or, if you are working outside England, documents specific to your context). What aspects of these documents do you identify as being of most use to your work and why?

Effective Mentoring Models

As alluded to earlier, there are a number of mentoring models which a mentor could adopt in order to support the growth and development of a beginning teacher. Attempts have been made to categorise different approaches to mentoring; for example Maynard and Furlong (1995) suggested that there are three categories of mentoring, the apprentice model, the competence model and the reflective model. The apprenticeship model argues that the skills of being a teacher are best learned by supervised practice, with guidance from imitating experienced practitioners. The competence model suggests that learning to teach requires learning a predefined list of competencies (the current Teachers Standards in England [DfE 2011] could be described as a competency model). In this model, the mentor becomes a systematic trainer supporting a beginning teacher to meet the competencies. In the reflective model, the promotion of reflective practice through mentoring is key. This requires a beginning teacher to have some mastery of the skills of teaching to be able to reflect upon their own practice and for the mentor to be a co-enquirer and facilitator rather than instructor. Task 1.4 asks you to look at three different mentoring models.

Table 1.1 Key external drivers influencing mentoring work

	Policy/guidance document	Author and date introduced	Key purpose
Teacher Standards Documents	Teachers' Standards (England)	DfE (2011)	Used to assess all student teachers working towards qualified teacher status (QTS) as well as newly qualified teachers completing their statutory induction period. 'Providers of ITT should assess trainees against the standards in a way that is consistent with what could reasonably be expected of a trainee teacher prior to the award of QTS' (DfE 2011, p. 6).
	The Australian Professional Standards for teachers (Australia)	Australian Institute for Teaching and School Leadership (AITSL) (2011)	The Standards are designed so that teachers know what they should be aiming to achieve at every stage of their career; to enable them to improve their practice inside and outside of the classroom. 'The Standards do this by providing a framework which makes clear the knowledge, practice and professional engagement required across teachers' careers' (AITSL 2011, p. 2)
Core Content requirements for Initial Teacher Education	ITT Core Content Framework	DfE (2019a)	This was introduced in 2019 to replace an earlier framework (DfE 2016a). Based on educational research, it defines a minimum entitlement for all trainee teachers, outlining both what they should have the opportunity to learn ('learn that') and have the opportunity to do ('learn how to'). It supports development in 5 core areas – behaviour management, pedagogy, curriculum, assessment and professional behaviours.
	Differentiated Primary and Lower Secondary Teacher Education Programmes for Years 1-7 and Years 5-10 (Norway)	Ministry of Education and Research (2010)	These regulations apply to universities and university colleges that provide primary and lower secondary teacher education. They aim to ensure that teacher education institutions provide integrated, professionally oriented and research-based primary and lower secondary teacher education programmes of high academic quality.
National or Regional Standards for Educators acting as mentors	National Standards for school-based initial teacher training (ITT) mentors (England)	DfE (2016b)	The standards were developed to bring greater coherence and consistency to school-based mentoring arrangements for student teachers. They set out the minimum level of practice expected of mentors. They are used to foster consistency in the practice of mentors, raise the profile of mentoring and build a culture of mentoring in schools
	The New York State Mentoring standards Albany (USA)	The State Education Department/ The University of The State Of New York (2011)	A set of standards that guide the design and implementation of teacher mentoring programmes in New York State through teacher induction.

(continued)

Table 1.1 Cont.

	Policy/guidance document	Author and date introduced	Key purpose
National or Regional guidelines for general coaching and mentoring practice	National framework for mentoring and coaching (England)	Centre for the Use of Resource and Evidence in Education (CUREE) (2005)	The framework was developed in order to help schools implement mentoring and coaching to assist with continuing professional development and other activities. It sets out ten principles based on evidence from research and consultation which are recommended to inform mentoring and coaching programmes in schools. The framework provides a tool for reflection on existing practice and further development and assists a mentor in self-regulation and monitoring of their own practice.
	NTC Continuum of Mentoring Practice (USA)	New Teacher Centre (NTC) (2011)	Designed to assist programme leaders as they seek to implement mentoring to support induction programmes that are capable of accelerating the development of beginning teacher effectiveness, improving teacher retention, strengthening teacher leadership and increasing pupil learning. "It presents a holistic view of mentoring, based on six professional standards. … The continuum of mentoring practice describes three levels of development, labelled Exploring/Emerging, Applying, Integrating/Innovating' (NTC 2011, p. 2).
Professional Development expectations for teachers	Early Career Framework (England)	DfE (2019b)	This is intended that this "builds on and complements" (DfE 2019b, p. 5) the core content framework (CCF) for ITT. Based on research, it outlines what early career teachers (those in their first two years of teaching) should be entitled to learn about and have opportunities to do during this induction period. Like the CCF it is structured around five core areas and is not used as an assessment framework.
	Standards for teachers' professional development (England)	DfE (2016c)	This is intended for 'all those working in and with, schools in order to raise expectations for professional development, to focus on achieving the best improvement in pupil outcomes and also to develop teachers as respected members of the profession' (DfE 2016c, p. 4). There is an emphasis on using the standards to support regular reflection on existing practice and discussion between all members of the teaching community. There are five parts to the standard which, when acted upon together, ensure effective professional development.
	Ohio Standards for Professional Development (US)	Ohio Department for Education (2015)	These define the essential elements of a strong professional learning system which is one way that school systems can support all educators and encourage improved teaching and learning.

Task 1.4 Three different mentoring models

- What are the features of practice for each of these models: apprentice, competence and reflective?
- Which features of these models do you use/want to use in our mentoring?
- When do/would you use each model of mentoring?

Maynard and Furlong (1995, p. 18) acknowledged that these three models exist but suggested that they should be taken together, in order to contribute to 'a view of mentoring that responds to the changing needs of trainees'. It is this recognition that mentoring practices and approaches evolve as a beginning teacher develops and the need for an examination of different stages of development that lead us to exploring three models of mentoring in more detail. We explore three well-known models (Daloz 2012; Katz 1995; Clutterbuck 2004), all of which focus on the need for the mentor to be flexible in their style and approach to best fit the needs of a beginning at any given stage of their development, in initial teacher education and/or their teaching career.

Daloz's (2012) developmental model identifies two key aspects that need to be present in order for optimal learning to take place: **challenge** and **support**. The challenge aspect refers to your ability as a mentor to question a beginning teacher to enable them to reflect critically on their own beliefs, behaviours and attitudes. The support aspect relies on you being able to offer an empathetic ear, actively listen and encourage a beginning teacher to find solutions in order to continue to develop and progress.

Daloz (2012) argues that a combination of high challenge and high support need to be offered by you as the mentor for a beginning teacher to learn effectively and to **'grow'** (high challenge + high support = **growth**). At the opposite end of this spectrum is what Daloz refers to as **'stasis'**. A beginning teacher's learning in this zone is very limited indeed as a result of their mentor offering low levels of challenge and support (low challenge + low support = **stasis**). Where challenge is high but support is low, a beginning teacher is likely to **'retreat'** from development (high challenge + low support = **retreat**). However, where challenge is low but support is high, a beginning teacher is unlikely to move beyond their present situation despite their potential for growth being on the increase. Daloz refers to this as **'confirmation'** (low challenge + high support = **confirmation**). You therefore need to be aware of both the level of challenge you offer and the level of support needed by the beginning teacher.

The second model is Katz's stages of development model (1995) which describes a model for professional growth in four stages:

1. Survival stage
2. Consolidation stage
3. Renewal stage
4. Maturity stage

During the first stage, '**survival**', a beginning teacher is likely to show signs of being very self-focused and just 'getting by' or coping from day to day. They are likely to experience their practice from a position of doubt and be asking questions like 'Can I get to the end of the week?' or 'Can I really do this day after day?' During this initial stage, a beginning teacher may show a reluctance to take responsibility for things and, instead, look to blame others, for example, the pupils, colleagues, the school. As a mentor, observing a beginning teacher during the survival stage, you are likely to see elements of confusion and a lack of any clear rules and routines in their lessons. The beginning teacher may also demonstrate little, if any, consistency in their approach to managing behaviour. Their teaching style is often very teacher-centric, and they show a reluctance to deviate from their 'script' in any way.

By the second stage 'consolidation' it is likely that a beginning teacher will have begun to implement clearer rules and routines into their classrooms. There is evidence of them starting to question their own practice and being more open to alternative ways of doing things. Whilst observing a beginning teacher at this stage, you are likely to notice that their classes are generally well managed and that the needs of the average pupil are predominantly well catered to. In addition, the beginning teacher is likely to demonstrate a greater awareness of individual pupils and their learning needs. However, they are unlikely to have gained a true grasp of how to support and cater for the needs of pupils within specific sub-groups, for example, special educational needs and disability (SEND), English as an Additional Language (EAL) and high achieving pupils.

The 'renewal' stage is the point at which a beginning teacher becoming much more self-aware and self-critical. They have generally mastered the basics and are now striving for ways in which they can improve their practice. They are looking for strategies and ideas of how to introduce more creative and innovative activities into their lessons. As a rule of thumb, at the 'renewal' stage, beginning teachers are often at their most self-motivated and are eager to contribute to departmental discussions, offer suggestions, design additional resources and/or become involved in the running of lunch time and after-school clubs.

The final stage of Katz's model 'maturity' is where a beginning teacher is demonstrating signs of developing their own beliefs, teaching style and strategies. They are regularly asking themselves a number of questions which support deeper levels of reflection, both in and on practice (Schön 1983). They are still looking to improve their practice and are still interested in new ideas and resources. However, their focus has shifted from an inwards perspective to a much broader one. They are now very much interested in the impact of their teaching on

---

Task 1.5 Responsibilities of the mentor and beginning teacher at each stage of Katz's stages of development model (1995)

In each of Katz's stages, there are responsibilities for both the mentor and the beginning teacher. Identify what you would do to support a beginning teacher at each stage.

---

their pupils' learning and progress. Task 1.5 focuses on the responsibilities of the mentor and beginning teacher at each stage of Katz's stages of development model (1995).

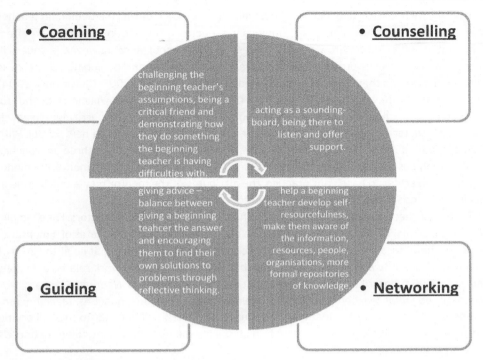

Figure 1.1 Helping to Learn Styles

Adapted from Clutterbuck's model of Developmental Mentoring (2004, p. 9)

And finally, Clutterbuck's (2004) model of developmental mentoring suggests that an effective mentor wants to draw on all four of the 'helping to learn' styles (guiding, coaching, counselling and networking; see Figure 1.1). Figure 1.1 shows that in any given mentoring relationship, a mentor may need to adopt a different style and/or approach to challenge and support a beginning teacher at various stages of their development. In developmental mentoring the beginning teacher sets the agenda based on their own development needs and the mentor provides insight and guidance to support the beginning teacher to achieve the desired goals. A more expert mentor will be able to select the right 'helping to learn' style for a beginning teacher's needs.

Task 1.6 Helping a beginning teacher to learn using Clutterbuck's (2004) model

- Consider which of the four 'helping to learn' styles you feel most comfortable with and why.
- Which do you use the least often and/or feel the least comfortable with and why?
- What could they do to overcome this?

Now complete Task 1.6 which looks at Clutterbuck's model.

Your ability to assess and identify the developmental stage in which a beginning teacher is operating at any given point, is a significant aspect of your role in becoming an effective mentor and ensuring growth takes places. Of equal importance, however, is your skill in adapting your own approach to fit the developmental needs of a beginning teacher. It is worth remembering that none of the three models (Daloz 2012; Katz 1995; Clutterbuck 2004) is linear in structure, and therefore, it is likely that a beginning teacher will move 'to and fro' between stages/zones, for example if teaching different aspects of the curriculum in which they have greater or lesser knowledge and/or confidence or starting at a new school. With each of the models considered earlier, it is possible to see elements of all three approaches to mentoring described by Maynard and Furlong (1995). Regardless of the mentoring model on which you prefer to base your practice, the attributes of the mentor play a crucial role in making decisions about the approach to mentoring.

There have been a number of attempts to characterise attributes of mentors. For example, Child and Merrill (2005) sought to generate an understanding of the attributes of a mentor in initial teacher education. Cho et al. (2011) described personal qualities that lie at the core of the mentor's identity and professional traits that relate to success in work-related activities. The DfE (2016b) described four separate, but related, areas in the *National Standards for School-based Initial Teacher Training (ITT) mentors*, that is personal qualities, teaching, professionalism and self-development and working in partnership. Ragins (2016) described the attributes of a mentor as an antecedent to high-quality mentoring, as something that needs

---

Task 1.7 Attributes of an effective mentor

1. Considering the context and models of mentoring outlined in this chapter, reflect on what you think the attributes of an effective mentor are. Attach a level of significance to each attribute, using three categories of significance: *essential*, *desirable* and *highly desirable*.
2. Having identified the attributes and the levels of significance, place five of the attributes in a prioritised list that best captures the ideal profile of a mentor of a beginning teacher.
3. Reflect on your own practice as a mentor how might to develop the attributes that you have prioritised.

---

to be in place before a mentor–mentee relationship begins. Task 1.7 asks you to consider the attributes of an effective mentor (see also Chapter 2).

Task 1.8 Mentor reflection: Reflecting on your mentoring practice

Having read this chapter, reflect how your understanding of definitions of *mentoring*, relevant policy and guidance documents and models of mentoring have/will impact on your practice.

Finally, Task 1.8 asks you to reflect again on your mentoring practice after having read this chapter.

Summary and Key Points

Effective mentoring is a complex and demanding task, but, as with any role that enables you to have a positive impact on the development of others, it is hugely rewarding. In this chapter, we have considered the importance of

- being aware of different definitions of mentoring.
- understanding the content in which you are carrying out your role and what moral, political or theoretical drivers might influence the education system that you work in and/or your work as a mentor.
- having a broad understanding of different models, or approaches to, mentoring in order to make decisions about how to carry out your role as a mentor.

Further Reading

Maynard, T., and Furlong, J. (1995) Learning to teach and models of mentoring. In T. Kerry, and A. Shelton-Mayes (Eds.), *Issues in Mentoring* Routledge, pp. 10-14.

This chapter should help to deepen your knowledge of the three categories of mentoring, the apprentice model, the competency model and the reflective models.

Cordingley, P., Higgins, S., Greany, T., Buckler, N., Coles-Jordan, D., Crisp, B., Saunders, L., and Coe, R. (2015) *Developing Great Teaching: Lessons from the International Reviews into Effective Professional Development*. Teacher Development Trust.

This should help you to gain an understanding of how mentoring fits into current ideas of effective continued professional development and learning.

References

Australian Institute for Teaching and School Leadership (AITSL). (2011) *The Australian Professional Standards for Teachers*. Education Council.
Centre for the Use of Resource and Evidence in Education (Curee). (2005) *National Framework for Mentoring and Coaching*. Curee.
Child, A., and Merrill, S. (2005) *Developing as a Secondary School Mentor: A Case Study Approach for Trainee Mentors and their Tutors*. Learning Matters.
Cho, C., Ramanan, R, and Feldman, M. (2011) Defining the ideal qualities of mentorship: A qualitative analysis of the characteristics of outstanding mentors, *The American Journal of Medicine*, *124*(5), 453-458.
Clutterbuck, D. (2004). *Everyone Needs a Mentor: Fostering Talent in Your Organisation* (4th ed.). CIPD.
Cordingley, P., Higgins, S., Greany, T., Buckler, N., Coles-Jordan, D., Crisp, B., Saunders, L., and Coe, R. (2015) *Developing Great Teaching: Lessons from the International Reviews into Effective Professional Development*. Teacher Development Trust.
Daloz, L.A. (2012) *Mentor: Guiding the Journey of Adult Learners*. Wiley.

Department for Education. (2011) *The Teachers' Standards*. Crown.

Department for Education (2016a) *Framework of core content for Initial Teacher Training*. Crown.

Department for Education (2016b). *National Standards for School-Based Initial Teacher Training (ITT) Mentors*. Crown.

Department for Education. (2016c) *Standards for Teachers' Professional Development, Implementation Guidance for School Leaders, Teachers, and Organisations that Offer Professional Development for Teacher*. Crown.

Department for Education. (2019a) *ITT Core Content Framework*. Crown. https://assets.publishing.service.gov.uk/government/uploads/system/uploads/attachment_data/file/974307/ITT_core_content_framework_.pdf

Department for Education. (2019b) *Early Career Framework*. Crown. https://assets.publishing.service.gov.uk/government/uploads/system/uploads/attachment_data/file/978358/Early-Career_Framework_April_2021.pdf

Driscoll, L. G., Parkes, K. A., Tilley-Lubbs, G. A., Brill, J. M., and Pitts Bannister, V. R. (2009) Navigating the lonely sea: Peer mentoring and collaboration among aspiring women scholars. *Mentoring and Tutoring: Partnership in Learning*, 17, 5–21.

Haggard, D. L., Dougherty, T. W., Turban, D. B., and Wilbanks, J. E. (2011) Who is a mentor? A review of evolving definitions and implications for research, *Journal of Management*, 37, 280–304. doi:10.1177/0149206310386227

Higgins, M. C., and Thomas, D. A. (2001) Constellations and careers: Toward understanding the effects of multiple developmental relationships, *Journal of Organizational Behavior*, 22, 223–247.

Katz, L.G. (1995) *Talks with Teachers: A Collection*. Ablex Pub. Corp.

Kroll, J. (2016) What is meant by the term group mentoring? *Mentoring and Tutoring: Partnership in Learning*, 24, 44–58.

Maynard, T., and Furlong, J. (1995) Learning to teach and models of mentoring. In Kerry, T., and Shelton Mayes, A. (Eds) *Issues in Mentoring*. Routledge.

Ministry of Education and Research. (2010) *Differentiated Primary and Lower Secondary Teacher Education Programmes for Years 1–7 and Years 5–10*. Ministry of Education and Research.

Montgomery, B.L. (2017) Mapping a mentoring roadmap and developing a supportive network for strategic career advancement. *SAGE Open*, April-June 2017, 1–13. doi:10.1177/2158244017710288

New Teacher Centre. (2011). *NTC Continuum of Mentoring Practice*. New Teacher Centre.

Ohio Department for Education. (2015). *Ohio Standards for Professional Development*. Ohio Department for Education.

Pollard, A. (2014). *Reflective Teaching in Schools* (4th ed.). Bloomsbury Publishing PLC.

Ragins, B. (2016). From the Ordinary to the Extraordinary: High Quality Mentoring Relationships at Work. *Organizational Dynamics*, 45, 228–244.

Schön, D. (1983). *The Reflective practitioner: How Professionals Think in Action*. Temple Smith.

The Chartered Institute of Personnel and Development [CIPD]. (2021) *Coaching and mentoring*. https://www.cipd.co.uk/Export/ToPdf?path=%252fknowledge%252ffundamentals%252fpeople%252fdevelopment%252fcoaching-mentoring-factsheet.

The State Education Department/The University of The State of New York (2011) *The New York State Mentoring Standards*. The State Education Department /The University of the State Of New York.

2 Subject-specific mentoring in religious education

Helen Sheehan

Introduction

There are many advantages to beginning teachers of religious education (RE) being mentored by subject specialists who can ensure that guidance, advice and feedback take into account the unique circumstances and pedagogical challenges of the subject. This is an area in which there is lively debate and discussion about the aims and purpose of the subject, the nature of knowledge and the different pedagogical approaches that might be employed. These issues impact on curriculum design, lesson planning and delivery. Therefore, it is crucial that beginning teachers are supported by a mentor who understands this context and can aid them in their development as subject specialists. Recognising what is distinct and unique within the subject is important for ensuring that professional conversations are focused and productive.

This chapter explores the ways in which you can use your knowledge, skills and experience to support a beginning teacher in their professional development as an RE specialist. It considers how you might support them in developing their substantive content knowledge, how you help them navigate the impact of wider issues on the RE curriculum and how you ensure that they develop their understanding of teaching and learning in a RE-specific context. Often the key to this is reflecting on what you already know and do and working out how you will articulate this to make what is implicit for you, explicit for your beginning teacher. Exploring how you might approach this will help you reflect on how you can develop your skills as an effective mentor of RE teachers.

By the end of this chapter, you should be able to:

- Reflect on the challenges that an RE mentor might face, and consider the issues in your context.
- Articulate the importance of subject-specialist mentoring in RE.
- Recognise the existing knowledge that you have of the context and content of the RE curriculum and articulate this in conversations with beginning teachers.
- Articulate how your wider professional understanding impacts your own practice in the RE classroom and find ways to explore this with your beginning teacher.
- Identify any areas where you would like to develop your own mentoring skills to ensure you are able to be an effective RE mentor.

DOI: 10.4324/9781003191087-3

Different contexts

It is the case that your priorities as an RE mentor may be influenced by your circumstances. This may be to do with you, the beginning teacher, the curriculum in your school or the context of your department. There are several possible scenarios in which a mentor might find themselves; in each situation, the subject-specific aspect of the mentoring is important, but the aspects of this that take priority may change. To help you consider this in more detail, Task 2.1 presents a series of case studies for you to read and reflect on, using the given questions to prompt your thinking.

Task 2.1 Dealing with complex circumstances

Case Study 1

Having graduated with a degree in theology and philosophy, Alison completed a School Direct programme to qualify as an RE teacher. She secured employment in the 11–16 school in which she completed a placement, and she has now worked there for five years. This year she has taken on the role of RE mentor for the initial teacher education (ITE) student assigned to their department which is made up of three specialist RE teachers. She is excited about this opportunity to develop her knowledge and skills. The student teacher that has been placed in her department has a degree in theology and religious studies and appears to have good subject knowledge in relation to world religions. However, they have admitted they lack confidence in teaching religious philosophy, which is covered in several units in Years 9, 10 and 11 on the school's curriculum.

Case Study 2

David is a history specialist who completed his Postgraduate Certificate in Education (PGCE) 9 years ago. He started his career in a small 11–16 school, but after 3 years he moved to his current post in an 11–18 school where, following an internal promotion, he is now head of humanities. In his career, he has taught RE in addition to history, but only at Key Stage (KS) 3. It has been a source of frustration that his school has not had an RE specialist up to this point, but due to increased pupil numbers they have now been able to appoint a new member of the team and they have managed to recruit an RE specialist who has just completed their PGCE course. As head of humanities, David has decided he should step into the mentoring role for the new member of his team.

Case Study 3

Aisha is a trained RE specialist with 12 years' experience, the last two in her current school, where she is head of RE within a large humanities faculty. The school has recently appointed a new member of staff who has just completed an RE PGCE course, and the head of humanities has asked Aisha to take on the mentoring role for this new colleague. They will be joining the faculty in September and will have 15 lessons of KS3 RE on their timetable per week as well as a Year 10 GCSE group. The new teacher is happy with their timetable, but they are a little anxious about having sole responsibility for a GCSE class for the first time.

Consider:

- What are the potential strengths and weaknesses of each of the three mentors?
- What are the challenges that they may face?
- What are the potential pitfalls that they need to avoid?
- What is the subject-specific priority for each mentor?

Each of the three mentors has experience as a strength. They have all spent several years in the classroom, and two of them – David and Aisha – have worked in more than one school. This may help them in their mentoring role as they are likely to have experienced different approaches, strategies and systems that may help them highlight for their beginning teacher different ways of approaching the challenges they face. Alison does not have this broader experience, and it may benefit her to be mindful of this, and perhaps ensure that the ITE student teaches some of her colleagues' classes to utilise the breadth of experience held within the department. Alison is also working with someone who lacks confidence in relation to their substantive knowledge in some areas of the curriculum. She will need to consider how she can support the beginning teacher to both develop their knowledge and their confidence over the course of the placement.

Aisha has considerable experience on which she can draw. As her beginning teacher gets to grips with the demands of their timetable, which is likely to be significantly heavier than the one they had at the end of their PGCE, Aisha may need to focus on supporting their planning. This may involve ensuring that the beginning teacher has a clear understanding of the RE curriculum in the school and how it sets out to build knowledge progressively over time. Aisha will also need to draw on her own expertise in teaching GCSE to support the beginning teacher in taking on the responsibility of their own GCSE group for the first time. It may be appropriate for her to share some of her own planning and in mentor meetings give time to discussion about how this will need to be adapted for the beginning teacher's own class.

David has the obvious challenge of mentoring a beginning teacher with whom he does not share a subject specialism. It is likely that, having taught some RE and led the subject, he has a good grasp of the curriculum in his school. However, without a qualification in RE, he may need to develop his knowledge in relation to current issues and thinking about the curriculum in RE to fully support his beginning teacher. He may also never have been introduced to or explored RE-specific pedagogical thinking. The danger is that the focus of his feedback and guidance is on generic teaching skills. Whilst this is important, he needs to support the beginning teacher in exploring how to use and develop these skills in the context of RE. David may find that he needs to do some reading and research about subject-specific pedagogy to ensure that he can engage in meaningful and supportive conversations with his new colleague.

The benefits of RE-Specific mentoring

Evidence indicates that not only is high-quality mentoring crucial for teacher development (Hobson et al., 2009), but it is also more effective when mentors are subject specialists (Hobson et al., 2007; Hobson & Malderez, 2013; Smith & Ingersoll, 2004). Sometimes, even subject-specialist mentors may feel that they lack the expertise to discuss the concepts, ideas and pedagogy that underpin their teaching with beginning teachers (Brown et al., 2015), but it is the case that they play a crucial role in supporting beginning teachers to develop pedagogical knowledge of the RE curriculum and the substantive knowledge required to teach it. Suggestions from ITE tutors or external course providers may be drawn from research or professional literature but are not necessarily tried and tested or grounded in the practice or context of a particular setting (Burn, 2007). Suggestions from members of the school's senior leadership team or others supporting beginning teachers may be generic in nature and not take into consideration the challenges faced in the RE classroom. Specialist RE mentors are uniquely placed to offer a "distinctive contribution" (Burn, 2007, p. 458) to the development of beginning RE teachers' substantive and pedagogical knowledge, as they support them with relevant, contextualised and subject-specific suggestions for practice.

Effective subject-specific mentoring requires engagement with the subject context. This may involve using your existing knowledge of the aims and purpose of the subject, your understanding of broader issues and your expertise in relation to different pedagogical approaches to inform and shape your approach to mentoring. For example, you may draw on your understanding of the aims and purpose of RE and current debates when discussing the rationale behind curriculum decisions with your beginning teacher or when you are supporting them with their medium- and long-term planning. Your knowledge of current thinking, substantive subject knowledge and awareness of different pedagogical approaches may help you structure conversations about short-term planning, influence the content of your lesson feedback or help you identify clear "next steps" when target setting.

Each of the mentors in the earlier case studies needs to think about how they support their beginning teacher to develop substantive and pedagogical knowledge in the context of RE, whilst also supporting them in applying research-informed approaches and whole-school initiatives in a subject-specific context. To do this, it is important that mentors are aware of the broader debates that influence and shape RE curricula and can identify what is distinctive and unique to RE within their practice and thinking. This may involve reflecting on what it is that you already know about the subject context, the curriculum in your school and the decisions you make every day about how best to teach RE so that you can distil this knowledge to share it effectively with a beginning teacher.

A shared sense of purpose

Establishing the aims and purpose of RE is acknowledged to be a complex discussion. As an experienced teacher you are likely to have your own, established perspective on these debates and be able to clearly articulate your own position. However, a beginning teacher may be only just starting to recognise this diverse range of opinions, or they may have developed their position, only to find that this is still sometimes challenged in conversations, training sessions, the resources they encounter or their wider reading. Task 2.2 offers an activity that you can work on with a beginning teacher to help you develop an understanding of the starting point of your beginning teacher and where their perspective lies in relation to your own.

Task 2.2 Developing a shared understanding

Independently, both you and your beginning teacher should write a few sentences to explain how you would articulate the aims and purpose of RE to another professional. Compare your responses and, together, consider the following questions:

- To what extent are your perspectives aligned?
- Discuss any differences; is there anything in your definition that the beginning teacher hadn't considered?
- Are there any points of disagreement, and if so, how are they likely to result in different approaches in the classroom?
- How do they compare to other statements of the aims and purpose of RE (e.g., contained within your agreed syllabus or in documentation published by Ofsted)?

It may be that the conversations resulting from Task 2.2 indicate that your views are aligned, and you share a very similar perspective on the aims and purpose of RE. However, it may also be the case that there are points of divergence in your thinking. If this is the case, you need to consider whether these are slight differences in emphasis that are unlikely to impact the experience of your pupils or whether the beginning teacher has an approach that is significantly different to the one taken by you and your department. Task 2.3 offers a case study to help you reflect on this and consider what your response might be.

Task 2.3 Differences of opinion

Natasha is a mature PGCE student who has previously been employed as a youth worker. Her passion is for supporting young people to develop into thoughtful, reflective adults who are aware of their own views on religious and moral questions. She thinks that RE should focus on discussion work so that her pupils have a chance to develop and express their own opinions; she places less value on pupils producing written work in which they can demonstrate their substantive knowledge of the world's religions. This perspective is at odds with the purpose of RE as it is understood by the department in her placement school. It is a large, well-established and successful department with good uptake and outcomes at GCSE and A level over many years. The team agree with Natasha that RE should prepare their pupils for the experiences of adult life, but they think this is best achieved by ensuring that they have good substantive knowledge of the world's religions that they are able to articulate and evaluate in both discussion and written work. They agree that it is important that pupils develop their own opinions, but they do not think this should be the main goal of RE.

Consider the following questions:

- What are the points of similarity between the two perspectives? What are the main areas of difference?
- If you were Natasha's mentor, how might you approach a conversation with her about this?
- What would your intended outcomes of the conversation be?
- How much freedom and flexibility can or should you give her to try things her way?

Conversations like the one proposed in Task 2.3 are rare. However, where there is divergence, it is important to become aware of the beginning teacher's position early in your working relationship and address it openly with the beginning teacher. These conversations are professional discussions in which one party is at the beginning of their career and may well find that their perspective changes and develops as they gain more experience. Nevertheless, a working relationship where this can be discussed openly will make for a stronger and more productive mentor–mentee relationship.

Developing subject knowledge

In 2019–2020, 40% of students enrolling on a PGCE course in RE had graduated in subjects other than theology or religious studies. Many had studied humanities subjects such as history, philosophy or sociology, but some came with qualifications in law, criminology or politics (National Association of Teachers of RE [NATRE], 2020). Whilst these degree qualifications are often related to RE and, in fact, may help beginning teachers approach this multidisciplinary subject, it is the case that as a mentor you may need to support them in developing their substantive subject knowledge. Often this is in relation to a particular religion or a particular concept. Task 2.4 presents an activity to help you consider how you might start to approach this with a beginning teacher (see Chapter 10 for a more detailed approach as you develop your work on this further).

Task 2.4 Developing subject knowledge

Discuss with your beginning teacher the gaps in their subject knowledge in relation to your curriculum (if you are working with an ITE student, this conversation could be based on the subject knowledge audit that it is likely they are expected to complete). Identify together a topic which they are due to teach but where they lack confidence and/or they need to develop their knowledge further.

Now undertake the following:

* Make a list of the books, websites, documentaries and podcasts that could be used to address this knowledge gap that you can share with them. Consider the accessibility and reliability of the resources you include.
* Design a reading task in which you identify one or two articles or book chapters that you would like them to read. Set aside some time in a mentor meeting to then discuss what they have learnt from the task.
* Identify a documentary or podcast that you can both make time to watch or listen to. Make some time afterwards to discuss it and share your thoughts.
* Ask the beginning teacher to incorporate some of this new knowledge or a new resource into the existing scheme of work.

Understanding the curriculum

Whilst developing accurate substantive knowledge is important, to focus solely on this is to focus on factual knowledge, which potentially does not engage with the broader understanding of religion that many curricula seek to develop in their pupils. If a beginning teacher only focuses on *what* they need to teach, at the very least they may not be paying sufficient attention to how this knowledge relates to the learning that proceeds and follows it. More than this, they may focus on an understanding of religion that does not acknowledge debates about truth claims, does not help pupils explore religion as it is lived around the world, does not introduce them to key concepts that underpin religious belief and fails to explore (and perhaps does not acknowledge) the meta-narratives that underpin belief.

Many agreed syllabi highlight key concepts that run through the curriculum. These are central ideas which help pupils understand the substantive knowledge that they encounter. They may be particular to a specific religion, or they could be concepts which are important in the study of more than one faith, such as belief, sources of wisdom and authority, worship and tradition. However, they may also be concepts which relate to human experience and about which religion seeks to offer understanding, concepts such as commitment, suffering, identity and questions about life after death (Ofsted, 2021). Beginning teachers need to be aware of the underlying concepts that shape the curriculum that they are teaching. In many schemes of work, these are concepts that underpin the curriculum at each key stage and about which there is the intention that pupils will develop a deeper and more nuanced understanding each time they are revisited. Beginning teachers need to develop an understanding of how these concepts have been addressed previously and how they might build on them in their own teaching.

Therefore, it is important that beginning teachers can identify the concepts that are explicitly addressed in your curriculum and that are fundamental to understanding a particular belief system. They must be aware of the ideas that you identified to be introduced in Year 7 because they explain something that is essential for understanding the curriculum in Years 8 and 9 and perhaps the GCSE specification. The identified concepts may differ from school to school; they will be based on the requirements specified by the syllabus being followed and will have been developed in the context of the school's own curriculum.

Beginning teachers must be aware of the key concepts encountered in the curriculum in their setting and conscious of the responsibility to build and develop these through their teaching. Task 2.5 suggests a way that you might work with a beginning teacher in your context to develop their understanding of this important aspect of the subject.

Task 2.5 Developing curriculum knowledge

Reflect on the knowledge required to teach the RE curriculum in your school. What substantive knowledge is required? Are there key concepts identified in the syllabus that you follow? Are there any key concepts that are central to your curriculum?

Ask the beginning teacher with whom you are working to also review the curriculum and then ask them the following questions:

- Which areas of substantive subject knowledge do you need to develop to teach this curriculum?
- What are the key concepts that underpin the curriculum? How and when will you have an opportunity to address them in your teaching?

In this discussion, guide them to develop their thinking, pointing out things that they may have overlooked or where they need to develop their knowledge or understanding further.

RE in a broader context

Beyond the support beginning teachers may require with developing their knowledge within the context of the subject, mentors also play a role in helping to induct them into the wider RE community. As well as introducing them to the structures that support RE beyond the school context, this also means making their developing understanding of wider RE debates relevant to their work in the classroom. There is always much to discuss within the wider RE community. Sometimes discussion and debate are prompted by external concerns (for example, focus in education on decolonisation of the curriculum or teaching about anti-racism). Sometimes the debate comes from within the community. Discussion about the aims and purpose of RE and pedagogical approaches all have the potential to impact classroom practice and these debates, that are regularly revisited, are likely to have impacted your curriculum. However, it can be a challenge to articulate for a beginning teacher the ideas embedded in your thinking that have been honed and developed over a long period. Consider the following debates and how they might impact mentoring a beginning teacher in your context:

- *RE or religion and worldviews (R&W)?* – In recent years, many RE departments around the country have changed the name of the subject on the school timetable in an effort to both remove any stigma that might be associated with the term *religious education* and also to try and more accurately reflect the content of the curriculum. More recently, the suggestion of the Commission on RE that the name of the subject in England should be changed to *R&W* (Commission on RE, 2018) has prompted renewed discussion in relation to this. Whilst many have written in support of this and the change of emphasis that it might encourage (Chater, 2020), the subject is still referred to in legislation as RE and the debate continues. Beginning teachers are likely to be aware of this. Does what you call the subject in your school in some way reflect the department's shared view about the nature and purpose of the subject? In an early meeting with your beginning teacher (perhaps as part of a conversation about the aims and purpose of the subject as discussed earlier) you should share with them your reasons for continuing to call the subject RE or adopting an alternative name. You should be able to articulate for them all the factors, both internal and external, that influenced your decision.

- *Pedagogical approaches* – The development of RE over the last 50 years has seen the emergence of a number of pedagogical approaches, each reflecting slightly different perspectives on the aims and intentions of the subject. Although some RE teachers may prefer one approach over another, the reality is that many RE teachers are aware of all these approaches and draw from several of them over time as they seek to develop their teaching in a way that engages their pupils and achieves their aims and objectives. Holt (2022) characterises this as the kaleidoscopic approach. More recently in England, Ofsted (2021) have acknowledged this range of possible pedagogical approaches but asserted that any single pedagogical model is not sufficient as some of them focus on a particular religion or prioritise particular 'ways of knowing'. At the same time, this Ofsted review of research (2021) noted other possible approaches (e.g. drawing on the academic disciplines of theology, philosophy and the human/social sciences to frame curriculum content). It is likely that beginning teachers will have been introduced to some of these ideas during their ITE courses. However, it is the role of a mentor to help a beginning teacher make links between theory and practice. What are the identifiable pedagogical approaches that are used consistently in your department? You must be able to articulate for a beginning teacher the rationale behind these approaches and, if there is no agreed approach, consider what advice might you give to a beginning teacher about developing and establishing a clear pedagogical perspective. These conversations should underpin discussion about medium- and short-term planning.
- *Curriculum content* – As many secondary schools in England are now academies, there is freedom for most RE departments to select the syllabus that they follow. However, when using that syllabus to develop the curriculum, teachers still have to make important decisions about what should be covered, when and in how much depth. Ofsted (2021) has challenged schools in England to consider whether representations of religion in the curriculum are both broad and deep, encouraging teachers to think about the pitfalls of both a thematic curriculum (one structured around themes such as 'festivals' or 'rites of passage'), which can be superficial and lead to misconceptions and a systematic curriculum (where the curriculum is composed of units where one religion or non-religious tradition is studied at a time), which does not allow pupils to see clearly areas of similarity, difference and overlap. Others share additional concerns. Holt (2019) makes the case for a curriculum that goes *"Beyond the Big Six Religions"* and others have expressed concern about the way that religions are either misrepresented or under-represented in school curricula (Insight UK, 2021). As a mentor, you need to help

beginning teachers understand the rationale that underpins your curriculum. You need to be able to articulate the way that knowledge builds as pupils progress through your schemes of work. You should also be able to justify your choices in relation to which religions are studied and when, and articulate what you have done to ensure breadth and depth in your representations of religion. Having shared this with your beginning teacher, you should then revisit this as you discuss with them their planning and teaching to help them reflect on how effectively they make connections between different parts of the curriculum and whether their presentations of religion have the required depth and breadth.

- *Curriculum time* – Many locally agreed syllabuses in England are constructed, based on an assumption that 5% of curriculum time will be given to RE. However, in a 2017 survey it was found that 44% of academies reported no timetabled RE (NATRE, 2017), and even in schools where RE is timetabled, there can still be issues with lack of curriculum time at KS3 and curriculum arrangements that offer no provision at KS4 to pupils who do not opt to sit a Religious Studies GCSE. Constraints of time can impact the construction and delivery of an ambitious curriculum, leaving RE departments to make difficult decisions about what to include and how to ensure progression in RE for all pupils. In your role as a mentor, you should be able to highlight any time constraints that have impacted the design of your curriculum and articulate for a beginning teacher how you have dealt with these. Going forward they may need support with working out how to plan teaching and learning for their own classes given these constraints.

These are all issues with which you are familiar and which you and your colleagues have considered and worked through in your context. However, whilst a beginning teacher may be familiar with some of the challenges, they need help to understand how day-to-day decisions in the classroom may be impacted by this context and any implications this might have for their own practice. To explore further, Task 2.6 suggests a way of approaching this conversation with trainees so that they understand their work in the context of the 'bigger picture'.

Task 2.6 The impact of broader debates

In an early meeting with your beginning teacher share with them your thoughts in relation to the debates outlined earlier, highlighting the position taken by you and your department. The following prompt questions may be useful in the discussion:

- Which pedagogical approaches are used in the department? To what extent is this aligned with the ideas that your beginning teacher has encountered in their ITE course or previous school placements?
- What is the process that shaped the curriculum at KS3? How were the units of work selected and what is the rationale behind their sequencing? How have you ensured depth and breadth?
- Have any recent publications (e.g. Ofsted guidance or Evidence Endowment Foundation research) informed the current developments? Have you or your

colleagues within the department engaged with any subject-specific continuing professional development that has influenced your thinking?

- How much time are you allocated at KS3 and KS4? Is this enough? If not, how has this influenced curriculum decisions? Even if you feel it is adequate, if you had more time, how would you use it?

Making conversations RE-Specific

A key skill required by RE mentors is the ability to help beginning teachers reflect on and articulate what is happening in the classroom and relate this to broader curriculum development initiatives. This includes understanding generic frameworks for teacher knowledge and assessment and being able to relate this to the development of pedagogical knowledge and skills in RE. Therefore, it is worth taking some time to consciously consider how to approach meaningful, subject-specific conversations. Task 2.7 presents a case study which allows you to consider how you might approach conversations through a subject-specific lens.

Task 2.7 Subject-specific conversations

Consider the case study and the questions that follow:

Nazish is mentoring an ITE student, Ben, who is completing university tasks throughout the duration of the placement. One of these tasks requires him to explore whole-school approaches to literacy and the impact these might have on his own teaching. He has asked Nazish if they can discuss this in their next meeting.

- What are the subject-specific issues Nazish needs to bring into the discussion?
- Are there any RE-specific ideas she needs to introduce?
- Are there any resources that she could recommend?

In the case study in Task 2.7, Nazish needs to reflect on the concept of 'disciplinary literacy' and what this means in the context of RE. Disciplinary literacy recognises that literacy skills can be subject-specific and that each subject has its own unique language (Collins, 2019). For example, many words used in RE that would be described by Beck et al. (2013) as Tier 3 vocabulary (low-frequency words which are limited to a specific subject or discipline) have their roots in other languages, such as Arabic, Hebrew or Sanskrit. Ben needs to explore strategies for supporting pupils in being able to recognise, define and use these terms accurately when both writing and speaking. There are many strategies that might be used to address this (Cox, n.d.), and Nazish could share with him some of the strategies commonly used in the department. Their conversation might also consider the challenges for a subject where high-stakes assessment relies on pupils' ability to write well. Frameworks used in the department for supporting pupils in their reading and analysis of longer texts, including passages from religious scripture, could be shared and discussed. Similarly, GCSE and A-level assessment objectives could be considered to support discussion regarding the characteristics of a well-structured examination response in religious studies. More generic frameworks may be helpful in this discussion (e.g. Quigley and Coleman, 2019), but the mentor has an important role to play in helping a beginning teacher see how these frameworks might apply to RE in their context.

Developing skills for mentoring

Recognising the importance of the RE-specific aspect of the mentoring role will require a reflexive approach as you begin to identify the knowledge and skills that you would like to develop. It may be that you wish to consider in more detail how to articulate aspects of your practice that have become 'second nature' to you. You are drawing on a wealth of knowledge and experience that allows you to perform classroom tasks and evaluate them easily, but the mentoring role requires that you now articulate these skills for, and teach them to, others. You may be working with a beginning teacher who is 'consciously incompetent'; they are aware that there are skills that they need to develop and can see that this must be addressed, but they don't always know how to approach this and are likely to make mistakes along the way. Or you may find yourself working with a beginning teacher who is 'consciously competent'; they have developed the required knowledge and skills, but they are still deliberate in their use and execution of this in the classroom and may need help to reflect on their practice and identify alternatives. As explored in Chapter 3, the relationship between you and the beginning teacher, and what they need from you, will change over the course of the time you are working together. However, at every stage, it is the case that you need to think about how to make the implicit explicit and ensure that conversations help the beginning teacher consider their work in the classroom through a subject-specific lens.

Going forward, it may be the case that you decide to engage in some continuing professional development to support you in developing your mentoring skills and there are many ways in which you could approach this. Some mentors may decide their focus is on building links with local universities so that they are in touch with changes to the ITE curriculum. Others may feel confident in this but wish to engage in some RE-specific continuing professional development or pursue further master's-level qualifications to develop knowledge and skills to ensure their mentoring is subject-specific. There may be others who have confidence in their RE knowledge but wish to engage in further training (perhaps leading to certification) to develop their understanding of mentoring processes. Just as every beginning teacher is different, so is every mentor and every context. The goal is to provide quality, subject-specific mentoring; but what each individual needs to support them in achieving this goal is different.

Summary and key points

This chapter has explored the importance of subject-specific mentoring and how experienced RE teachers in a mentoring role can draw on their knowledge and experience to help beginning teachers develop as RE specialists.

- It is important that mentoring is subject-specific. A specialist RE mentor is uniquely placed to provide support that is both relevant to the context and understands the subject-specific concerns of beginning teachers.

- In situations in which there is no RE specialist to take on the mentoring role, it may be that the mentor is from another humanities discipline. Where this is the case, the mentor should be aware of some of the key issues and pedagogical debates within RE so that advice and guidance do not become generic.
- Each mentor, each beginning teacher and each school context is different. It is important that mentors can recognise the opportunities and challenges of a given situation to ensure that they provide appropriate support for a beginning teacher.
- Debates in RE can lead to different understandings of the aims and purpose of the subject and different classroom approaches. It is important to work through this with beginning teachers to acknowledge different perspectives and develop a shared understanding as the basis of your working relationship.
- Mentors need to consider what is distinctive and unique about RE. Their role is to support beginning teachers as they develop their skills as subject specialists; this requires knowledge of not only substantive RE curriculum content and pedagogy but also wider debates in RE and subject-specific responses to broader education debates and initiatives.
- Factors that can impact the design and implementation of the RE curriculum are well understood by experienced RE specialists, but beginning teachers may need support from their mentors in understanding these issues and how they might impact on their work in the classroom.
- Taking on a mentoring role presents an opportunity to develop your own knowledge and skills further. However, each mentor needs to decide for themselves the focus of such development.

Further resources

Hutton, L., & Cox, D. (2021). *Making every RE lesson count: Six principles to support religious education teaching*. Crown House Publishing.

This text considers some evidence-informed approaches to classroom practice in an RE context. It effectively demonstrates how to look at teaching and learning through an RE lens.

RE: ONLINE – www.reonline.org.uk/

This website offers essays to support the development of subject knowledge. These are a useful resource when working with beginning teachers who have gaps in their knowledge that they wish to address. There is also a section of the website to support professional development which may be of interest to both you and beginning teachers.

References

Beck, I. L., McKeown, M. G., & Kucan, L. (2013). *Bringing words to life: Robust vocabulary instruction* (2nd ed.). Guilford Press.
Brown, T., Rowley, H., & Smith, K. (2015). *The beginnings of school led teacher training: New challenges for university teacher education*. Manchester Metropolitan University.

Burn, K. (2007). Professional knowledge and identity in a contested discipline: Challenges for student teachers and teacher educators. *Oxford Review of Education*, 33(4), 445–467. https://doi.org/10.1080/03054980701450886

Chater, M. (2020). *Reforming religious education: Power and knowledge in a worldviews curriculum*. John Catt Educational Ltd.

Collins, K. (2019, July 5). *What do we mean by 'disciplinary literacy'?* Evidence Endowment Foundation Blog. https://educationendowmentfoundation.org.uk/news/eef-blog-what-do-we-mean-by-disciplinary-literacy

Commission on Religious Education. (2018). *Religion and worldviews: The way forward. A national plan for RE*. Religious Education Council of England and Wales.

Cox, D. (n.d.). *Closing the word gap: Activities for the classroom–Religious Education*. Oxford University Press.

Hobson, A., Ashby, P., Malderez, A., & Tomlinson, P. D. (2009). Mentoring beginning teachers: What we know and what we don't. *Teaching and Teacher Education*, 25(1), 207–216. https://doi.org/10.1016/j.tate.2008.09.001

Hobson, A., Malderez, L., Tracey, L., Homer, M., Mitchell, N., Biddulph, M., et al. (2007). *Newly qualified teachers' experiences of their first year of teaching: Findings from Phase III of the becoming teacher project*. University of Nottingham.

Hobson, A. J., & Malderez, A. (2013). Judgementoring and other threats to realizing the potential of school-based mentoring in teacher education. *International Journal of Mentoring and Coaching in Education*, 2(2), 89–108. https://doi.org/10.1108/IJMCE-03-2013-0019

Holt, J. (2019). *Beyond the Big Six Religions: Expanding the Boundaries in the Teaching of Religion and Worldview*. University of Chester Press.

Holt, J. (2022). *Religious Education in the Secondary School. An introduction to Teaching, Learning and the World Religions* (2nd ed). Routledge.

Hutton, L., & Cox, D. (2021). *Making every RE lesson count: Six principles to support religious education teaching*. Crown House Publishing.

Insight UK. (2021). *A report on the state of Hinduism in Religious Education in UK schools*. https://insightuk.org/wp-content/uploads/2021/01/Hinduism-in-RE_Project-report.pdf

Malderez, A., Hobson, A. J., Tracey, L., & Kerr, K. (2007). Becoming a student teacher: Core features of the experience. *European Journal of Teacher Education*, 30(3), 225–248. https://doi.org/10.1080/02619760701486068

National Association of Teachers of RE. (2017). *The state of the nation: A report on religious education provision within secondary schools in England*. https://www.natre.org.uk/uploads/Free%20Resources/SOTN%202017%20Report%20web%20version%20FINAL.pdf

National Association of Teachers of RE. (2020). *Number of RE trainee teachers increases–To their highest in a decade*. https://www.natre.org.uk/news/latest-news/number-of-re-trainee-teachers-increases-to-their-highest-in-a-decade/

Ofsted. (2021). *Research review series: Religious education*. https://www.gov.uk/government/publications/research-review-series-religious-education/research-review-series-religious-education

Quigley, A., & Coleman, R. (2019). *Improving literacy in secondary schools: Guidance Report*. Education Endowment Foundation. https://d2tic4wvo1iusb.cloudfront.net/eef-guidance-reports/literacy-ks3-ks4/EEF_KS3_KS4_LITERACY_GUIDANCE.pdf?v=1635355220

Smith, T. M., & Ingersoll, R. M. (2004). What are the effects of induction and mentoring on beginning teacher turnover? *American Educational Research Journal*, 41(3), 681–714. https://doi.org/10.3102/00028312041003681

3 The Changing Nature of the Mentor-Beginning Teacher Relationship

From Modelling to Co-enquirers

Sjay Patterson-Craven

Introduction

Mentoring beginning teachers can be incredibly rewarding. Aside from the professional development opportunities it provides for you, it is a chance to support, encourage and guide a beginning teacher at the outset of what is a hugely rewarding career. Effective mentoring can not only provide a beginning teacher with the practical teaching and learning skills needed for the classroom but also contribute to the development of their professional self and shape their sense of identity and agency as a beginning teacher (Izadina, 2015). Ineffective mentoring, however, can drive beginning teachers from the classroom, and without a chance to develop their sense of teacher self, they can leave the profession altogether (Hammerness, 2008). Thus, whilst the role of mentoring beginning teachers can be incredibly challenging, with great power comes great responsibility. Whether you are new to the position or it's been some time since you last mentored, this chapter outlines some broad definitely 'dos' and some definitely 'don'ts' and suggests some possibly/maybes along the way.

At the end of this chapter, you should be able to:

- Recognise how the relationship between mentor and beginning teacher may change and the key features of each stage.
- Reflect on how effective mentoring can enable beginning teachers to develop their sense of professional self.
- Have an awareness of some practical strategies which you can utilise when mentoring a beginning teacher.

Mentoring: What Is It, and What Is It Not?

Before we go any further, let us clarify what mentoring is and is not:

- Mentoring is fundamentally about helping beginning teachers to develop their practice, learn from an experienced mentor and discover who they are as professionals both inside and outside of the classroom. It involves an immense amount of patience, time, support (both professionally and personally) and humility on the part of both the mentor and mentee.
- Mentoring is not teaching by proxy (Roberts and Graham, 2008) and such an approach should be actively discouraged. Be open to hearing about different approaches, different educational values and/or different ideas about the purpose of religious education (RE).

DOI: 10.4324/9781003191087-4

- Mentoring is about giving beginning teachers the space and opportunity to develop their sense of teacher self. This is just as important as ensuring they can plan a lesson.
- Mentoring is not about creating a teacher who is the 'finished product'. Resist putting any such expectations on the relationship and/or having others expect this of you.
- Mentoring is an opportunity for you to learn from someone at a different stage of their career.

Task 3.1 provides an opportunity for you to reflect on your own experiences of being mentored and how you might use this as you step into a mentoring role.

Task 3.1 Mentoring reflection: Reflecting on your experience of mentoring

Think back over your career to date and reflect on the following questions:

- What experiences have you had of being mentored?
- What do you feel makes someone an effective mentor? What are the factors which may contribute to the effectiveness of a mentor?
- What do you want to achieve as a mentor? Think about both you and the beginning teacher you are mentoring when reflecting on this question.

The Development of the Mentoring Relationship: Furlong and Maynard (1996)

Terms such as *coach* or *facilitator* are often used in place in the term *mentor*, but this is somewhat inaccurate as each term denotes a different relationship between you and the beginning teachers you will work with. Whilst dated, Furlong and Maynard's (1996) work is useful as an overview of the stages of professional relationship which will occur over the course of your mentoring relationship from model to coach to critical friend and then co-enquirer. Task 3.2 introduces the model to be considered throughout this chapter and allows you to consider what the key terms mean to you and how the relationship may change or develop over the course of your mentorship.

Task 3.2 Reflecting on the stages of the mentor/beginning teacher relationship

Look at Figure 3.1 which shows the Furlong and Maynard model. You may want to look back to your answers from Task 3.1 to help you consider the following questions:

- What do you initially understand by the term *model*, *coach*, *critical friend* and *co-enquirer*?
- If you have mentored before, which model of mentoring (if any) have you used?
- At first glance, do you think the Furlong and Maynard model is a useful one?

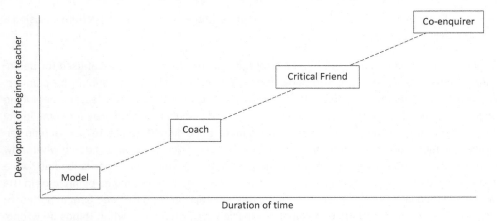

Figure 3.1 The stages of the mentor/beginning teacher relationship

Adapted from Furlong and Maynard (1996)

The Model

Imagine a young child learning to ride a bike. At this early stage, you are doing most of the riding, modelling what you do, how you do it, and the impact it has. Thus, no matter if they are a few days into their initial teacher education or have several terms as an early-career teacher under their belt, initially you will be demonstrating not only high-quality teaching and learning in RE but also the expectations and standard operating procedures of your setting. During the modelling stage, you are 'setting out your stall', and at this stage, the power rests with you as the model of good practice, showing the beginning teacher not only how things are done, be it in your setting or as an example of good RE, but also why things are done in that way. For example, how and why do lessons follow a certain cycle? Why do pupils stand behind their chairs when they enter the classroom? How and when do you ask for hands-up? To develop as reflective practitioners, beginning teachers at all stages of their careers need to be consistently encouraged to unpick not only *what* happens in a classroom but *why* and the modelling stage is where this process starts as well.

Given the spotlight which is on you at this stage of the relationship, you may need to adapt your practice so that you are purposefully performing rather than just going through the usual day-to-day moments in your classroom. Those of you who have passed an examination for your driving licence will know the difference between casually glancing in the mirror before executing a manoeuvre and explicitly showing the examiner that you are using your mirror ("Look at me looking!"). This is a helpful analogy to use during this stage as you are making the modelling explicit for the purpose of instruction and induction. For beginning teachers at the very outset of their career, you may want to consider talking them through such fundamentals as the following:

- How to organise and structure your workload, including your planning and marking.
- The way in which transitions are managed in the classroom including the start and end of lessons.

- The 'language' or 'teacher talk' used in your setting when giving instructions or using a behaviour system.

Team planning and teaching are helpful strategies at this stage and be be utilised for beginning teachers at all levels. It can allow you to model how the lesson should be planned, delivered, and evaluated, and can be a relatively safe option if you don't feel the beginning teacher is ready for the full responsibility of a class. It can also pave the way for some initial joint reflection after the lesson. Whilst there is much to be gained from it, team-teaching can present some challenges if not managed appropriately. Be clear on who is doing what; how is the lesson being divided up? What is one person doing whilst the other is leading? As a mentor, try to avoid 'stepping in' if you feel that something is not going as planned or in the way you would like. Despite good intentions, this will only serve to damage beginning teachers' confidence and rob them of a valuable experience of what to do when things go wrong. When done well, team-teaching can be a supportive and useful tool by which to model the basics, develop collaboration between professionals and redress the power balance between mentor and beginning teacher.

Lesson planning at this stage of the relationship can also be complicated. Inexperienced beginning teachers at the start of their initial teacher education course may be required to complete a lesson planning proforma in which they detail the lesson structure and the assessment opportunities to help scaffold their skill development as they learn the principles of effective planning. For experienced teachers, lesson planning is not necessarily about the completion of a proforma, and it may be some years since you completed a physical lesson plan. However, as the model, you will still need to ensure you are demonstrating how a lesson is planned effectively so that beginning teachers can see what it means to 'plan and teach well-structured lessons' (Teachers' Standards, 2012). This may involve making implicit thinking processes explicit via joint-planning exercises; what is the learning goal or goals? What will proof of learning look like? How will your teaching be adapted? Why are you assessing in that manner? A beginning teacher may be totally inexperienced when it comes to lesson planning, or they may have already developed their own style and approach to planning. In either instance, there is no single approach to lesson planning, so your focus should be on modelling how to effectively plan in a manner which is not onerous rather than advocating for one specific template, style or cycle.

It may also be the case that you are one of the few qualified RE teachers which the beginning teacher has worked alongside, so there is a responsibility on you to model not just good RE, but what it means to a professional outside of the classroom. Such considerations are likely to be covered in the competencies or standards which are relevant for the country in which you are teaching. You should also avoid involving beginning teachers in department or school 'politics' or informal gossip. For example, you may not agree with a particular policy in your school or setting, but your role as a mentor is to model professional behaviours and induct beginning teachers into the expectations of the profession and the school in which they are working or training to teach. Once they are more experienced, such conversations can provide opportunities for critique and development of practice, but this may not be appropriate at this stage of the relationship.

For more experienced beginning teachers, it should be expected that they have some understanding of the importance of such matters but they will need to be inducted into the procedures and systems of your setting so make sure you are modelling the expectation correctly so they can be clear on what is expected of them in their own practice and ensure they are continually developing in accordance to whatever competencies they are expected to meet.

Task 3.3 invites you to consider the different aspects of being a teacher in your setting and how this might impact you as a mentor.

Task 3.3 The model

Thinking about all the different aspects of being a teacher in your setting, make a list of the following:

- What are the non-negotiables that you will need to model and therefore induct your beginning teachers into?
- What are the practices or habits you want them to avoid and therefore need to be mindful of *not* modelling?
- What are the areas for flexibility, freedom, agency or autonomy? How could you support or facilitate their development in this area?

The Coach

Thinking again of our child learning to ride their bike, being a coach means attaching some stabilisers and encouraging them to have a go for themselves, albeit with you keeping one hand on the seat. This stage can include those teaching for the first time or those who may have some experience already but who are new to your school or setting. In either case, this development in your relationship comes with it a shift in power; it no longer resides solely with you as the 'expert' but instead is distributed a little more equally between you as the experienced mentor and the relatively inexperienced beginning teacher.

The focus at this stage of the relationship moves from modelling the 'basics' of teaching (the relationships, rituals and routines, etc.) and towards systematic feedback for their developing teaching competencies and skills. The importance of formative feedback and the setting of targets becomes increasingly important to help beginning teachers develop in the classroom and as reflective practitioners. Your role is not only one of encouragement and support but also in the creation of an environment which encourages risks and in which failures are not viewed as a poor reflection on them (or you). As a mentor, allow them the space and opportunity to exercise their own agency, to teach in a way which reflects their own values or their own identity – even if this is at odds with the RE which is normally taught in your school or setting. It is only through trial, error and reflection that beginning teachers will grow and develop as practitioners. Your role at this stage is to guide them through the highs and the lows and assist them in developing their practical knowledge alongside finding an approach which works for them as beginning professionals.

For those undertaking their initial teacher education, this period is often characterised by them taking increasing responsibility for several classes. They may still be doing some targeted observations (e.g. focusing on specific strategies or pupils) and/or team-teaching, but much of their time is spent developing their solo teaching with you as a coach alongside them, providing consistent, structured and formative feedback. Although you may find that your workload shifts slightly, your focus as a mentor shifts to coaching the beginning teacher through some of the practicalities of teaching and demonstrating effective RE pedagogy, thus the importance of modelling this from the outset. Don't forget how difficult some of the basics of teaching can be at the very start. It is not uncommon for inexperienced beginning teachers to spend hours planning a single lesson that lacks any real creativity or adaptation. There is nothing wrong with 'safe' RE lessons, especially at the outset and for many, this is part of them testing out what they feel comfortable with in their own classroom; however, they also need to develop confidence in demonstrating how different pupils learn (Department for Education [DfE], 2019; Carter, 2015). Take the opportunity to work alongside them to develop more engaging or challenging lessons with a greater degree of adaptive teaching. The same is equally true for those who may be a little more experienced but who still need work on furthering the basics. Regardless of what stage they are at, beginning teachers should have a reduced teaching load so they can take advantage of opportunities to make use of team planning, team-teaching and observations of other expert colleagues. Good teaching and learning exist everywhere, and lots can be learnt from going to see what adaptive teaching looks like in English or how behaviour is managed in physical education (PE).

If there is an expectation that certain competencies are met, such as the Teachers' Standards (DfE, 2011), it is worth bearing in mind that these are usually to be met at the conclusion of the initial phase not throughout. Beginning teachers will therefore either be working towards the expected standards or have only just met them. Your coaching will need to reflect this developmental approach.

Practical strategies used to support development at this stage may include the following:

- *Meet on a regular basis for structured, formative, and constructive meetings.* Agree a regular time to meet which is going to be productive yet which also takes account of both your teaching workloads and any other responsibilities you may have. Agree a focus and ensure that your meetings are structured and developmental and provide an opportunity for professional dialogue rather than just being a catch-up. Meet in a space where you won't be interrupted or disturbed and where 'safe' conversations can be had. Avoid staffrooms or busy planning rooms; instead, book an empty classroom or meeting room where you can both be assured of a quiet and conducive space for professional discussion.
- *Encourage and scaffold professional dialogue.* Coaching in this context is not about giving out the answers or troubleshooting; rather, it is about encouraging and supporting beginning teachers in the spirit of professional enquiry. Inexperienced beginning

teachers often struggle to reflect and will only want to hear your judgement as the 'expert'. Whilst this can be tempting (and often much quicker!), this is a conversation to be *crafted* during your mentorship and may need some scaffolding at the start. Lesson observation feedback which starts by asking, "How do you think that went?" can quickly and unhelpfully focus only on areas for development and ignore areas of success. Such conversations also give beginning teachers an easy way out to say, "Oh, I don't know . . . what do you think?" It is important that you *hear* what they are saying rather than just waiting for a point to interject. Keep conversations focused on the question of learning, unpicking what makes learning effective and how this links to current educational research, rather than focusing on what you want to say.

- *Set realistic and achievable goals*. Whilst this may seem obvious, it is worth remembering that beginning teachers are just that, *beginners*, and there is nothing wrong with setting what may feel like very mundane targets. For example, to have the books set out at the start of the lesson or to use the school sanction system consistently. Starting with small, achievable goals can often be the best way forward, especially if all involved are struggling to see the wood for the trees! As the coaching relationship develops the targets themselves should develop as well. Ensure that they are mutually constructed and that there is an opportunity for beginning teachers to scaffold and set their own targets. The targets should enable them to develop as professionals regardless of the school or setting they are in, make clear what success will look like and identify what the impact of meeting such targets will have on pupils' learning. Targets should always provide opportunities for developing skills rather than be a 'to-do list' of tasks.

The Critical Friend

Mentoring as a critical friend means removing the training wheels but keeping one hand on the seat as they pedal under their own steam. Whilst your role so far may have seemed like a flurry of activity, getting them up and running with the basics in place, the next stage of development sees you coming alongside the beginning teacher and holding up a critical mirror to their practice. Over time, they should be encouraged to hold up the mirror themselves, allowing them to exert a little more power and develop their own voice as professionals. Criticality is not about being *critical* in the negative sense of the word. Whilst there is a place for this, and such conversations will need to be crafted with care, it is about encouraging beginning teachers to adopt a different view or perspective on things and be prepared to do things in a way which is unfamiliar but which may produce equally good or better results. This involves posing difficult, and sometimes uncomfortable questions. As with all stages of a teacher's professional development, teaching should always be research-informed. If this is something which has been lacking up to this point, this is the moment for you to model such practice and engage beginning teachers at all stages in appropriate research. The suggested text by Hendrick and Macpherson (2017) is a good starting point for such conversations, and Task 3.4 invites you and your beginning teacher to identify an approach from the research and trial this within your own RE context.

Task 3.4 Making greater use of research in classroom-based practice

- Allow the beginning teacher to identify an area of practice which they would like to develop. This may be derived from some recent feedback, as part of a performance management target or an area which they feel needs some development or enhancement.
- Broker an opportunity for them to develop in this area with a view to having them trial a new approach in their practice. This may involve identifying a colleague who has expertise in this area and who is happy to be observed, directing them to relevant texts (such as Hendrick and Macpherson, 2017), or exploring evidence-based approaches via a resource such as the Teaching and Learning Toolkit available via the Education Endowment Foundation (2021).
- Having implemented the new approach in their practice, review with them what they have learnt and have them critique the approach they trialled. How successful was it? What impact did it have on learning? How could the approach be utilised in the future?

For those of you mentoring a beginning teacher during their initial teacher education phase, be on the lookout for the 'one-trick pony', someone who is very comfortable with the same strategies and rarely strays outside of their comfort zone. Whilst they may have a slightly bigger bag of tricks, the same may be true for those with a little more experience. With lessons planned, pupils taught and behaviour managed, the danger at this stage is that beginning teachers can feel they have 'mastered' teaching and thus start cutting corners with tasks which they perceive as no longer useful or which are too time-consuming. Lesson planning may lack systematic or informed approaches, adaptive practice may be limited to word banks and/or extension questions and feedback may be perfunctory rather than formative. Believing that in performing the *act* of teaching, they *are* teachers, bad habits can creep in, and they may need reminding about the importance of their own development as practitioners and thus encouraged to reflect, implement and evaluate new approaches. Even if this means trying approaches which they have previously found unsuccessful, unpicking why something hasn't worked is just as important as unpicking why it has.

A suitable strategy at this stage may be to video record the beginning teacher teaching a lesson, presuming appropriate permissions are in place to protect the identity of pupils. The approach is useful for several reasons. The recorder can be set up at the outset of the lesson and requires no further involvement from either of you, thus leaving them to teach and you to be elsewhere. It is an exact recording of what happened in the lesson, unaffected by the influence of either the teacher or the observer, and most significant, it provides a valuable resource for the beginning teacher to observe their own practice and encourage reflection on practice. This can be done in a variety of ways, depending on their level of teaching experience:

- The beginning teacher watches the recording back on their own, making notes either on the lesson as a whole (possibly making use of an observation proforma or checklist) or on a specific aspect (e.g. feedback). The recording is then watched by both of you, and feedback is shared.
- The mentor and beginning teacher watch the recording together, critiquing and evaluating at key moments. It may not be appropriate to do this for the whole lesson, so you may want to agree on a specific focus beforehand (e.g. effective use of recall).
- More experienced beginning teachers are given the responsibility to watch and critically reflect on the recording in their own time. Thoughts and points for action are shared with the mentor at an agreed time.
- If both are comfortable, the mentor records themselves teaching and offers this up for either professional critique (in a manner similar to co-enquiry) or as a development of the modelling approach previously discussed, ensuring that the focus is on unpicking *why* something was done rather than just *what*.

The Co-Enquirer

Like teaching a child to ride a bike, there comes a point when the stabilisers come off, the hand holding onto the seat is doing so less frequently, and they are motoring along at their own speed with only the occasional fall. The co-enquirer aspect of your mentorship sees the balance of power shift almost to a balanced equilibrium between you and the beginning teacher who is now a co-enquirer to effective practice. Whether they are coming to the end of an initial phase or undertaking an enhanced period of probation, as a co-enquirer they not only have the workload and responsibilities which come with being a qualified teacher, they are also increasingly autonomous and independent professionals, responsible for their own development. Whilst you are still there as a mentor, you are needed less and less for the practical day-to-day matters and instead have a more equal and open relationship with them, not dissimilar to that which you may have with your other less experienced colleagues.

At this stage, beginning teachers undertaking their initial teacher education will be responsible for a much greater teaching and marking load, they may be involved in departmental planning, working with those outside of the immediate department, and may have even secured their first teaching post. They will continue to benefit from formative mentoring; however, conversations may deal with the wider questions of educational value and purpose rather than just the practical application of lesson design. Similarly, those with a little more experience, whilst still beginners, will be operating much more as a fully fledged member of their own departments; this may even include some additional responsibilities, such as leading on planning for a year group or Key Stage.

As co-enquirers, you will be embarking on a new stage in your relationship: learning together as professionals and from each other. Your mentoring at this stage may go beyond didactic or structured reflective feedback, and instead, you are increasingly engaging beginning teachers in the co-construction of knowledge. For those coming to the end of their initial teacher education period, there is much less focus on you having 'the answers' and you need to be open to your relationship taking on this new dimension, recognising the beginning teacher as someone who is able to partake in conversations and reflections on a more sophisticated and professional level. As co-enquirers they should be able be able to set their own targets and proactively seek opportunities for development. They may be transitioning to a new setting or a new post in their current one, and as mentor, your role is to prepare them for this transition where more will be expected of them. Long term, the maintenance of your relationship may prove to be both personally and professionally fulfilling for all involved and contribute to the network of professional support to which you both belong.

A useful strategy at this stage may be to undertake some small-scale practitioner-based research together as co-researchers. Work together to identify a problem or phenomena to explore, research and trial interventions before evaluating the subsequent effectiveness for further actions. This can assist with the development of professional knowledge not just for those directly involved in the research but also for other practitioners in similar contexts. Such research can form the basis of further study, such as an MA or a PhD/EdD, and thus provide further development opportunities for both of you.

Task 3.5 invites you to take stock and plan your approach to mentoring by considering the approaches or strategies you may utilise at each stage of the mentoring relationship and review the Continuing Professional Development [CPD] resources available to you (such as key texts or recording equipment). The task suggests you familiarise yourself with the frameworks or competencies relevant to the stage at which your beginning teacher will be working.

Task 3.5   Taking stock and planning your mentorship

Having read through the four stages outlined in this chapter (model, coach, critical friend, co-enquirer),

- Construct a list of approaches, methods, or strategies which you would like to implement in your mentoring. Consider the purpose of each, the research which underpins it and how approaches could be developed and built on through the stages of model–coach–critical friend.
- Familiarise yourself with the necessary guidance, structures, frameworks or competencies as appropriate to the stage of development for the beginning teachers you are working with. Identify areas which you will need support with and/or those areas for which you will need to undertake some further research/development.
- Review the CPD resources in your setting/department with a specific focus on developing beginning teachers, including any texts or research to which you have access (RE:ONLINE - www.reonline.org.uk/ - may be a useful starting point if you want to explore RE-specific research and support the development of subject knowledge). Identify resources you are going to draw from in your mentoring and where there are any current gaps.

Summary and Key Points

This chapter has explored the relationship which may exist between the mentor and the beginning teacher and how this relationship may evolve and shift throughout the duration of the mentoring.

- The nature of the relationship between you and your beginning teachers is a fluid and dynamic one that affords opportunities for both to learn from each other.
- It may be helpful to consider the relationship between mentor and beginning teacher as one which transitions through four stages: model, coach, critical friend and co-enquirer.
- Effective mentoring should allow beginning teachers to learn from an experienced RE practitioner whilst still developing their knowledge, expertise, identity and agency as a teacher.
- Modelling, team planning, team teaching, video recordings of practice and practitioner-based enquiry are all suggested strategies to facilitate effective mentoring.

Further Resources

Gravells, J. and Wallace, S. (2017). *Mentoring: Getting it right in a week*. Critical Publishing.

This short and accessible book provides practical mentoring strategies in 'bite size' chunks. Suitable for those at all stages of mentoring who want to pick up hints and tips.

Hendrick, C. and Macpherson, R. (Ed.) (2017). *What Does This Look Like in The Classroom? Bridging The Gap Between Research and Practice*. John Catt Educational Ltd

Not related to mentoring but an accessible guide to current educational research regarding effective teaching and learning in the classroom. Suitable for those at all stages of mentoring who want to better explore research informed practice for the purpose of developing their mentorship and unpicking the 'why' from the 'what'.

References

Carter, A. (2015). *Carter Review of Initial Teacher Training (ITT)*. https://assets.publishing. service.gov.uk/government/uploads/system/uploads/attachment_data/file/399957/ Carter_Review.pdf

Department for Education (DfE). (2011). *The Teachers' Standards*. https://assets.publishing. service.gov.uk/government/uploads/system/uploads/attachment_data/file/1040274/ Teachers__Standards_Dec_2021.pdf

Department for Education (DfE). (2019). *Early Career Framework*. https://assets.publishing. service.gov.uk/government/uploads/system/uploads/attachment_data/file/978358/ Early-Career_Framework_April_2021.pdf

Education Endowment Foundation. (2021). *Teaching and Learning Toolkit*, [Online]. https:// educationendowmentfoundation.org.uk/education-evidence/teaching-learning-toolkit

Furlong, J. and Maynard, T. (1996). *The growth of professional knowledge: Mentoring student teachers*. Routledge.

Gravells, J. and Wallace, S. (2017). *Mentoring: Getting it right in a week*. Critical Publishing.

Hammerness, K. (2008). "If you don't know where you are going, any path will do": The role of teachers' visions in teachers' career paths. *The New Educator*, 4 (1), 1–22. https://doi. org/10.1080/15476880701829184

Hendrick, C. and Macpherson, R. (Eds.) (2017). *What does this look like in the classroom? Bridging The Gap Between Research and Practice*. John Catt Educational Ltd.

Izadina, M. (2015). A closer look at the role of mentor teachers in shaping preservice teachers' professional identity. *Teaching and Teacher Education*, 52, 1–10. https://doi.org/10.1016/j.tate.2015.08.003

Roberts, J. and Graham, S. (2008). Agency and conformity in school-based teacher training. *Teaching and Teacher Education*, 24(6), 1401–1412. https://doi.org/10.1016/j.tate.2008.01.003

4 Understanding yourself
Positionality and mentoring

Helen Bromley and Summan Rasib

Introduction

Positionality refers to a reflective understanding of your own starting point. As well as understanding your own worldview, for a religious education (RE) teacher, this may include acknowledging the academic background from which you have approached RE teaching, your own cultural and moral beliefs and your perspective with regard to the purpose and place of the subject within the curriculum. Some elements of your own positionality may be obvious to you, while others may be more unconscious; it may be complex, fluid and multi-dimensional. Bryan and Revell (2011) found that far from having neutral positions, teachers are a product of their own background, experiences, faith and education. It is important that both you and the beginning teacher with whom you are working are clear about your positionality and that beginning teachers have considered the extent to which they should reveal elements of this in the classroom. It is particularly important as many beginning teachers are of the social media generation where openness may be a cultural norm (van Manen, 2010). They will need support in this process and in thinking about how they would respond to the question often asked of RE teachers: 'What do you believe?'

This chapter is designed to give you the space to consider what your own positionality is and to think about how you share elements of this with your beginning teacher. It will also provide some guidance regarding how you may create opportunities for beginning teachers to identify their own positionality, become more reflective and develop a professional understanding of how much to share with their pupils.

By the end of this chapter you should:

- Be aware of your own positionality and the impact of this when working with beginning teachers.
- Have reflected on the place of your own personal worldviews in the classroom and the extent to which you should guide your beginning teacher to share their own position.
- Have considered how a teacher's own positionality may impact pedagogical and subject knowledge preferences.
- Have considered the impact of positionality when teaching about moral issues.

Worldview and positionality

Worldview is a term that has a variety of meanings and that is used in different ways (Chater and Donnellan, 2020). The report of the Commission on RE distinguishes between

DOI: 10.4324/9781003191087-5

institutional worldviews (which are shared among groups and may be embedded in institutions) and personal worldviews. The latter are described as "a person's way of understanding, experiencing and responding to the world", and it is noted that "a person's worldview is likely to influence and be influenced by their beliefs, values, behaviours, experiences, identities and commitments" (Commission on RE, 2018, p. 4). Given this, having clarity about your own worldview is significant for then being able to reflect on your positionality and the impact this has on your classroom practice. Flanagan summarises the advantages of engaging in reflection on this. She argues that worldview consciousness has a number of benefits, namely that it aids "greater 'self-illumination'; countering bias; enhancing knowledge and critical thinking; enriching dialogue; and developing an understanding of others" which can make us more effective RE teachers (Flanagan, 2019, p. 10). She also claims that our own prejudice and bias are likely to be unconscious but may surface in response to perceived threats which could produce negative responses (2019, p. 11). This means that, if a teacher is challenged in the classroom during a heated discussion, the unconscious element of their positionality may surface. Therefore, a high level of awareness and reflexivity is important so that a teacher can be in control of what they share and when. By becoming more 'worldview conscious' yourself, you may be better prepared to help your beginning teacher achieve the same whilst ensuring an understanding for themselves that worldviews may be differing and divergent. Task 4.1 offers a way of reflecting on your own worldview and, in time, a similar approach could be used to support your beginning teacher to do the same.

Task 4.1 Mentor reflection – Your personal worldview

Either read some of the accounts from the *Voices from Religion and* Worldviews section of the RE:ONLINE website or look at the personal reflections in the Theos Report on Worldviews (Cooling et al., 2020, p. 89 onwards). Both sources offer autobiographical reflections on individuals' worldviews and should stimulate your thinking so that you can respond to the following questions:

- If you were to create your own autobiographical reflection, what would it include?
- What has influenced and formed the worldview that you currently have?
- How present is your worldview in your classroom when you are teaching?
- How much of your own worldview perspective will share with your beginning teacher?

Understanding your own positionality

Having considered how you would define your worldview, it is useful to pause and reflect on how this impacts on your positionality in relation to your work in the classroom. There are likely to be elements of your worldview that are particularly pertinent to your role, shaping your thinking about the aims and purpose of RE and your pedagogical approach. For an RE teacher, reflecting on your personal perspective is likely to involve identifying your "personal beliefs, experiences of and attitudes to religions" (Jackson and Everington, 2017, p. 13). This may extend to include your personal approach to RE, your academic background, your moral and cultural viewpoints and your pedagogical preferences. Task 4.2 offers some questions you can reflect on for yourself to help you articulate your own position. In due course, you may choose to share your answers with your beginning teacher to engage them in a similar discussion.

Task 4.2 Mentor reflection - Your positionality

Reflect on your own teaching career and consider the following questions:

- How would you define your own positionality (your personal beliefs, experiences of and attitudes to religions)?
- How does this impact on your classroom practice?
- How does this influence your teaching style?
- Has this changed throughout your career?
- To what extent would you be comfortable informing your beginning teacher of your personal standpoint and how this impacts your delivery?

The impact of worldview and positionality on beginning teachers

It will be important in your work as a mentor that, having reflected on your own worldview, the way that this has influenced your own positionality and how it impacts on your classroom practice, you are willing and able to help beginning teachers consider and address some of the same questions for themselves. One way in which you might find that their positionality either consciously or unconsciously impacts their work in the classroom is in the perspective it gives them about the purpose of the subject. It is important they reflect on this as it is likely to influence the approach they take to planning and teaching in RE.

Dinham and Shaw (2015) consider the purpose of RE and argue that the subject has become too burdened with the job of ensuring community cohesion, a social function that should not be the task of RE alone. RE should be about the study of religions and beliefs as a basis for well-informed engagement with religion and belief encounters throughout life. They report that pupils are keen to learn about diversity and about a wide range of religious beliefs so that they understand "what people do in everyday lives" (Dinham and Shaw, 2015, p. 9). They found that teachers are concerned with the need to ensure depth in the knowledge they present in their lessons whilst also ensuring that pupils have space for a personal, spiritual and moral development. Therefore, teachers were occupied with the tension between the academic and personal purposes of RE. This is where your guidance will be important for your beginning teacher as they become aware of their position and the position of their pupils and begin to develop an understanding of how to balance this personal perspective with the development of academic understanding of religions and beliefs.

As a mentor, you can support this process by having important discussions with your beginning teacher about the context within which they are training. Beginning teachers will have a range of starting points and views about the purpose of their role, and this may be one of the first ways in which they are conscious of their personal position impacting their work in the classroom. This may also be made more complex by the school context in which they find themselves. Jackson and Everington (2017) consider a range of possible perspectives which highlight the diverse experiences trainee teachers may have and three examples are outlined in the following. Task 4.3 offers an opportunity to reflect on these examples to help you consider how you might approach conversations about the purpose of RE in your context with your beginning teacher.

- A beginning teacher may be in a faith school which is aligned with their own beliefs and where they consider their purpose to be vocational. In this situation, it is possible for a beginning teacher to confuse vocation and profession and struggle with the balance between commitment and neutrality as they develop their own understanding of the interaction between the two (Conroy, 2016).
- A beginning teacher may find themselves in a church school where many pupils in fact do not have a faith or where their faith perspective is different from that held by the school. For example, a Muslim teaching in a Church of England school may have to teach concepts of God such as the Trinity. Rather than being vocational, this teacher may consider the purpose of RE to ensure that worldviews are taught in an accurate way, even when these concepts may contrast with their own beliefs.
- Third, to take an example from Everington and Sikes (2001), consider the experience of an atheist who is struggling to reconcile personal anti-religious views with the role of an RE teacher who is able to represent religions in an impartial manner. In this case, with some support to reflect on his own perspective, this individual was able to identify that for him, the role of religious education was to combat prejudice and racism; focusing on this goal enabled him to overcome a profound concern that he was 'living a lie' as an atheist teacher of RE (Jackson and Everington, 2017).

Task 4.3 Helping beginning teachers explore their perspective on the purpose of RE

Prior to meeting with your beginning teacher reflect on the previous examples which outline a range of possible scenarios. Then consider the following:

- How would the three beginning teachers in the preceding examples fit into your department? Is it possible that any issues would arise?
- To ensure clarity about the approach taken by your department, when you first meet your beginning teacher how will you explain to them the ethos of your school and the approach taken to delivering the RE curriculum?
- What do you consider the purpose of RE to be? How you would articulate this for a beginning teacher?

In a meeting with your beginning teacher:

- Ask them to articulate for you what they consider to be the purpose of the subject.
- Ask them to reflect on and identify the ways in which this position has been shaped by their worldview and positionality.
- Discuss how this aligns with the approach taken in your department.

Having explored with your beginning teacher their motivation for teaching RE, it is useful for you both to think about how different academic backgrounds may influence pedagogical and curriculum choices. As a complex subject with a range of approaches you will have developed your own teaching style and preferred methods of delivery for teaching RE. This may have been influenced in part by your academic journey to teaching the subject. This is clear when we struggle to deliver material prepared by other teachers, without understanding the thought process behind their planning, and find ourselves out of our pedagogical comfort zone. The balanced RE approach (Chipperton et al., 2018) reminds us that RE may draw from the disciplines of theology, philosophy and social sciences. When mentoring beginning teachers, there may be times when it is clear which of these disciplines the teacher has come from. For example, a philosophy graduate may plan lessons using an approach which favours criticality and questioning, whereas the priorities and approaches of a theology graduate may differ. Encourage your beginning teacher to observe different members of the department teaching and discuss with them afterwards if they could see the emphasis on different lenses and whether this is in line with the different academic backgrounds of your colleagues. Another useful exercise may be to encourage your beginning teacher to use different lenses in their planning and discuss with them whether they are conscious of having a preferred approach and whether there is a benefit to having an increased awareness of this.

As well as impacting teaching styles, positionality can also influence curriculum choices. Flanagan (2019) argues our positionality may have a considerable impact on the curriculum content we select. As we consider what we put in and leave out of the curriculum, or what we emphasise, this may become clearer. Do we just choose the palatable elements of religion to teach and avoid the controversial? For example, do we choose to focus on what is good in religion, highlighting aspects of religious teaching, such as the 'golden rule', whilst failing to engage with more difficult debates about religious perspectives on sexuality or gender (Flanagan, 2019, p. 11)? If your beginning teacher has the opportunity to be involved in curriculum planning, encourage them to reflect on the choices we make about what to include. Explain to them the decisions you have made as a department and the rationale for these.

Sharing personal positions with pupils

Many beginning teachers have relatively recent experience of undertaking an academic study of religion or worldviews in a higher education (HE) setting and, on such courses, a level of neutrality is usually encouraged or even required. However, in the school setting our pupils often have a personal perspective on their learning which interacts with our own, and this can be even more apparent in a faith school. Therefore, beginning teachers can experience a contrast between the approach taken in schools and the neutral stance adopted in HE that they may have been used to as an undergraduate. As teachers they are occupying a liminal space between the world of childhood and adolescence, occupationally becoming separated from the adult world (Conroy, 2016). Further to this, many beginning teachers may be of the social media generation who may view intimacy and openness as "cultural norms, reinforced on a daily basis by reality TV shows, 'Facebook,' and 'Twitter'" (Everington, 2012, p. 394).

Sharing experiences can be seen as part of everyday life and where this is done effectively while maintaining proper professional distance, it can play a significant part in making RE real and relevant (Everington, 2012). As your beginning teacher is starting to develop their professional identity, if there are times when the personal and professional self cannot be separated, you may have an important role in guiding them to ensure that they do not abandon proper distances but that they consider what may be gained from being impartial rather than neutral in the classroom. As you work with them in co-planning and in your reflective discussions, encourage an understanding of the boundaries between the personal and the professional. Discuss with them the extent to which they plan to share elements of their own lives, encourage them to articulate reasons for these choices. Encourage them to consider the following questions: is what they are sharing age appropriate? How does it support the lesson? Is it more advantageous to share this information than to leave it out of their lesson? Task 4.4 suggests a way of opening up these conversations based on their observations of more experienced colleagues teaching.

Task 4.4 Using observation to consider positionality in the classroom

Arrange for your beginning teacher to observe you (or another host teacher) and ask them to consider the following questions:

- Did the teacher share their personal position with the pupils? If so, at what point of the lesson?
- Was the personal position shared before or after substantive content was taught?
- How has this enhanced or supported student understanding?
- What are the potential advantages and disadvantages of this?
- If the teacher's personal position was not clear, do you think enhanced the lesson or was this a missed opportunity?

Discuss your observations with your beginning teacher during your mentor meeting. Aim to help them understand the rationale for the choices that were made.

Benefits of sharing personal positions

Everington (2012) would suggest that rather than adopting a position of neutrality, where teachers' and pupils' views are set aside, a good teacher of RE should include personal viewpoints in their delivery. As a mentor, you may agree with this approach or may choose to keep your personal beliefs private. Whilst this may be different in faith schools, generally the extent to which the private is to be made public in the classroom is a professional choice for teachers. Therefore, having an awareness of possible benefits and drawbacks of sharing personal perspectives can help you to guide your beginning teacher. Teachers can be impartial without concealing their personal beliefs and many argue that this openness can create trustful teacher–pupil relationships. For example, a Muslim teacher may be able to answer questions honestly from their own perspective about arranged marriage, challenging misconceptions from pupils and increasing understanding of diversity. The same teacher answering questions about prayer and fasting may have a similar impact and lead to more productive pupil–teacher relationships than if they refuse to be drawn on their own personal experience. These conversations can bridge the gap between the life-worlds of pupils and religious material in textbooks. Revealing some of our personal perspectives may make RE real and relevant and encourage pupil engagement. It may also increase pupils' understanding of difficult concepts and of diversity. Everington illustrates the benefit of teachers using themselves as a resource to combat misconceptions: 'They thought all religious people were aliens until I told them how I celebrate Christmas the same way they do (Sikh trainee)' (Everington, 2012, p. 349). Beginning teachers will need support from their mentors to develop the skills to do this successfully to ensure that the personal examples are not the only thing that pupils remember. In lessons in which personal perspectives are shared, you may want to encourage your beginning teacher to plan a retrieval task which focuses on the substantive content taught so there is a balance in what they remember. You may also wish to use task 4.5 which suggests a way of working with your beginning teacher to help them think about making the personal professional.

Task 4.5 Reflecting on the place of positionality: benefits and drawbacks

Discuss with your beginning teacher the following questions in a mentor meeting:

- When is it appropriate to bring your own views into the classroom?
- Could this help pupils' understanding of the difference between religion and culture?
- How might this help tackle misconceptions?

Following this discussion, arrange to observe your beginning teacher in a lesson in which they plan to share personal examples or some aspect of their personal perspective. In the conversation that follows the observation, consider the following:

- How comfortable/confident was the beginning teacher in sharing personal examples?
- In what ways did the decision to approach the lesson in this way support the learning?
- Where there any drawbacks? Would the beginning teacher do things differently next time?
- How did they ensure that the personal examples were not the only thing that the pupils remembered? What strategies were used to keep the focus on the content of the lesson?

Another potential benefit of sharing personal positions is in the opportunity this presents to explore the relationship between religion and culture. At times, some beginning teachers who have a faith may find it difficult to differentiate between which parts of their own beliefs are religion and which are culture or tradition. They may believe that their individual faith perspective is representative of their faith as a whole. Jackson and Everington (2017) illustrate this highlighting that a Christian teacher might unconsciously present a particular aspect of Christian teaching as "the accepted meaning" (p. 14) rather than as one interpretation. For example, teacher who themselves had a Roman Catholic education might not realise that they have developed classroom activities that assume all pupils have a belief in God. However, as they develop as a teacher and share their personal perspectives when appropriate, they may find that this creates an opportunity for an increased understanding of their own beliefs and of the difference between religion and culture which, when shared with pupils, can enhance understanding. For example, a Muslim teacher teaching the Qur'an may develop an academic understanding of their own religious text which may challenge them to consider which parts of their own worldview come from their sacred text and which are cultural. As you observe and co-plan with your beginning teacher, ensure you encourage rigour in their subject knowledge. Consider planning with them the personal examples they will use in advance so you can discuss the extent to which these may have a personal, cultural context. When they draw on anecdotal examples ad hoc in lessons, allow time to encourage reflection on the place of these and again the extent to which they are cultural or religious.

Encouraging your beginning teacher to share their personal perspective may also help them model what Ofsted calls 'personal knowledge' in RE. According to Ofsted, personal knowledge is where pupils "build an awareness of their own presuppositions and values about the religious and non-religious traditions they study" (Ofsted, 2021). Allowing space for this may also develop skills in the beginning teacher to encourage their pupils to have an attitude of critical enquiry, in evaluating sources of information as they consider the positions of others (Jackson and Everington, 2017). Use Task 4.6 to help you to unpack the concept of 'personal knowledge' with your beginning teacher.

Task 4.6 Planning task – *Nobody Stands Nowhere*

- Watch the short, animated film *Nobody Stands Nowhere* (Downe, 2021) with your beginning teacher (see Further Resources).
- After watching the film, consider with them the definition of *personal knowledge* given earlier. What are the presuppositions and values that they bring to their study of religion?
- Discuss how your beginning teacher might plan a lesson using this resource to encourage reflexivity and the development of personal knowledge in their pupils.

Drawbacks of sharing personal positions

It may be the case that an over-reliance on personal perspectives could reduce the rigour of the content taught. Furedi (2010) reminds us that we must not be overly concerned with the 'pedagogy of motivation'. Focusing principally on motivating students and harnessing their interest may lead us to focus too much on over-simplification through just using life knowledge (Everington, 2012, p. 351). Similarly, Acevedo et al. (2015) write about the danger of a narcissistic approach to education which systematically privileges the learner's subjectivities, experiences and various self-positionings as sources of knowledge over academic standards which they claim may lead to learners putting forward positions which they are unable to support using academic content. As suggested earlier, you might encourage beginning teachers to reflect on the purpose of their use of personal knowledge to avoid this pitfall. You may find that discussions about positionality become more relevant once good classroom relationships and routines are established. Where trainees are considering adding personal perspectives to lessons before good relationships are established with pupils, ensure that you have discussed this with them in your mentor meetings.

Beginning teachers should also be provided with opportunities to reflect on the dangers of encouraging an unprofessional relationship in which teacher or pupil sharing is of a personal nature or involves manipulation by either party. A skilled teacher will grow to understand the difference between impartiality and neutrality. Impartiality involves organising teaching and learning without discrimination, allowing for freedom of expression within limits (Jackson and Everington, 2017, p. 10). As mentioned before, the world of social media may encourage more sharing of the personal than is beneficial in their role as teacher of RE. Another concern is that they may hold beliefs that are difficult for their pupils to process so they may need to consider in advance how they will present or defend their own viewpoints should pupils question them or whether they would prefer to detach themselves from certain discussions.

Task 4.7 provides a useful context for discussing this with your beginning teacher. This is based on the school experience in which a beginning teacher was teaching the emotive concept of hell in Islam and was not prepared for the impact her own commitment to her religion may have on her pupils.

Task 4.7 Case study

Read the following scenario and consider the questions that follow:

Aneeka has taught a General Certificate of Secondary Education (GCSE) lesson on the Muslim concepts of heaven and hell. Her pupils were particularly interested in Qur'anic descriptions of the afterlife, particularly the description of hell as a burning fire. However, some pupils became distressed by this and asked Aneeka if she believed this was true. Aneeka informed students that, as a Muslim, she did. This left pupils feeling a little unsettled and seeking reassurance that this alarming image of hell is not real.

- What questions you might ask Aneeka to encourage her to reflect on this lesson?
- Considering Aneeka's own positionality, what could she have done differently?
- Would the experience of teaching this lesson have been different for someone holding a different worldview?

Share this scenario with your beginning teacher. In your discussion, ask them to consider whether there was anything Aneeka could have done differently. They should also be encouraged to reflect on whether their own positionality or worldview could ever lead them to a similar situation.

Moral issues in the classroom

Perhaps the most obvious area where beginning teachers may need support in reflecting on their own positionality and the purpose of sharing this in the classroom is when delivering material related to moral issues. Classroom discussions may provoke strong personal reactions from pupils and the need for consideration of arguments from all sides. This can be more complex in a faith school where emphasising specific perspectives may be encouraged. Here the teacher has the difficult task of doing this in a way which is sensitive to the needs of the faith community and to the variety of perspectives held by pupils. However, beginning teachers in any setting may need support in considering the place of their own perspective and whether they choose to be neutral or impartial in class discussions. They may need support in reflecting on the framework within which their own moral views are formed and recognising that this may be a product of their worldview rather than being a norm. Support of your beginning teacher is important to ensure they plan ahead to avoid these difficult moments in delivering moral issues content. To structure this support, you might try some of the following approaches:

- Identify topics that address moral questions with your beginning teacher in advance and consider which aspects may be sensitive.
- Encourage them to examine what their place may be in these discussions as well as sharing with them decisions you have made when teaching these topics.
- Ask them to consider and plan the questions they will ask pupils and focus particularly on the wording of these questions.
- Ensure they understand the context of the class they are teaching so they are aware of any topics which may trigger an emotional response in their pupils, as well as encouraging them to consider this for themselves.
- Invite them to consider the answers pupils may give to these questions and discuss with them how they may respond to ensure balanced discussion.

The final tasks in this chapter – Tasks 4.8 and 4.9 – present an opportunity to use some of the previous suggestions as you support your beginning teacher to deliver lessons that focus on moral issues.

Task 4.8 Joint observation

Set up a joint observation during which you and your beginning teacher both observe a colleague teaching about moral issues. Focus on the extent to which they share their position with their pupils. You could both use the following questions as prompts:

- Did the teacher share their own perspective on the issue?
- How did the teacher allow lots of perspectives to be heard?
- Did the lesson explore the ways in which pupils' own worldviews will impact their perspective?
- Were there any difficult moments? If so, how did the teacher diffuse them?

   Afterwards, in addition to considering your observations in relation to the preceding questions, consider together the type of language used by the teacher to ensure their own positionality did not influence the views of their pupils. If you can, schedule some time for you both to talk to the class teacher to get their perspective on your observations.

Task 4.9 Co-planning lesson based on a moral issue

- Work with your beginning teacher to plan a lesson focusing on a moral issue that allows pupils to explore their personal knowledge.
- Discuss during this process, how this lesson may be structured to allow pupils to move from their own viewpoint to understanding the viewpoints of others.
- Discuss with your beginning teacher the extent to which they plan to remain impartial in the delivery of this lesson and how their plan and resources will allow them to do this.

Summary and key points

This chapter has encouraged you to identify and articulate your own worldview and positionality. It is hoped that this will enable you to support your beginning teacher as they consider this for themselves and explore the impact this might have on their teaching.

- Take the time to consider your own position with respect to your worldview, approach to RE, academic background and moral and cultural influences and decide how much of this you will share with your beginning teacher.
- Encourage reflexivity in your beginning teacher so they can become aware of their own worldview and positionality and the role these may play in their approach to teaching.
- Support your beginning teacher in developing their own professional identity as they decide how much of their personal perspective should enter their classroom.
- Encourage a high level of self-illumination as you work with your beginning teacher in their planning and teaching so they can develop a clear understanding of how their positionality may impact their practice.

- Think about how you can support a beginning teacher to prepare lessons that address moral issues so that they can consider their own perspective and how this might impact on their approach to the lesson.

Further resources

Downe, E. (2021). *Nobody Stands Nowhere*. Theos Think Tank. https://www.reonline.org.uk/resources/telling-my-worldview-story/

This is a short video that you could encourage your beginning teacher to watch so they consider where they 'stand' as they think about their own positionality. It is also a useful resource they could consider using with pupils as they work on how to develop reflexivity in their classroom.

Cooling, T., Bowie, B., and Panjwani, F. (2020). *Worldviews in Religious Education*. Theos. https://www.theosthinktank.co.uk/cmsfiles/Worldview-in-Religious-Education---FINAL-PDF-merged.pdf

The personal reflections section in this report is useful for exploring responses from a diverse range of worldviews.

Spencer, N. (Host). (2021, July 6). What does "being spiritual" actually mean? In conversation with Rowan Williams (No. 16) [Audio podcast episode]. In *Reading Our Times*. Theos Think Tank – www.theosthinktank.co.uk/comment/2021/06/28/what-can-we-learn-from-the-east

This podcast picks up some of the themes explored in this chapter about the importance of reflecting in individual perspectives and considering what it may mean to different individuals to be spiritual.

Voices from Religions and Worldviews – www.reonline.org.uk/resources/voices-from-religion-and-worldviews/

This is a collection of responses to questions from a diverse range of worldviews. Beginning teachers could engage with this resource to improve their understanding of the worldviews of others and to consider how they may respond to these questions themselves.

References

Acevedo, S., Aho, M., Cela, E., Chao, J., Garcia-Gonzales, I., MacLeod, A., Moutray, C., and Olague, C. (2015). Positionality as Knowledge: From Pedagogy to Praxis. *Integral Review*, 11(1), 28–46.

Addai-Mununkum, R. (2018). Teacher Identity, Positionality and (Mis) Representation of Religion in the Ghanaian School Contexts: Insider/Outsider Case Study Perspectives. *American Journal of Qualitative Research*, 2(2), 40–59.

Bryan, H. and Revell, L. (2011). Performativity, Faith and Professional Identity: Student Religious Education Teachers and the Ambiguities of Objectivity. *British Journal of Educational Studies*, 59(4), 403–419. https://doi.org/10.1080/00071005.2011.602328

Chater, M. and Donnellan, L. (2020). What Do We Mean By Worldviews? In Chater, M. (Ed.), *Reforming Religious Education: Power and Knowledge in a Worldviews Curriculum* (pp. 115–130). John Catt Educational Ltd.

Chipperton, J., Georgiou, G., Seymour, O., and Wright, K. (2018). *Key Principles of a Balanced Curriculum in RE*. The Church of England Education Office. https://www.churchofengland.

org/sites/default/files/2018-03/Key%20principles%20of%20a%20balanced%20 curriculum%20in%20RE_0.pdf

Conroy, J. (2016). Religious Education and Religious Literacy – A Professional Aspiration? *British Journal of Religious Education*, 38(2), 163–176. https://doi.org/10.1080/01416200. 2016.1139891

Cooling, T., Bowie, B., and Panjwani, F. (2020). *Worldviews in Religious Education*. Theos. https://www.theosthinktank.co.uk/cmsfiles/Worldview-in-Religious-Education---FINAL-PDF-merged.pdf

Commission on Religious Education. (2018). *Religion and Worldviews: The Way Forward. A National Plan for RE*. Religious Education Council of England and Wales.

Dinham, A. and Shaw, M. (2015). *RE for REal: The Future of Teaching and Learning about Religion and Belie*f. Goldsmiths, University of London.

Downe, E. (2021). *Nobody Stands Nowhere*. Theos Think Tank. https://www.reonline.org.uk/ resources/telling-my-worldview-story/

Everington, J. (2007). Freedom and Direction in Religious Education. The Case of English Trainee Teachers and Learning from Religion. In Bakker, C. and Heimbrock, H. (Eds.), *Researching RE Teachers. RE Teachers as Researchers* (pp. 111–124). Waxmann.

Everington, J. (2012). 'We're All in This Together, the Kids and Me': Beginning Teachers' Use of Their Personal Life Knowledge in the Religious Education Classroom. *Journal of Beliefs & Values*, 33(3), 343–355. https://doi.org/10.1080/13617672.2012.732815

Everington, J. and Sikes, P. (2001). "I Want to Change the World": The Beginning RE Teacher, the Reduction of Prejudice and the Pursuit of Intercultural Understanding and Respect. In Heimbrock, H., Scheilke, C., and Schreiner, P. (Eds.), *Towards Religious Competence: Diversity as a Challenge for Education in Europe* (pp. 180–203). Lit Verlag.

Flanagan, R. (2019). Implementing a Ricoeurian Lens to Examine the Impact of Individuals' Worldviews on Subject Content Knowledge in RE in England: A Theoretical Proposition. *British Journal of Religious Education*, 43(4), 472–486. https://doi.org/10.1080/01416200. 2019.1674779

Furedi, F. (2010). *Wasted: Why Education Isn't Educating*. Continuum.

Jackson, R. and Everington, J. (2017). Teaching Inclusive Religious Education Impartially: An English Perspective. *British Journal of Religious Education*, 39(1), 7–24. https://doi.org/ 10.1080/01416200.2016.1165184

McCain, N. (2017). Religious Education as a Safe Space for Discussing Unsafe Ideas. In Castelli, M. and Chater, M. (Eds.), *We Need to Talk about Religious Education* (pp. 169–185). Jessica Kinsley Publishers.

Ofsted. (2021). *Research Review Series: Religious Education*. https://www.gov.uk/government/ publications/research-review-series-religious-education

Spencer, N. (Host). (2021, July 6). What does "being spiritual" actually mean? In conversation with Rowan Williams (No.16) [Audio podcast episode]. In *Reading Our Times*. Theos Think Tank. https://www.theosthinktank.co.uk/comment/2021/06/28/what-can-we-learn-from-the-east

Van Manen, M. (2010). The Pedagogy of Momus Technologies: Facebook, Privacy, and Online Intimacy. *Qualitative Health Research*, 20(8), 1023–1032. https://doi.org/10.1177/10497 32310364990

5 A skills audit
Your knowledge, skills and understanding as a mentor

Helen Sheehan

Introduction

Although taking on a mentoring role can add to an already heavy workload, it can also be a joy and a great opportunity for continuing professional development (CPD). The first four chapters of this book have focused on you as a mentor, encouraging you to think about the nature of the role, the approaches you can take and how it might change over time. Consideration has also been given you to as a mentor of beginning religious education (RE) teachers. This has focused on making the implicit, explicit, drawing on your own knowledge and expertise to support a beginning teacher so that skills and knowledge that are instinctive to you can be developed and become second nature to them too. You have also been invited to reflect on questions around positionality and your worldview to help you consider how this might impact your mentoring and how you might support a beginning RE teacher to reflect on the same issues.

This chapter offers an audit to help as you step into or develop the mentoring role. For some, this will be a first opportunity to engage in this work, others will have lots of experience on which to draw and be looking to develop their practice, and some may be returning to the role after time away and looking to refresh their thinking and skills. The chapter starts by reviewing the content already covered in Chapters 1 to 4 and gives you an opportunity to think about your level of confidence in relation to the ideas explored there. Following on from this the remaining sections of the chapter are designed to help you think about the next steps in your own professional development, whatever your level of experience.

By the end of this chapter, you should:

- Have audited your knowledge and responses to the content covered in Chapters 1 to 4.
- Have reflected on whether you consider yourself to be a 'beginning mentor', or a mentor with experience who is looking for ways to develop your knowledge and skills.
- Considered the focus of your own 'next steps' to develop your mentoring skills.

Mentoring in RE: An audit

A first step in considering your level of expertise in mentoring is to consider your confidence in relation to the content of the first four chapters of this book. Table 5.1 picks up on aspects of mentoring explored in Chapters 1 to 4 and asks you a series of questions based on this. Task 5.1 invites you to respond to these questions and use them to both establish your level of preparedness and identify your strengths and areas for development.

DOI: 10.4324/9781003191087-6

Table 5.1 Mentoring in RE Audit

Aspect of Mentoring in RE	Mentor Skills	Fully Prepared	Mostly Prepared	Need to Learn More
Models of mentoring	Do you have a clear idea about how you define mentoring and how you see your role? Can you identify different approaches to mentoring that might be adopted at different points in a beginning teacher's journey? Have you considered how the context that you work in impacts on your role as a mentor? Are you conscious of different models of mentoring and how your approach fits within them?			
Subject-specific mentoring in RE	Have you identified your strengths as a mentor (subject knowledge, experience, support from colleagues, etc.) and considered how you might bring these to the role? Have you considered your own areas for development as an RE mentor (e.g. in relation to experience, subject knowledge, etc.) and identified strategies you might use to mitigate these? Can you articulate the vision for RE that is shared by your department? Have you reflected on how you handle conflict and/ or differences of opinion in relation to the purpose of RE? Are you familiar with resources that you could use with a beginning teacher to develop their substantive subject knowledge in RE? Do you feel confident in discussing current debates in RE? Can you identify the RE-specific issues in more generic aspects of teaching and learning (e.g. disciplinary literacy, adaptive teaching, etc.)?			
The changing nature of the mentor– beginning teacher relationship: from modelling to co-enquirers	Have you reflected on your own experiences of being mentored and considered how you might use your experiences in the role? Have you had experience mentoring before that has allowed you to experience being a model, coach, critical friend and co-enquirer for another professional? Can you 'unpack' your own teaching to identify for a beginning teacher the routines that you follow unconsciously (e.g. organising your workload, managing transitions, giving clear instructions)? Are you aware of any habits in your own teaching that you do not want a beginning teacher to emulate? Can you identify the classroom practices that your beginning teaching must adopt?			

(continued)

Table 5.1 Cont.

Aspect of Mentoring in RE	Mentor Skills	Fully Prepared	Mostly Prepared	Need to Learn More
	Have you thought about the practicalities of the mentoring role (e.g. when and how you will set aside time for a weekly meeting)?			
	Do you have prior experience with setting targets for others? Are you confident in setting subject-specific targets?			
	Are you confident in encouraging your beginning teacher to engage with research to help inform and develop their classroom practice?			
Understanding yourself: Your positionality as a mentor	Can you confidently articulate your own worldview and how this impacts on your classroom practice?			
	Have you worked with colleagues whose worldview is different to your own? If so, can you use this experience to prepare to be a mentor?			
	Do you feel able to help a beginning teacher to reflect on their own worldview and develop their ability to articulate this?			
	Are you confident that you can help a beginning teacher see how their worldview might impact their classroom practice and support them to recognise this?			
	Have you co-planned lessons before? Are you confident in your ability to model the thinking that underpins your planning for a beginning teacher?			

Task 5.1 Auditing your knowledge and skills

Having read the first four chapters of the book, consider your responses to the questions in Table 5.1. Are you fully prepared, mostly prepared, or do you need to learn more?

As you look back at the completed table, consider where the majority of your responses lie. Does this reflect how you feel about your knowledge and skills as a mentor?

Research indicates that one of the ways in which teachers benefit from taking on a mentoring role is through the opportunity to engage in self-reflection or critical reflection on their own practice (Hobson et al., 2019). To support deeper reflection on your responses in Task 5.1, Task 5.2 encourages you to produce answers to some of the questions to help you identify your own areas for development.

Task 5.2 Mentoring journal

To help you engage with self- or critical reflection, start a mentoring journal which you can use throughout your time as a mentor to record your own reflections and ideas as you develop your skills. As you progress through the period when you are working with your beginning teacher you may write reflections, make notes of resources or research that you come across which could be useful in your work with them or write down tasks you come across in this book which you intend to use. It may also be an appropriate place to record your own thoughts and reflections following your weekly meetings.

   Begin your journal by producing written responses to some of the questions in Table 5.1. Pick at least one question from each of the four sections which will generate responses that you think might be particularly helpful as you start to work with your beginning teacher. For example, ask yourself:

- How will the context in which I work impact my role as a mentor?
- What is the vision for RE that is shared by our department? Can I easily articulate this for a beginning teacher?
- What are my potential areas for development as a mentor?
- How will I bring my own experiences of being mentored to the role?
- How do I articulate my worldview, and can I identify how this impacts on my classroom practice?

It is unlikely that anyone feels fully prepared in relation to all aspects of their readiness to take on a mentoring role. Even very experienced mentors are likely to be conscious that there are always new ideas and research that are impacting on classroom practice, and they may be reflecting on how to draw on this when working with beginning teachers. However, there will be those who are about to mentor a beginning RE teacher for the first time and have more immediate concerns about how to help beginning teachers plan lessons and about what they should say in post-observation discussions. The rest of this chapter focuses on how you might seek to develop your skills, whatever your level of experience.

Developing the skills of new mentors

As explored in Chapter 3, for new mentors a good starting point would be to consider carefully what a beginning RE teacher needs at each stage in their development so that you can think about the difference between supporting an initial teacher education (ITE) student and someone in the early years of their career. To do this effectively, it is important that you speak to your beginning teacher about their prior knowledge and experience so that, from the outset, you have a clear understanding of the kind of support they will need from you. Task 5.3 suggests a way that you might approach this conversation.

Task 5.3 Establishing priorities

In your first meeting with your beginning teacher gather answers to the following questions:

- What prior experience do they have in the classroom?
- Do they have any other experience that is relevant to teaching (e.g., experience as a youth worker or a previous role that involved training others)?
- What are the areas of strength and weakness within their subject knowledge? What help do they feel they need to address the weaknesses? Would they be willing to share expertise in areas of strength?
- At this stage do they have any understanding of wider debates in RE?
- Are they able to articulate their own worldview and positionality in relation to the RE curriculum?

Having used an early conversation to establish your starting point, the next step might be to focus on practicalities. It is likely that you have been asked to take on a mentoring role because of your skills in the classroom but, as a mentor, you now need to think about how to make the implicit, explicit; you need to 'unpack' the things that you do unconsciously to help a beginning teacher understand the processes involved in teaching RE. Essentially you need to learn how to 'think aloud' (Feiman-Nemser, 1998). This may mean ensuring that you can articulate curriculum decisions that have already been made, but it will also mean being able to talk the beginning teacher through the process of lesson planning, thinking carefully about how you manage the transition from you as the class teacher to them as the class teacher and considering how you approach observations and post-observation discussions.

If these are the areas that are currently the focus of your attention, Task 5.4 suggests how you might start to address this.

Task 5.4 Dealing with practicalities

Set aside some time to read Chapters 11 to 14 of this book. These chapters focus on lesson planning, lesson delivery, observations and post-observation discussion in the context of teaching RE. You may wish to focus on just one or two of these.

In light of the needs of your beginning teacher (as identified in Task 5.3) decide on the opportunities or support you will put in place for them in the first few weeks. For example:

- How will you help an ITE student plan their first lessons? What resources will you give them? Will you need to do some co-planning to model the process? What will be the nature of your early observations?
- With a qualified early-career teacher how soon will you go and observe them teaching? Will this be the first step (so that you can assess their needs and engage in target setting), or will you do some co-planning with them in advance of this?

Another potential practicality is ensuring that the beginning teacher has a good understanding of your school, its ethos and its systems. Any mentor needs to consider this, but if you are teaching in a faith school, you may wish to read Chapter 8 before you start working with your beginning teacher. This chapter highlights some of the challenges beginning teachers might experience in such a context, and you may wish to think this through in advance to support their induction into your school and RE department.

Focusing on religious education

If you have dealt with key practical issues and are looking to develop your skills further, it may be that exploring different models (Chapter 1) or stages (Chapter 3) in mentoring has been helpful to you. Being more conscious about what you are doing and why it might be effective can give a clearer sense of purpose to your role as a mentor.

Having developed confidence in supporting beginning teachers with their planning, conducting observations, and engaging in post-observation discussion and target setting, a next step might be to focus more clearly on what it means to mentor specifically in the context of RE. This could involve developing your mentoring practice to ensure that support with planning and post-lesson discussion specifically focus on subject-specific issues, ensuring that questions of pedagogy and lesson content are explored as well as the more generic 'craft' aspects of teaching. This might also mean ensuring that conversations are set into a broader context so that the beginning teacher fully understands the curriculum content and sequencing, and the external factors and research that have influenced curriculum design and how this might impact their own planning and teaching. Task 5.5 helps you think about how you might achieve this.

Task 5.5 Making your mentoring RE-specific

Revisit Chapter 2 and then read Chapters 6, 7 and 9. These chapters consider how to support a beginning teacher as they navigate the complexities of teaching religion and worldviews and support you in reflecting on how you conceptualise and present knowledge in your own teaching.

Look through the tasks in those chapters and, based on the needs of your beginning teacher, identify some tasks you could complete with them that will help ensure that the focus of your conversations is RE-specific. Make a note of these in your mentoring journal.

When engaging with RE-specific issues another area you will need to consider is that of subject knowledge. You may be working with a beginning teacher who is being expected to audit the development of their subject knowledge (this is likely to be the case if you are working with a trainee on an initial teacher education programme). However, every RE teacher has gaps in their knowledge or areas in which they would like to improve their knowledge. Chapter 10 specifically considers this, and you should use this chapter to help you reflect on how you can offer support to a beginning RE teacher as they address this.

Subject knowledge can become particularly important when you are supporting a beginning teacher as they work with examination classes. Gaining this experience can be problematic for beginning teachers in RE; not all schools have lots of examination groups, and the pressure to ensure the best possible results for all pupils means that taking on responsibility for these classes can put a lot of pressure on both the beginning teacher and the mentor who is supporting them. Therefore, a useful 'next step' might be to think about this more explicitly and reflect on how supporting beginning teachers in their work with examination classes might be different to supporting beginning teachers working at Key Stage 3. Chapter 15 offers guidance with this; if your beginning teacher has GCSE or A level groups on their timetable you may wish to read this chapter before they take on the classes so that you can think in detail about how you want them to prepare for this responsibility.

Developing the skills of experienced mentors

Experienced mentors are likely to have encountered lots of possible scenarios, both good and bad, in their time in the role. You may be in a position in which you are not only confident in supporting beginning teachers with their planning and delivery and in observing lessons, but you are also able to help them understand how their lessons sit in the broader context of the curriculum, link to the aims and purpose of the subject and can develop disciplinary as well as substantive knowledge. In addition to this, you may also have developed a great deal of skill in supporting beginning teachers as individuals through the ups and downs of their early classroom experiences. The value of this is not to be underestimated; this experience gives mentors good instincts when it comes to dealing with problematic or challenging situations or when pushing a good beginning teacher to develop their skills further.

However, even experienced mentors want to further their knowledge (perhaps particularly in relation to educational research) and develop their skills. Experience can give you the confidence to try out new strategies and approaches in your mentoring practice. For example, when you reflect you may realise that, in post-observation discussions, you generally lead the discussion and do most of the talking! If this is the case the opportunity to explore further approaches like educative or ONSIDE mentoring (see Chapter 14) may be welcome as an opportunity to try and do things in a new way.

There may also be aspects of your own practice that you are seeking to develop and find that sharing your experiences of this with a beginning teacher can be a valuable learning opportunity for them. For example, if you are making changes to your curriculum, rather than simply sharing outcomes, discussing your developing ideas with the beginning teacher can effectively model the thought processes that underpin curriculum design. Alternatively, you may be seeking to develop a particular aspect of your own pedagogical approach. Sharing this with a beginning teacher and seeking to develop this in their own practice can benefit you both. For example, Chapter 16 demonstrates how a particular aspect of effective RE teaching - in this case teaching controversial issues - can be considered on its own terms with the intention of developing confidence in a particular aspect of classroom practice. This may not be a particular area of focus for you, but this chapter exemplifies how a particular aspect of pedagogy can be examined and then explored in detail with a beginning teacher. Consider whether you currently have a focus for the development of your own teaching practice that could usefully be shared with a beginning teacher.

It may also be the case that an experienced mentor continues to take on the role because they have a particular interest in professional development and supporting less experienced colleagues. As already noted in Chapter 2, it may be that you wish to develop this aspect of your work further and engage in CPD or with educational research to explore mentoring or a particular aspect of RE in greater detail. Chapter 17 suggests different ways in which you might do this and support a beginning teacher to engage in a similar way (e.g. through further study, wider reading, engagement with websites or podcasts, etc.). It is worth taking some time to consider why you are a mentor and what you get out of the role to help you reflect on whether it would be helpful for you to engage in CPD or current research to support this aspect of your work. Tasks 5.6 allows you to reflect on this for yourself.

Task 5.6 Next steps in mentoring

Chapter 17 includes lots of suggested CPD opportunities and identifies ways to engage in more depth with the wider subject community and recent research.

- Read through this chapter and make a list of resources, research or CPD opportunities that you would like to follow up on.
- Consider how you might make use of this list. Can some aspect of it be incorporated into your own professional development targets? Are some of them things that can be explored with your beginning teacher? Is there anything that you wish to pursue, with the sole intention of developing your own knowledge and understanding further?

Mentoring as professional development

Even though it is likely that taking on a mentoring role will add to your already considerable workload, it is an opportunity for you to develop your own practice, both as a teacher and as a mentor. There is evidence to indicate that the role has a positive impact on both personal and professional development, giving mentors the opportunity to gain new ideas and perspectives and, as a result, develop their own teaching (Hobson et al., 2019). In their research, Walters, Robinson and Walters (2019) noted three ways in which the role impacted on mentors personally:

- Teaching identity – mentoring required mentors to consider who they were as teachers.
- Teaching practice – mentoring presented opportunities for mentors to reflect on their own classroom practice.
- Professional development – mentors found that the opportunity for collaborative working and ongoing discussion about teaching and learning was not only valuable for their mentees, but it also provided them with a professional development opportunity.

As you continue your mentoring journey hold these potential benefits in mind. Continue to reflect on how you see yourself as a teacher and mentor (and whether this changes in any way). Also note any ways in which your own teaching is impacted by your regular conversations about teaching and learning in RE and identify any benefits or positive outcomes of the opportunities you have for collaborative working. It is important that you can recognise how being a mentor is developing you personally and professionally whilst you, in turn, are supporting the professional development of beginning RE teachers.

Summary and key points

You should take time to consider yourself in the mentoring role. The provided audit will help you reflect on the skills and knowledge that you currently have and those you need to develop to support beginning RE teachers, but you should also think about what you might gain from taking on the role.

- Consider what you understand the role of a mentor to be, and if it would help you, explore further some of the definitions and ideas explored in the literature.
- Whatever your level of experience, it is important to reflect on how you want to develop your knowledge and skills for mentoring beginning RE teachers.
- New mentors may feel it most helpful to focus on the practical aspects of mentoring as they learn how to make the implicit, explicit through sharing their thought processes with beginning teachers.
- As mentors develop their skills, they should reflect on what it means to be a mentor of beginning RE teachers and how they can develop beginning teachers as subject specialists.
- Experienced mentors can build on their extensive skill set by exploring new models of mentoring and focusing on the development of RE-specific pedagogical knowledge and research.
- It is important that mentors are aware of the wider support that is available for both them and beginning teachers.

Further resources

Chater, M. (Ed.) (2020). *Reforming Religious Education: Power and Knowledge in a Worldviews Curriculum*. John Catt Educational Ltd.

This is an example of an RE-specific text which might be of value if you are keen to develop the support you offer a beginning teacher in thinking about wider issues in the RE curriculum. There is also a supporting blog site (https://reformingre.wordpress.com/); some posts model RE teachers 'thinking aloud' as they share the rationale behind their own curriculum design.

Hughes, H. (2021). *Mentoring in Schools: How to Become an Expert Colleague Is an All-Encompassing Guide to Becoming a Valued in-school Mentor*. Crown House Publishing.

If you are a new mentor, it may be helpful to look at a general text designed to support mentors in their role. This book is one such example, written for mentors in England to align with the Core Content Framework and Early Career framework. If you are working outside England, you may wish to look for something similar aligned to your own context.

References

Chater, M. (Ed.). (2020). *Reforming Religious Education: Power and Knowledge in a Worldviews Curriculum*. John Catt Educational Ltd.

Feiman-Nemser, S. (1998). Teachers as teacher educators. *European Journal of Teacher Education*, 21(1), 63–74. https://doi.org/10.1080/0261976980210107

Hobson, A., Ashby, P., Malderez, A., & Tomlinson, P. (2009). Mentoring beginning teachers: What we know and what we don't. *Teaching and Teacher Education*, 25(1), 207–216. https://doi.org/10.1016/j.tate.2008.09.001

Hughes, H. (2021). *Mentoring in Schools: How to Become an Expert Colleague Is an All-Encompassing Guide to Becoming a Valued In-School Mentor*. Crown House Publishing.

Walters, W., Robinson, D., & Walters, J. (2020). Mentoring as meaningful professional development: The influence of mentoring on in-service teachers' identity and practice. *International Journal of Mentoring and Coaching in Education*, 9(1), 21–36. https://doi.org/10.1108/IJMCE-01-2019-0005

SECTION 2
The complex picture
Religious education and worldviews

6 What Are We Doing and How Do We Do It?

A Skills and Knowledge Audit for a Multidisciplinary Study

Kate Christopher

Introduction

Beginning teachers will possess different degrees of subject knowledge regarding religions and worldviews and will have had different experiences of religious education (RE). This chapter proposes that an initial conversation about the aims of the subject can provide a baseline for auditing both subject knowledge and teaching approaches. Confident teaching develops over time but starts with a clear vision. RE carries both academic aims and social, ethical and personal aims. Beginning teachers need to know what knowledge and skills pupils are progressing in, and what overall purpose lies behind the planning. Far from being abstractions, by initially considering the various aims of RE, how they differ and the knowledge and skills to arise from these aims, a baseline of clarity can be provided on which a coherent curriculum progression can be built over time.

This chapter also introduces thinking around the idea of a multidisciplinary approach to religion and worldviews for you to discuss with your beginning teacher. A consideration of the benefits for teaching and learning of a multidisciplinary approach further consolidates thinking around aims and outcomes. An audit should allow many opportunities to address, through examples, the fundamental question, what are we doing and how do we do it? Answers to this question provide a clear vision upon which knowledge and skills can be built.

At the end of this chapter, you will be able to:

- Support beginning teachers in identifying the difference between academic and personal aims.
- Enable beginning teachers to envisage how aims can be met through choice of substantive knowledge and learning activities.
- Help beginning teachers to articulate what sort of teaching input will result in what sort of pupil outcomes.
- Work with beginning teachers to identify theological, philosophical, ethical and historical thinking and what this looks like in practice

Why Start with Aims?

The aims and expectations of RE have shifted over the decades in England and Wales. In Task 6.1, you will read the history of the aims of RE with your beginning teacher (see Table 6.1). You are probably aware that in 1944, RE, or religious instruction (RI) as it was known, was

DOI: 10.4324/9781003191087-8

introduced as Christian moral nurture, but over the decades, it has become increasingly multifaith and academic. The value of this helping beginning teachers to understand this lies in allowing them to gain a sense of where the subject has come from and ensure they are working to embody a current vision of religious education.

Task 6.1 The aims of religious education

If you are working in England and Wales, you and the beginning teacher with whom you are working should read the history of the aims of religious education in Table 6.1. Different jurisdictions have different histories, but the general point about dual aims can still be made. However, if you are outside England and Wales, you may wish to focus your discussion on your own context.

Task 6.2 presents discussion questions to follow up on this reading task.

Table 6.1 A Very Brief History of the Aims of RE

1944 Education Act.	Aims
Religious Instruction (RI) was established as part of the compulsory, non-academic school curriculum. Academic aims were not set. RI included the classroom subject and collective worship. Parents had the right to withdraw their children under the right to freedom of worship because the aims were faith nurture.	Christian moral education
The subject was a branch of the Sunday School movement. The aim was to create a society based on Christian values. Teachers were usually local Christians, often ordained.	
By the 1960s Secondary school teachers found that RI did not meet students' thirst for discussion about life, purpose and meaning. A shift occurred within the subject, driven by teachers, to introduce more philosophical and ethical topics.	Moral and philosophical discussion
By the 1970s there was a growing interest from students and teachers to explore non-Christian faiths, including Humanism. This began in Birmingham and spread across the country. Local faith representatives advised on the local syllabus.	Non-Christian religions
Religious Studies as an academic discipline influenced the teaching of RE in schools, driven by Ninian Smart, Professor of Religious Studies at Lancaster University. **Ethnographic** approaches were applied to the study of world religions in school; looking at practices, beliefs and diversity as outsiders rather than insiders.	To understand religion as a global phenomenon.
1988 Education Reform Act	**Aims**
Christians on the political right in Parliament argued strongly against the move to multifaith RE. They felt the original, spiritual aims of the subject were being abandoned. The shift towards multifaith RE had come from within the RE profession, often advanced by Christian teachers.	Christian moral education Multifaith RE.
The 1988 Act enshrined multifaith RE in law, giving rise to a statutory need for SACREs. Schools were required to emphasise Christianity as the basis of British religious heritage.	Learning about multiple religious beliefs as outsiders.

(continued)

Table 6.1 Cont.

The right to withdrawal was retained. Faith schools continued to teach within their denomination. RE was left outside the National Curriculum. Ninian Smart's '7 dimensions of religion' (1968); all religions possess dimensions- ritual, stories, institutions, philosophies, etc.	Religion as a global phenomenon

Dual Aims	Aims
Different approaches to RE developed although they were rarely operational at the level of the classroom. For example;	
• David Hay (2000) developed an 'experiential' approach connecting children's own spiritual selves with experiences within the religious traditions.	Spiritual connection
• Bob Jackson (2000) developed an ethnographic approach looking at the reality of culture and identity as well as beliefs in religion.	Religion as a phenomenon
The two most influential approaches to RE were developed by Hull and Grimmitt:	
• John Hull (2000): all religions are connected by a common spiritual thread; religions are different ways of achieving salvation/ enlightenment/ liberation/ redemption.	The benefits of all religions
• Michael Grimmitt (1987): his work informed Agreed Syllabus design through the dual aims. His 'Human Development' model: combining children's own meaning-making with acquiring external knowledge about religion.	1) Acquiring information 2) Benefitting from religious ethics
AT1: learning *about* religion AT2: learning *from* religion	

Task 6.2 Discussion of aims over time

After reading this brief history, discuss these questions:

1. What were the original aims of the subject in 1944?
2. Who wanted to change to a multifaith approach? Which group resisted this change?
3. What are the 'dual aims'?
4. In your view, should the dual aims be superseded by something new or upheld as still educationally valuable?

This historical view shows that the subject carries two broad aims; academic and personal aims. The academic aims describe the knowledge, understanding and skills pupils will gain over time. This is the content or knowledge base of the subject; the information students will explore and engage with and the skills of comprehension, enquiry and analysis they will develop. The personal aims describe students' developing sense of self, attitude to others and the growing ethical and political awareness of a young adult. Whether the discussion is about euthanasia or climate change, students will have many opportunities to encounter different views and develop their own. The personal aims describe engagement with wider moral and political diversity and questions about citizenship, identity and how to live in the world.

In the next two tasks (Tasks 6.3 and 6.4), beginning teachers will reflect on these two broad aims of religious education, the academic and the personal, which are not always clearly defined or delineated. Each aim carries a different outcome; the pupils' developing understanding of an event or concept is an academic aim, the development of the pupil's sense of self, ideas about justice or view of reality is a personal aim. When the nature of RE's two aims and their implications for learning outcomes are not clear, it can be hard for a new teacher to judge whether aims have been achieved. Therefore, an initial conversation about the aims and purposes of the subject can provide clarity from the outset. Task 6.3 provides a way of approaching this conversation, and Task 6.4 highlights questions that may help you develop this discussion further.

Task 6.3 Prioritising aims

Potential aims of the subject are given below.
  Aims of religious education:

- Know and understand the histories of different religions
- Know and understand key beliefs and practices in different religions
- Engage with different views, beliefs and ways of life
- Reflect on the process of encountering difference and diversity
- Be able to define words like 'religion' and 'worldview'
- Listen to others and share own view
- Know and understand connections between religious traditions
- Know and understand the major groups or denominations in the religions studied
- Articulate ethical stances or convictions
- Recognize stereotypical or misrepresentative views of people or beliefs
- Reflect on own opinions or views

Draw a scale with 'most important' at one end and 'least important' at the other and ask beginning teachers to write the aims on this scale, reflecting their views.

Task 6.4 Identifying aims

Look at the aims selected in Task 6.3 as the most important. Are they academic or personal aims or a mixture of both? Discuss the nature of the aims with beginning teachers; what seems to be their vision for the subject?

Select one or two academic aims and one or two personal aims. Discuss *how* these might be met in the classroom. What sort of input would be needed to meet these aims? What teaching activities would help achieve these aims?

Starting with a discussion of aims allows new teachers to categorise what subject knowledge and teaching skills they need to develop. Being able to discern between the academic and the personal aims offers an initial chance to consider what they are doing and how they will do it. Of course, beginning teachers will be as worried about behaviour management as curriculum design, but a coherent curriculum, designed to meet a clear aim that stretches and engages students, also supports behaviour management. If the teacher knows what they are doing and why, they can work on getting better and better at meeting this aim. Confusion about practical aspects of the lesson such as where the glue and scissors are, who should be sitting where, or what the purpose of the lesson is, are all chinks in a beginner teacher's armour. Over time, practical matters of equipment and seating plans will be resolved with habit, but unclear aims will continue to sow confusion.

Learning Outcomes

After conversations about the different aims of religious education and the history of the subject's aims over time, you will be ready to focus with the beginning teacher on what this means in terms of learning outcomes.

Building on your conversation from the preceding four tasks, you will begin to explore with beginning teachers how different aims of the subject will look in terms of pupil outcomes. You have already introduced beginning teachers to the idea of two aims, the academic and the personal. In this section two additional aims are brought into focus to allow a more complex picture of aims to build. These are interpersonal aims, relating to how pupils interact with each other in the classroom and social aims, meaning a connection between what is learnt in the classroom and wider social issues.

In the first of three tasks in this section, you will discuss in general how different learning aims require different types of activities to achieve them (Task 6.5). You will then take the time to look together at one section of your own curriculum and consider what tasks are set to achieve what pupil outcomes (Task 6.6). This will allow a conversation with the beginning teacher about planning and progression and could provide a platform for critical engagement with the idea of curriculum design.

Task 6.5 Teaching techniques

With your beginning teacher read the learning outcomes below and the techniques that might be employed to achieve these outcomes. Can the beginning teacher identify any more? Use this as a stimulus to discuss more widely the idea that different outcomes will require different types of activities and information.

Learning outcomes	Techniques to achieve this outcome
Interpersonal: Focus on conversation and discussion, allowing pupils to learn in a shared environment	Talking and listening techniques Class rules that allow a respectful environment Techniques requiring groups to collaborate and co-create Opportunities for pupils to hear other view and share their own, and to explore where personal worldviews might come from.
Academic: Focus on understanding, exploration and analysis of substantive knowledge.	Activities which test knowledge and understanding Connecting small pieces of information to a wider concept. Framing information against a wider background Research or analysis in response to an enquiry question Uncovering influences that have shaped the world today
Social: Focus on helping pupils develop a sense of wider society through their learning	Learning about political or economic contexts as well as beliefs Opportunities to make connections between lived social contexts and what is learned, for example, learning about structural racism, identifying examples in students' own experience. Opportunities to navigate different social situations.
Personal: Focus on pupils developing their own view, conclusion or reflection in response to substantive knowledge.	Opportunities to explore ethical or personal questions, such as through case studies or first-person accounts. Opportunities to voice justified support or opposition to a stance. Finding out about others' ethical views, exploring how these views came to be held. Making connections between academic ethical thinking and real-life examples.

Task 6.6 Aims in the curriculum

After discussing in general what sorts of activities and input might lead to different outcomes for pupils, it will be valuable to think in more specific terms about the curriculum the beginning teachers will be working with.

Choose one or two units of work your beginning teacher will be delivering. Look at the unit plans together and consider the following:

What aims – academic, social, interpersonal and personal – are visible?
Using highlighters, note where different aims are found in the curriculum

Now that the intended aims of a particular unit of work have been considered, Task 6.7 asks the beginning teacher to explore how these aims can be met. This presents beginning teachers with a valuable opportunity to develop their critical engagement with curriculum design.

Task 6.7 Evaluation of planning

Returning to Task 6.6, with the identified aims at hand, consider together the following questions:

- What aims are planned to be met, using what activities and input? Is there any disconnect between what is claimed and what is achieved?
- Is there additional substantive knowledge that should be included to help meet an academic aim?
- Are there activities that need to be adapted to help meet a personal, interpersonal or social aim?

Giving beginning teachers time and space to think about a purpose for religious education and prepare their toolboxes to meet this purpose offers clarity from the outset. As well as auditing their own knowledge and skills in relation to general aims and specific examples, they will begin to categorise what knowledge and skills they want to focus on developing.

RE's two broad aims, the academic and the personal, reflect its peculiar role in school and society. A subject about people, community, change, identity, and diversity seems to carry expectations wider than the acquisition of knowledge, speaking to pupils' own political and ethical development and society's hopes for the next generation. However, these two aims can lead to confusion. Should both be upheld in all situations, does one take priority at certain times, do they sometimes compete? Is the purpose to understand, or is it to somehow respect an aspect of religion and belief? These are questions you might address through your conversations with beginning teachers. You might find that some beginning teachers are more inclined to prioritise personal aims, and others prioritise academic aims. Either way, the chance to arrive at a clearer understanding of what is to be achieved and how is of enormous benefit.

Multidisciplinary Religious Education

There is an increasing interest in a multidisciplinary approach to religious education. This can be seen in a recent review of current research around religious education by the English schools' inspectorate, Ofsted (2021). For example, the review suggests that pupils need to possess two types of knowledge:

- 'knowledge of well-established methods and processes and other tools of scholarship that are used to study and make sense of global and historical religion/non-religion
- knowledge of the types of conversation (or "modes of enquiry" or "scholarly discourses") that academic communities have about religion/non-religion.'

These are described as 'disciplinary knowledge' ('Ways of Knowing in RE', citing Bowie, 2019). Thinking about the disciplines, or the 'forms of knowledge', is found in philosophy of education. Philosophy of education is a field of educational studies which applies the precise, analytical thinking of philosophy to what is happening in education. Philosophy of education asks questions about aims and how they are to be achieved, so you could suggest to your beginning teachers that in thinking about aims you are engaging in philosophy of education.

Philosopher of education Paul Hirst justified the use of the disciplines in school-level education in an influential 1972 paper. The 'disciplines', or 'forms of knowledge' as Hirst terms them, refer to the academic disciplines such as history, maths, physics or philosophy. Hirst describes the disciplines as forms of knowledge because each is an attempt to make sense of an aspect of the world, whether the past, literature, the physical world, living organisms, human interaction and so on. Each discipline has evolved to investigate and understand one of the ways we can know about the world and takes its shape from the nature of the object of study. Students of the disciplines learn to think in disciplinary terms, meaning they learn to think like a historian, a philosopher or a scientist. Richard Kueh describes disciplinary knowledge as 'the sum total of the tools, norms, methods and modus operandi of the way in which humans go about exploring a field of human knowledge that has its own set of conventions' (Kueh, 2020, p. 138).

Following this line of thought, it is important that beginning teachers consider examples of disciplinary thinking in religious education. They should explore thinking in theology, history, philosophy and ethics (although ethics is, strictly speaking, a branch of philosophy). Some, such as Georgiou and Wright, include the social sciences, which they take to include history, as disciplines relevant to religious education (Georgiou and Wright, 2018). Religion and worldviews operate in multiple dimensions, personal, communal, cultural and institutional. Because of this, more than one discipline is utilised to make sense of religion and worldviews, hence the interest in a multidisciplinary study. Beginning teachers need to be thinking about how they approach this in the classroom.

A Knowledge and Skills Audit for Multidisciplinary Religious Education

In this final section, we consider what a multidisciplinary approach could look like in practice. In discussion with your beginning teachers, it might to help to think of utilising the different disciplines as like looking through different lenses. If you look at substantive knowledge through a historical lens you will ask questions about historical context, reliability of sources or powerful influences that shaped events. If you look at the same substantive knowledge through a theological lens, you will be asking different questions, about authority and how beliefs shape what people do.

The following tasks present an opportunity for you to support your beginning teacher in thinking about how pupils might develop their skills within these disciplines. In each case, activities and learning content for the primary phase have been given to help them think about progression within the disciplines; even though your beginning teacher is working in the secondary phase, considering the knowledge and skills gained at primary school has worth for them. With your beginning teacher, work your way through the tasks that follow.

In each case, read the descriptions of the different types of thinking and what they might look like in practice. This will then open up a conversation with your beginning teacher, allowing you to identify disciplinary thinking in your schemes of work.

Please note that, to complete these tasks, you will need a copy of your schemes of work which you can annotate together. You will also need highlighters in **four** colours. Task 6.8 starts with a focus on theology.

Task 6.8 Theology

Complete these alongside beginning teachers or set as a self-study task, as you see fit.

1) Read the description of theological thinking and examples of what this could look like in practice in Table 6.2.
2) Identify examples of theological thinking in the schemes of work. The following approach might be helpful:
   - Highlight theological thinking in one colour to be compared to philosophical, ethical and historical thinking in subsequent tasks.
   - Identify the **content** that supports theological thinking: What information illuminates beliefs, ways of seeing or conceptions of reality?
   - Identify the **activities** that support theological thinking: What are pupils asked to do as they make sense of beliefs and worldviews?

The aim is for your beginning teacher to be able to identify theological thinking in a scheme of work. Therefore, you will want to select a scheme of work that permits this.

THEOLOGY

Looking at religion through a theological lens will feel most familiar. Most religious education resources present this way of seeing religion. Theology relates to beliefs and doctrines and the ways of living these inspire. Theology is the 'inner' view of a religion or worldview, the beliefs about the universe and humanity and about purpose and meaning that make each particular worldview unique. Religions and worldviews are connected, but a theological lens can show what distinguishes one worldview from another. For example, Christianity shares monotheism with Judaism and Islam, but belief in the Trinity is unique to Christianity.

When looking through a theological lens the aim is to grasp the core concepts that underpin a tradition. Theology explains what sets traditions apart and what gives meaning to those inside.

Read the examples in tables to gain a clear understanding of what theological thinking looks like in religious education.

Table 6.2 Looking Through a Theological Lens

Looking Through a Theological Lens

Key beliefs
Planning should enable key beliefs to be made visible, such as through festivals or practices.

Plan for an increasingly complicated understanding of beliefs across the years, where the basic building
   blocks feed into a richer understanding.

Example: Christian belief in the Incarnation
Primary phase: Christians give gifts at Christmas, Christians believe God gave Jesus as a present to
   humanity, Christmas remembers Jesus' birth. Learn the word 'Incarnation', break down its meaning.
   Connect to Christmas beliefs and traditions. Reflect on what the Incarnation means for Christians.
Lower Secondary: learn what two different Gospel authors say about Jesus' death and resurrection.
   Connect to belief in the Incarnation. How does each Gospel author see the Incarnation?
Upper Secondary: there is a danger at this level that theological concepts can be presented in the
   abstract, which can prevent students from exploring them at any depth. Find a hook or angle that
   frames the beliefs in a manner that will allow students to critically engage with the concept. Enquiry
   questions are a good way of doing this. Enquiry questions ask students to show their knowledge, but
   also to offer their own analysis as they engage in theological thinking. Examples:

   If Jesus wasn't crucified, would Christianity exist?
   Should non-Muslims be allowed on Hajj?
   Is Hinduism polytheistic?
   Is Christianity polytheistic?
   Should Buddhism be called a religion?

Diversity
Looking at differences in and across traditions can enable a richer understanding of key beliefs.
   Questions such as below explore issues of multiple and universal belief;

   Do differences in religious practice reflect differences in belief?
   What do all members of the faith or worldview seem to agree on?

Tasks 6.9, 6.10 and 6.11 follow the same pattern as Task 6.8 (theology). These tasks allow your beginning teacher to consider philosophical (Task 6.9), ethical (Task 6.10) and historical (Task 6.11) thinking and what they look like in practice. You might find these are less frequently utilised in your planning, but there will be certain topics or questions in which each of these types of thinking is present.

As for Task 6.8, you will need schemes of work containing these types of thinking to allow your beginner teacher to consider them in practice. Even if these disciplines are only employed in one or two lessons, it will be helpful to have a concrete example to consider. You will also need your three remaining highlight colours.

Task 6.9 Philosophy

Complete these alongside beginning teachers or set as a self-study task as you see fit.

1) Read the description of philosophical thinking and suggested classroom examples in Table 6.3.
2) Identify examples of philosophical thinking in a scheme of work.

- Highlight philosophical thinking (in a different colour than theological thinking).
- Identify the **content** that supports philosophical thinking.
- Identify the **activities** that support philosophical thinking.

PHILOSOPHY

Philosophy is a search for what can be said to be true or, at least, reliable. Religion offers theories of truth and can therefore be looked at through a philosophical lens. Religions can be described as 'meta-narratives'; they provide an account of the nature of the universe and humanity which stand over (*meta* is Greek for 'beyond') smaller questions such as about how we should live. Mundane questions about work, sex, marriage, family, politics, education, morality, and so on are answered by religious traditions in particular ways depending on the overarching metanarrative about what the universe is and where humans stand in it. The metanarrative itself can be considered in philosophical thinking.

Table 6.3 Looking Through a Philosophical Lens

Looking Through a Philosophical Lens
Philosophy is a consideration of what arguments and information is reliable. Two examples of philosophical questions are:
What is this belief based on? *Why do people believe this to be true?*
With younger students: Philosophy tends to be rather abstract, a form of thinking that is not straightforward for younger students who are building up their understanding of the world. However, even with younger students, questions about *how we know* can be explored. Primary phase: ask pupils to say something they know is true. Talk about why they know it is true. Ask them to prove that the chair they are sitting on is really there. Some pupils in the class might be rather lost, some might enjoy it. Even if the conversation is inconclusive, you will be showing pupils that such questions can be asked. Lower Secondary: As pupils' understanding of beliefs and practices grows, take the time to explain the roots of these sources of truth for believers. For example, Muslims revere the Qur'an and follow its teachings because they believe the words are given from God. To be able to explain *why* this source has authority is to engage in philosophical thinking about authority and reliability generally. Upper Secondary: Religion answers philosophical questions based on a particular view of the universe and humanity. Diverse traditions within religion offer different answers. Answers to philosophical questions are also drawn from non-religious sources.
To engage in philosophical thinking in the classroom is to place religious answers to philosophical questions on a wider framework. This is to go beyond the religious answer itself and investigate what the answer is based on. For example, questions about the origins of life and the universe are answered in different ways. There are answers drawn from physics and evolutionary biology, as well as answers drawn from religious sources. The enquiry questions below allow students to go beyond the answers, and consider what they are based on:
What type of thinking is religious thinking? What is it based on? *What type of thinking is science thinking? What is it based on?* *What can religion tell us? What can religion not tell us?* *What can science tell us? What can science not tell us?* *Are science thinking and religious thinking complementary or incompatible?*

Task 6.10 Ethics

Complete these alongside beginning teachers or set as a self-study task, as you see fit.

1) Read the description of ethical thinking and suggested classroom examples in Table 6.4.
2) Identify examples of ethical thinking in a scheme of work.
   - Highlight ethical thinking (in a third colour).
   - Identify the **content** that supports ethical thinking.
   - Identify the **activities** that support ethical thinking.

ETHICS

Ethics is a type of philosophical thinking, and as such belongs in the category of philosophy. However here a separate Ethics section is given as ethical thinking, whether in personal, social or intellectual terms, is a significant proportion of the religious education curriculum. Ethical thinking is concerned with how we should live, right and wrong, fairness and justice. Religion offers answers to ethical questions, as do non-religious philosophies. All human societies ask and answer ethical questions, therefore ethical thinking places religious answers to ethical questions on a wider framework.

Table 6.4 Looking Through an Ethical Lens

Looking Through an Ethical Lens
Read these examples of ethical thinking.
Where can you identify ethical thinking in your own curriculum? Are there gaps where ethical thinking would be of benefit? What sorts of activities allow ethical thinking?
Lower Secondary: explore questions of how we ought to live that apply to all humans, before considering religious answers to these questions.
Make a distinction between religious moral guidance and personal moral commitments. Religious guidance stems from particular beliefs, such as in the afterlife and judgment. Personal morality is an individual's own sense of what is right and wrong.
Consider non-religious answers to ethical questions and where these stem from, such as the idea of human rights or environmental ethics.
Upper Secondary: Place religious moral guidance on a wider ethical framework. For example;
How far is fighting for justice a practical matter, and how far a moral matter?
Do you have to want to help others, can you do it by accident?
Should the environment have the same moral status as humans?
Students might ask why, if religious teachings preach love and generosity, there is so much evidence of religious abuse. If you have placed human behaviour on a wider ethical framework, you can address questions such as this.
For example: gender discrimination
Explore sexism in its own right before looking at religious teachings. Through well-chosen case studies explore gender discrimination around the world, such as child marriage, bans on abortion, the gender pay gap, girls denied access to school, and so on. Having explored the shape and nature of gender discrimination, the ways religion either reproduces or disrupts these norms can be explored.

Task 6.11 History

Complete these alongside beginning teachers or set as a self-study task, as you see fit.

1) Read the description of historical thinking below and suggested classroom examples in Table 6.5.
2) Identify examples of historical thinking in a scheme of work.
   - Highlight historical thinking (in a fourth colour).
   - Identify the **content** that supports historical thinking.
   - Identify the **activities** that support historical thinking.

HISTORY

Religions have rich and diverse histories; they are rooted in places, language and culture; they are influenced by geopolitical pressures; and they, in turn, shape nations, continents and societies. Much of these contexts will be explored through historical thinking. Exploring the historical context of religion and belief offers a richer understanding.

Table 6.5 Looking Through a Historical Lens

Looking Through a Historical Lens
Consider these potential historical contexts that could add richness and texture to understanding people, culture and traditions. Are there other historical contexts that your beginner teachers suggest would add a deeper understanding to a religion or worldview in the curriculum?
Origin stories: explore the times and places where a religion was born, such as 7th-century Arabia (Islam) or the 1st-century Roman-occupied Jewish world (Christianity).
Cultural histories: trace groups of people, such as South Asian communities who came to Britain after the partition of India and World War II. Where did they originate, what aspects of their language, culture and beliefs have found a home in Britain, how far has the worldview changed through life in Britain?
Formative histories: to understand current aspects of religion and worldviews it is sometimes necessary to devote some time to past events in order to make sense of the present. For example, explore the succession crisis in early Islam that led to the Sunni and Shi'a split. Teach the Great Schism, the Protestant Reformation or the Evangelical revivals to understand why there are diverse Christian churches.

In taking the time to consider different types of thinking in practice you will enable your beginning teacher to understand what is meant by a multidisciplinary study. As they audit their knowledge and skills, they can categorise these into types of thinking, or disciplinary lenses, as they develop in experience, understanding and confidence.

Summary and Key Points

It is important that beginning teachers explore the broad aims of RE to allow them to identify how different aims can be met through well-chosen activities and substantive knowledge.

They also need to develop an understanding of disciplinary approaches in the classroom to ensure awareness of the different types of thinking that can result.

* Identifying religious education's two broad aims, the academic and personal, provides a base layer of clarity for beginner teachers.
* Beginning teachers need to understand that substantive knowledge and activities will be shaped by intended outcomes.
* A multidisciplinary approach to religion and worldviews provides richness and texture when making sense of the body of knowledge that makes up the RE curriculum.
* Familiarity with these structural matters can assist a beginning teacher in auditing their knowledge and skills and identifying how they want to develop.
* Noting the different outcomes, purposes, processes and disciplines of religious education can provide clarity of aims for a beginning RE teacher from the start.

Further Resources

Commission on Religious Education. (2018). *Religion and Worldviews: The Way Forward. A National Plan for RE*. Religious Education Council of England and Wales.

This report represents a paradigm shift, describing the thinking behind the move to 'religion and worldviews'. It also sets out a helpful history and report into the current state of the subject.

Conroy, J., Lundie, D., Davis, R., Baumfield, V., Barnes, P., Gallagher, T., Lowden, K., Bourque, N., & Wenell, K. J. (2013). *Does Religious Education Work? A Multi-dimensional Investigation*. Bloomsbury Publishing.

This multidimensional study provides an illuminating glimpse into the recent state of religious education, raising questions about aims, diversity and local determinism.

Chater, M. (ed.). (2020). *Reforming Religious Education: Power and Knowledge in a Worldviews Curriculum*. John Catt Educational Ltd.

Each chapter is written by a different teacher or scholar, making sense of worldviews thinking in their own contexts. A blog site supports the book, representing teachers' ongoing development of worldviews in the classroom (https://reformingre.wordpress.com/).

Culham St Gabriel's blog site - https://reonline.org.uk/blog/

This educational trust offers a large and growing collection of blogs from many authors exploring current thinking in education, religion, and worldviews and what it means in practice. The blogs are hosted on their website, RE:ONLINE.

References

Bowie, B. (2019). The implicit knowledge structure preferred by questions in English religious studies public exams. In Biesta, G. & Hannam, P. (Eds.), *Religion and Education: The Forgotten Dimensions of Religious Education* (pp. 112–123). Leiden Brill.
Chater, M. (ed.). (2020). *Reforming Religious Education: Power and Knowledge in a Worldviews Curriculum*. John Catt Educational Ltd.

Commission on Religious Education. (2018). *Religion and Worldviews: The Way Forward. A National Plan for RE*. Religious Education Council of England and Wales.

Conroy, J., Lundie, D., Davis, R., Baumfield, V., Barnes, P., Gallagher, T., Lowden, K., Bourque, N., & Wenell, K. J. (2013). *Does Religious Education Work? A Multi-dimensional Investigation*. Bloomsbury Publishing.

Copley, T. (2008). *Teaching Religion: Sixty Years of Religious Education in England and Wales* (updated edition). University of Exeter Press.

Cox, E. (1966) *Changing Aims in Religious Education*. Routledge and Kegan Paul Ltd.

Culham St Gabriel's blog site. n.d. Available at: https://reonline.org.uk/blog/

Georgiou, G. & Wright, K. (2018). Re-dressing the balance. In Castelli, M. & Chater, M. (Eds.), *We Need to Talk About Religious Education: Manifests for the Future of RE* (pp. 101–114). Jessica Kingsley Publishers.

Grimmitt, M. (1987). *Religious Education and Human Development: The Relationship between Studying Religions and Personal, Social and Moral Education*. McCrimmon.

Hay, D. (2000). The religious experience and education project: Experiential learning in Religious Education. In Grimmitt, M. (Ed.), *Pedagogies of Religious Education; Case Studies in the Research and Development of Good Pedagogic Practice in RE* (pp. 70-87). McCrimmon.

Hirst, P. (1972). Liberal education and the nature of knowledge. In Dearden, R. F. Hirst, P., & Peters, R. S. (Eds.), *Education and the Development of Reason*. Routledge & Kegan Paul. https://www.taylorfrancis.com/chapters/edit/10.4324/9780203861165-25/liberal-education-nature-knowledge-hirst

Hull, J. (2000). Religion in the service of the child project: The gift approach to religious education. In Grimmitt, M. (Ed.), *Pedagogies of Religious Education; Case Studies in the Research and Development of Good Pedagogic Practice in RE* (pp. 112-129). McCrimmon.

Jackson, R. (2000). The Warwick Religious Education Project: The Interpretive Approach to Religious Education. In Grimmitt, M. (Ed.), *Pedagogies of Religious Education; Case Studies in the Research and Development of Good Pedagogic Practice in RE* (pp. 130-152). McCrimmon.

Kueh, R. (2020). Disciplinary hearing: Making the case for the disciplinary. In Chater, M. (Ed.), *Reforming Religious Education: Power and Knowledge in a Worldviews Curriculum* (pp. 131-147). John Catt Educational Ltd.

Loukes, H. (1961). *Teenage Religion*. SCM Press Ltd.

Ofsted. (2021). *Research Review Series: Religious Education*. https://www.gov.uk/government/publications/research-review-series-religious-education/research-review-series-religious-education

Smart, N. (1968). *Secular Education and the Logic of Religion*. Faber and Faber Ltd.

7 Helping beginning teachers develop religious literacy through their classroom practice

Kathryn Wright

Introduction

Religious literacy is a very complex term, but most agree that there is a convincing case for helping children and young people become knowledgeable about religion and worldviews, including religious beliefs and practices, as they shape contemporary societies (Biesta, Aldridge, Hannam and Whittle, 2019). Understanding others' worldviews, developing self-understanding and being able to participate in a diverse, global community are essential elements of religious education (RE) in all schools. The Commission on RE (2018) states,

> Young people today are growing up in a world where there is increasing awareness of the diversity of religious and non-religious worldviews, and they will need to live and work well with people with very different worldviews to themselves.
>
> (p. 3)

In addition, the importance of a religiously literate workforce has been cited in the McKenzie-Delis Packer Annual Review November 2020. One of the recommendations in the report is the value of knowing about and understanding religious diversity, as well as being open and transparent about diversity and inclusion in the workplace. Therefore, being religiously literate is essential for the beginning teacher themselves particularly as they will be teaching about a range of religious and non-religious worldviews and interacting with colleagues who have different worldviews to their own. Second, and the primary focus of this chapter, is the importance of developing religiously literate young people through classroom practice. Beginning teachers are required to have secure subject knowledge and curriculum knowledge to motivate pupils and teach effectively and anticipate common misconceptions within the subject. As a mentor, you play a vital role in supporting your beginning teacher in fulfilling these expectations through your own reflective practice, conversation and observation.

The aim here is to take a pragmatic approach and consider how you can support beginning teachers to develop not only their own religious literacy but also that of the young people they teach through their classroom practice. It is hoped that the approach taken alongside the suggested tasks and questions is appropriate for beginning teachers working in any context, whether the school has a designated religious character or not. Using the

DOI: 10.4324/9781003191087-9

broad terms *religious literacy* and *religion and worldviews* mean the principles outlined can be applied in schools within and beyond the United Kingdom. The question we are asking is, 'What might a classroom in which beginning teachers and pupils demonstrate a high level of religious literacy look like?' Through this chapter, we use the phrase 'religiously literate classroom' as shorthand. At the end of the chapter, we reflect on ways in which you, as a mentor, can support beginning teachers to develop a more religiously literate classroom and engage with scholarship in this field.

By the end of this chapter, you should be able to:

- Identify different ways in which you can support beginning teachers to develop religious literacy through effective planning and classroom interactions.
- Use a range of tasks to challenge beginning teachers about the ways in which they are developing religious literacy in classroom practice.
- Reflect on your own and support beginning teachers in developing religious literacy and engagement with scholarship in this field.

Religious literacy – a working definition

It is important for mentors to have clarity about the meaning of religious literacy. As noted, it is potentially contentious, but the following definition has served me well when working with primary and secondary teachers over the last few years:

> The ability to hold balanced and well-informed conversations about religion and worldviews.
>
> (Norfolk Agreed Syllabus, 2019, p. 4)

In this definition there is an implied assumption that pupils will have knowledge and understanding of religion and worldviews but that they will, most importantly, be able to apply this in and through their daily lives. Some might call this wisdom. Are pupils able to contribute wisely to the public sphere in relation to religion and worldviews? Are pupils able to make wise decisions about how they engage and interact with those who hold different worldviews to their own?

In this definition and throughout this chapter, I use the phrase 'religion and worldviews'. This phrase provides a useful way of thinking about our approach to the subject and promotes a broad understanding of religious literacy which includes both religious and non-religious worldviews. The following summary of the Commission on RE (2018) proposed statement of entitlement provides a helpful reference point:

> Pupils are entitled to be taught, by well qualified and resourced teachers, knowledge and understanding about:
>
> 1. what religion is and worldviews are, and how they are studied;
> 2. the impact of religion and worldviews on individuals, communities and societies;
> 3. the diversity of religious and non-religious worldviews in society;
> 4. the concepts, language and ways of knowing that help us organise and make sense of our knowledge and understanding of religion and worldviews;

5. the human quest for meaning, so that they are prepared for life in a diverse world and have space to recognise, reflect on and take responsibility for the development of their own personal worldview

(RE Policy Unit [NATRE, REC, RE Today], 2020)

To become religiously literate therefore means to not only know about and understand religion and worldviews (substantive knowledge or content) but also know about and use a range of methods and tools when studying (ways of knowing), as well as recognise and reflect on one's own personal worldview (personal knowledge). These three forms of knowledge are advocated in the Ofsted Research Review 2021. This rounded approach to understanding religious literacy is of paramount importance because it not only enables pupils to become well-informed and hold balanced views but roots RE in well-established academic traditions. One of your roles as a mentor is to promote the value of scholarship with your beginning teacher, modelling this through your own engagement with the ongoing debate. Task 7.1 is designed to help you enter into conversation with your beginning teacher to come to some shared understanding of what you might mean by religious literacy.

Task 7.1 My understanding of religious literacy

Discuss the following questions with your beginning teacher:

*   To what extent do you agree with the working definition from the Norfolk Agreed Syllabus 2019?
*   In what ways are the three types of knowledge (substantive, ways of knowing and personal) helpful in articulating a broad understanding of religious literacy?

Where appropriate, you might encourage your beginning teacher to have conversations with pupils about the meaning of religious literacy and/or about the importance of an education in religion and worldviews for life in the real world. You may wish to use some of the pupil blog competition pieces (2021) which demonstrate this and are available on the RE:ONLINE website (http://www.reonline.org.uk).

Developing religious literacy: Disciplinary knowledge

Planning with beginning teachers is an essential element of your role as a mentor as you work with them evaluating their independent short-, medium- and sometimes long-term planning. In order to develop religious literacy, an understanding of disciplinary knowledge, or ways of knowing, as a framework for planning can be helpful. It can support you and your beginning teacher in designing teaching and learning episodes, sequencing of knowledge and understanding, resources, vocabulary and assessment for learning opportunities.

Christine Counsell (2018) has described disciplinary knowledge as a curricular term for what pupils learn about how substantive knowledge (or content) was established and organised. A discipline is widely understood to have an intellectual history, a body of knowledge founded on core concepts and theories, an object of investigation which might be shared across disciplines, specific terminology and language, particular methods of enquiry and particular grounds on which valid truth claims are made. Disciplinary knowledge in religion and worldviews is about understanding the different ways of knowing in our subject, such as theology, philosophy, history, anthropology, sociology and so on. It is about intentionally enabling pupils to participate in and understand discourse around this.

As mentors, it is important to establish a balance of disciplinary approaches across a key stage to ensure that pupils are equipped with a range of methodological approaches. You also need to ensure your beginning teachers understand this rationale to support them in the planning process. It enables the beginning teacher to understand different perspectives utilised in the school subject which may be different from the degree course they undertook. For example, a beginning teacher may have completed a degree in philosophy and may be less aware of methods used by theologians or social scientists. An awareness of different perspectives supports a balanced approach to religion and worldviews. We may use a theological method such as looking for internal consistency or coherency in texts, approaching the study of a worldview ontologically. In contrast, we might explore the wider human questions raised about a particular religious practice considering identity, power and the lived experience of adherents through a sociological focus. These approaches might be more phenomenological. Methods of study may include quantitative data observation, survey and interviews. A philosophical approach might explore religion and worldviews epistemologically, logically and ethically. Pupils may employ the use of evidence and sources and insights from Eastern philosophical traditions. Task 7.2 asks you to consider a scenario where a beginning teacher is perhaps reluctant to move beyond her own sociological specialism, thus missing potential opportunities for pupils to gain theological perspectives.

Task 7.2 Considering questioning through reflective practice

Read the following example and consider why Antonia, who has a sociology degree, may be reluctant to engage pupils with Christian texts.

Antonia has taught a series of lessons with Year 8. The enquiry question being studied was, 'To what extent does the lived reality of Anglican Christians reflect the authoritative understanding of teachings and practice in the Church of England?' She has employed a range of largely sociological methods such as in-depth interviews with adherents of an Anglican Christian worldview, analysis of census data and an ethnographic study based on the local parish church. However, Antonia was reluctant to engage pupils with interpreting authoritative Christian texts which would have provided a more theological dimension to learning.

How might you encourage Antonia to make pupils aware of the different ways in which sociologists and theologians validate knowledge? For example, as Antonia's mentor, you might suggest some texts for her to read and have a conversation about them together to build her confidence. You might also suggest she consider some of the methods outlined by Bowie (2020).

Opening up the different disciplinary dimensions with your beginning teacher may help them to see beyond their own degree specialism. As mentors equipping beginning teachers with the knowledge and understanding of these disciplinary fields is an important element of supporting religious literacy. In addition, providing pupils with the knowledge of well-established methods, processes and tools of scholarship that are used to study religion and worldviews, as well as having knowledge of the types of scholarly conversations that academic communities hold is highlighted in the Ofsted Research Review 2021. Task 7.3 invites you to work with your beginning teacher to reflect on planning, thus increasing their understanding of this important aspect of religious literacy.

Task 7.3 Reflecting on disciplinary framing

Reflect on your current curriculum and the different disciplines that underpin each scheme of learning. You might take one year group and ask your beginning teacher to reflect on a different one. The following questions could be used to stimulate a conversation about curriculum planning:

- How are you explicitly planning for pupils to learn about different ways or knowing/ disciplinary knowledge, for example in reference to different types of questions and disciplinary fields?
- How is the learning sequenced (in medium-term planning) to ensure pupils develop their understanding of different ways of knowing?
- What different tools or methods are included in planning to ensure pupils develop a balanced approach to the study of religion and worldviews, for example interpreting texts, observation, interviews, analysis of data, use of source material?

Developing religious literacy: Selecting and resourcing substantive content

For pupils to become religiously literate, representations of religious and non-religious worldviews should be as authentic and accurate as possible. As a mentor, your beginning teacher will look first to you for guidance in this area. Teachers make choices when deciding what content to include, whether this be developing substantive knowledge over time through well thought out schemata, or in individual lessons where specific examples are chosen. In considering the 'what' of the curriculum it is important to consider the intent of a scheme of learning and increasing depth of understanding, thus ensuring continuity and progression. You make professional judgements which are often implicit; as a mentor, you can make these decisions more explicit in conversation with your beginning teacher. For example, you will be able to guide your beginning teacher to the locally agreed syllabus (or equivalent) to determine any overarching principles in terms of content selection.

However, most beginning teachers will be able to choose the resources they use in their own individual lessons under your supervision. These resources should reflect both the lived reality of the worldview as well as current scholarship. Resources which support this might include the subject knowledge resources on the RE:ONLINE website, many of which reflect the divergence within religious and non-religious worldviews. The same website has examples of personal worldview stories, as well as authentic responses from adherents to commonly asked questions about a range of topics. However, more than 10 years ago, a project led by a team from the University of Warwick (Department for Children, Schools and Families, 2010) examined materials available to schools for teaching and learning in religion and worldviews and made recommendations particularly in relation to accuracy, balance and appropriateness of representation of religious traditions. These points have been raised again in conversations about decolonising the curriculum. To illustrate this notion of diverse voices, if we consider a Year 9 medium-term plan different sources could be used to offer a range of authentic voices on the concept of sacredness. These might include short extracts from Peter Berger, Rudolf Otto or Émile Durkheim as well as excepts from religious texts; 'sacred' artefacts or places; a visit to a place of worship; podcasts or film material of people talking about the 'sacred' (e.g. Theos Think Tank's 'The Sacred' Podcast and True Tube (www. truetube.co.uk) extracts about nature and the environment being sacred). Task 7.4 invites you to enter into a discussion with your beginning teacher about resources used for a specific scheme of learning.

Task 7.4 Reviewing resources

Invite your beginning teacher to review resources for a scheme of learning they will be teaching with you to ensure accurate representation and diversity of authentic voices are included.

As you review you may consider the following questions:

- Are the curriculum examples, content and resources showing accurate representations and authentic voices? If one view is being presented, is this made clear to pupils?
- Do the resources and content examples recognise the complexity and internal divergence within a particular worldview with accuracy and sensitivity?
- Do the resources provide a sense of the lived reality of the worldview being studied? For example, in medium-term planning, is there an opportunity for pupils to encounter people from different worldview perspectives or visit places of worship?
- Are primary sources (e.g. sacred texts) being used when exploring theological questions? Is the beginning teacher confident in their handling of these texts?

To support beginning teachers' developing religious literacy, you might consider hosting visitors from different worldviews, and/or meeting with them through an online virtual platform. You might arrange visits to local places of worship for your beginning teachers to help them understand the importance of authentic representation, and engage in conversation about what it means to be an adherent of a particular worldview. Supporting beginning teachers in developing correct and accurate pronunciation of specialist religious terminology is a vital element of religious literacy. It builds their knowledge and gives them confidence in the classroom. Helping beginning teachers introduce this in the classroom with pupils is then a natural progression. For example, you might use the RE Definitions website (http://re-definitions.org.uk/) to help improve pronunciation and understanding of the word *TeNaCh* within a Jewish worldview before the beginning teacher studies this concept and the structure of the word with pupils. Or you might encourage the beginning teacher to investigate the etymology of some religious concepts, for example a theological concept such as salvation, which has its roots in the Latin *salvare* or *salvus*, which means 'safe' or 'healthy'. Task 7.5 brings together the disciplinary dimension and effective resourcing as a focus for an observation to be undertaken by you as a mentor to support pupils' depth of understanding.

Task 7.5 Reflecting on an observation

Set up a lesson observation in which you observe the beginning teacher with a focus on the effective use of examples and resourcing to ensure depth of understanding. You may want to consider these questions as you observe and reflect on the lesson.

- Do the content examples and resources chosen enable pupils to develop a depth of understanding of the worldview being studied? What are the strengths and limitations of the chosen examples and resources?
- Which disciplinary perspective is the focus of the lesson? Do the chosen examples and resources reflect this focus?

Developing religious literacy: Pedagogical choices

As a mentor you will no doubt have evolved your own pedagogical approaches over time. It is important to be self-aware, acknowledge your own preferences and be open to challenge from your beginning teacher. This section advocates an approach to pedagogy which supports the development of religious literacy. You may want to reflect on it yourself, as well as discuss it with your beginning teacher. The ontological, 'lived' nature of pedagogy has been written about previously in other studies (e.g. Wright, 2017). This is relevant in this context, as it is the teacher who creates space, seeks encounters and listens for wisdom (Wright, 2017, p. 229). It is about your presence as teacher/mentor and a sense of being in the classroom which is of fundamental importance as you live out and model these three principles of pedagogy to develop religious literacy:

- Creating space: This is a purposeful, safe and subversive space and is essential for the other two principles to be applied. In order to achieve, this the space must be shaped by values and by being intellectually open, inclusive and affirming. The space should allow for solitude and silence as well as collaboration. The space should not be concerned with time limits but be slow and deep.

- Encountering others: This is characterised by the notion of encounters being open and transformative. In order to achieve this the encounters should be humble and authentic, rooted in reality. For them to be effective, the encounters are required to enable deep, theological engagement to take place.
- Listening for wisdom: This brings the two other principles together by providing the purpose for the space and means of encounter. Listening for wisdom takes place through narrative and engagement with story, through enquiry into theological concepts and through relationships.

(Wright, 2017, p. 267)

In practical terms, to create space means considering the hospitable nature of the learning environment, using collaborative and dialogic approaches yet allowing for silence and slowing down the learning. To foster true encounters means spending time with and researching worldview communities to understand and learn from them. It means the use of hermeneutical approaches and application of contact theory (Wright, 2017, pp. 253-254). To listen for wisdom means not overloading learning, allowing everyone to learn from each other's stories (Wright, 2017, pp. 263-264). In practical terms, this means employing a range of strategies to support collaborative learning, such as those identified in the *RE and Good Community Relations Toolkit* (National Association of Teachers of RE [NATRE], 2017). This might include the jigsaw approach which allows different views to be shared or use of techniques such as 'ouch' and 'oops' when discussing a controversial topic. Task 7.6 invites you to reflect with your beginning teacher on the notion of pedagogy as hospitality. You may also want to discuss whether the environment created for the beginning teacher themselves is a hospitable one. This places you, as mentor, in a potentially vulnerable position, but it is an important question to reflect upon as you consider yourself as a 'host'.

Task 7.6 Considering pedagogy as hospitality

Sit down with your beginning teacher, and together reflect on a recent day in school and lessons you have both taught in light of the principles of pedagogy put forward here by Wright (2017). This provides an opportunity to model reflective practice with your beginning teacher and open up conversation about pedagogy in a creative way.

- How are your classrooms organised to provide a hospitable space where relationships can be fostered and listening prioritised?
- Do your pedagogical approaches support collaboration and dialogic talk?
- Were pupils given the opportunity to work in a range of pairs/groups to explore different personal worldviews?
- Were pupils given the opportunity to listen to different worldview stories, including their own, if they wish to share them?

Together, you might consider what steps you need to take to ensure that both the physical and non-physical spaces are hospitable and review again a few weeks later.

Developing religious literacy: Positionality and reflexivity

When pupils study this subject and when teachers plan and deliver lessons, they do so from a position. As a mentor you have a position, which is most likely different to that of your beginning teacher. Nobody is neutral; everyone stands somewhere. Some may describe this as a personal worldview which is influenced by prior knowledge, experiences, culture and identity. Enabling pupils to recognise, reflect on and develop their own personal knowledge is interwoven with the other two forms of knowledge – substantive and disciplinary (Wright, 2021). Self-awareness and reflexivity are vital elements of becoming religiously literate for you, your beginning teacher and the pupils. Task 7.7 is based on the animation *Nobody Stands Nowhere* (Downe, 2021) and encourages you to share your own worldview story with your beginning teacher.

Task 7.7 Considering positionality

Watch *Nobody Stands Nowhere* with your beginning teacher and reflect together on your own positionality, sharing honestly and openly with one another. Consider how the film might be used with pupils as well as the wider implications for classroom practice. You might use the following questions to stimulate your conversation:

- How comfortable do you feel sharing your own worldview with one another?
- Are you aware of the presence of minority and sometimes hidden worldviews present in your classroom? Do you make efforts to ensure the classroom is an inclusive and open space? Are pupils able to agree to disagree well?
- How are pupils encouraged to show respect for one another and the worldview(s) they are studying?
- How are you creating safe, yet challenging, spaces for rigorous discussion and critical enquiry?
- How do you challenge assumptions and recognise that no one is 'neutral'?

Some years ago, I started a session for primary beginning teachers with the word *religion* on the screen and asked them to write down the first thing that came into their minds. They were then invited to share this and consider their own positioning in relation to this word. At the time, there was much discussion about how helpful this was and how important. Everyone in the classroom has a view about religious and non-religious worldviews, and we need to acknowledge this. Ruth Flannagan writes extensively about working with teachers to help them consider and understand their own worldview (Flanagan, 2021).

Beginning teachers are to be role models creating a culture of mutual trust and respect. The Religious Education Council produced a helpful Code of Conduct (RE Council of England and Wales, 2009), giving some principles and exemplifications for teachers of RE. For example, it is important that you support beginning teachers by carefully acknowledging the divergence within organised worldviews, such as the Islamic tradition. Encourage them to use phrases such as 'some Muslims' or 'in this particular example . . .'. This provides pupils with a range of views whilst helping them understand that they will never be able to comprehensively cover all of them. The aim is for pupils to understand there is a difference of opinion, and modelling this language for beginning teachers supports their, and their pupils', religious literacy.

How can the beginning teacher develop their own religious literacy?

Throughout this chapter, I have provided opportunities for you and your beginning teacher to consider your own religious literacy. For example, I have already referred to the ontological nature of being or becoming a teacher. If teachers are to embody a pedagogical approach, and through their presence advocate for religious literacy, then it makes sense for them to develop their own religious literacy as well. In this final section, I will outline some further ways in which beginning teachers can develop their own religious literacy.

The most important way of supporting beginning teachers in becoming more religiously literate is to be in conversation; to acknowledge that it is good to talk about our own positioning, and those of others, in professional contexts. Reading groups and professional communities of practice can support beginning teachers in developing reflexivity. You can encourage beginning teachers to join university research groups, local teacher networks and professional associations such as the National Association of Teachers of Religious Education (NATRE). One of the best ways to encourage participation is to get involved in these communities yourself and model through your own learning.

Second, it is essential that you and your beginning teachers engage with up-to-date research about religion and worldviews. There are several ways in which teachers at all stages of their careers can engage in and with research. For example, a number of theology and religious studies departments, such as the University of Chester, have run online webinars linked to A-level topics. RE:ONLINE hosts a regular 'research of the month' feature, offering a vlog, text and questions for the teacher to ask themselves and discuss with others. A research library also contains an extensive set of summarised journal papers, reports and articles. Various recorded 'in conversation' events, as well as self-study courses, are available through the same website focusing on research, curriculum, subject knowledge and community relations. As a final activity, Task 7.8 challenges you to reflect on a recent piece of research and discuss it with your beginning teacher, considering the impact it may have on your professional practice in the future.

Task 7.8 Being a member of a professional, scholarly community

Choose a piece of scholarly input to share with your beginning teacher. You could use one of the 'Research of the Month' pieces (www.reonline.org.uk/research/research-of-the-month/), a journal article or paper or a chapter from a book.

As you choose a suitable piece, reflect personally on the following questions:

- How am I engaging in scholarly conversations with other professionals?
- To what extent am I aware of the latest research about religion and worldviews?

After you have discussed the scholarly piece with your beginning teacher, you might conclude by asking them the following:

- Are they confident enough to answer questions arising from pupils about this topic?
- What impact do they think this might have on their classroom practice?
- How can they continue to engage in scholarly conversations once they qualify as a teacher?

Summary and key points

A classroom in which beginning teachers and pupils demonstrate a high level of religious literacy is dynamic and creative. It is a space in which you can support the beginning teacher to do the following:

- Plan learning sequences with different ways of knowing in mind and make well-informed choices about the subject content.
- Carefully consider the resources they use to ensure reliable, accurate and authentic representation of religion and worldviews.
- Create a hospitable space where everyone acknowledges that no one is neutral.

Foundational to these three strands, is an awareness that you and your beginning teacher are always learning. This is demonstrated through your ongoing participation in the religion and worldviews field of scholarship.

Further resources

Beista, G, Aldridge, D, Hannam, P, & Whittle, S. (2019). *Religious Literacy: A way forward for Religious Education?* Brunel University and Hampshire Inspection and Advisory Service. https://www.reonline.org.uk/wp-content/uploads/2019/07/Religious-Literacy-Biesta-Aldridge-Hannam-Whittle-June-2019.pdf

A paper which informs discussion about religious literacy and its potential value.

RE:ONLINE – www.reonline.org.uk

A comprehensive website with resources to support practical teaching, subject knowledge and expertise, as well as a research library and recorded event material.

National Association of Teachers of RE (NATRE). (2017) *RE and Good Community Relations: A toolkit for teachers of RE.*

This toolkit presents theory-based resources and ideas for how to best promote community relations in RE classrooms. Designed in collaboration with teachers and researchers, the activities aim to improve young people's intergroup attitudes and help them develop some of the skills necessary to navigate the increasingly diverse world in which they are growing up. www.natre.org.uk/uploads/Additional%20Documents/The%20Shared%20Space%20 Folder/teachers%20toolkit%20final%20April%202018.pdf

References

Biesta, G., Aldridge, D., Hannam, P., & Whittle, S. (2019). *Religious literacy: A way forward for religious education?* Brunel University and Hampshire Inspection and Advisory Service. https://www.reonline.org.uk/wp-content/uploads/2019/07/Religious-Literacy-Biesta-Aldridge-Hannam-Whittle-June-2019.pdf

Bowie, R. (Ed.) (2020). *The practice guide: Classroom tools for sacred text scholarship.* Canterbury Christchurch University.

Brown, A. (2021, May 26). *Writing towards an anti-racist RE curriculum.* [Video] RE:ONLINE. https://www.reonline.org.uk/research/in-conversation/

Commission on Religious Education. (2018). *Religion and worldviews: The way forward. A national plan for RE.* Religious Education Council of England and Wales.

Counsell, C. (2018). Taking curriculum seriously in 'Impact: Designing a curriculum: Developing strategies to support access to knowledge'. *Journal of Chartered College of Teaching,* Issue 4, 6–9.

Department for Children, Schools and Families. (2010). *Materials used to teach about world religions in schools in England.* University of Warwick.

Downe, E. (2021). *Nobody stands nowhere.* Theos Think Tank. https://www.reonline.org.uk/resources/telling-my-worldview-story/

Flanagan, R. (2021). Teachers' personal worldviews and RE in England: a way forward? *British Journal of Religious Education,* 43(3), 320–336. https://doi.org/10.1080/01416200.2020.1826404

McKenzie-Delis Packer Annual Review. (2020, November). https://www.dialglobal.org/review

National Association of Teachers of RE. (2017). *RE and Good Community Relations: A toolkit for teachers of RE.* https://www.natre.org.uk/uploads/Additional%20Documents/The%20Shared%20Space%20Folder/teachers%20toolkit%20final%20April%202018.pdf

Norfolk County Council. (2019). *Norfolk agreed syllabus for religious education.* https://www.schools.norfolk.gov.uk/teaching-and-learning/religious-education-agreed-syllabus

Ofsted. (2021). *Research review series: Religious education.* https://www.gov.uk/government/publications/research-review-series-religious-education

RE Policy Unit (NATRE, REC, RE Today) www.retoday.org.uk. (2020). *A National Plan for RE in England.* https://www.natre.org.uk/uploads/Additional%20Documents/A%20National%20Plan%20for%20RE%20-CoRE%20summary%20final.pdf

Wright, K. (2017). A Pedagogy of Embrace: A Theology of Hospitality as A Pedagogical Framework for Religious Education in Church of England Schools. PhD diss., University of East Anglia.

Wright, K. (2021, May 25). Weaving a knowledge tapestry. *RE:ONLINE.* https://www.reonline.org.uk/2021/05/25/weaving-a-knowledge-tapestry/

8 Mentoring beginning RE teachers in faith schools

Mark Plater

Introduction

This chapter explores the mentoring of beginning religious education (RE) teachers in schools which have an affiliation to a particular religion or religious denomination. Although some have contested the term *faith schools* to describe all schools with a religious foundation, it is used in this chapter since that is the legal term used by the British government for this category of schools. So, in this chapter, the term *faith school* is taken to mean any school that in its Foundation Deeds, or in its intention and practice, gives religious faith a central role in the curriculum and ethos of the institution. The chapter begins by looking at why such schools exist in the first place and then outlines the range and variety of such institutions, showing how the task of mentoring might vary from one school to another, depending on not only the purpose for the existence of the school but also how the subject of RE is placed within the wider curriculum. In some faith schools for instance, the RE teacher will serve a role which is little different from that of any other teacher, whereas in others, they will be core to the foundational intention or purpose of the school. In the latter, they might be expected to not just uphold the teachings of the faith that is being passed on to the pupils but also to be instrumental in nurturing the faith and religious lifestyle and worldview of the whole community, both within and beyond the specific school community.

Although the focus is largely on faith schools in England, much of what is written may apply to faith schools in other countries. Therefore, if you are working in a country other than England, you are encouraged to relate the content of the chapter to your own context. The first part of the chapter is designed to enable you to support a beginning RE teacher to understand the context of faith schools in general as well as being aware of the specific faith school in which they are working. The second part focuses more specifically on aspects of mentoring a beginning teacher in a faith school in which the teaching of RE is regarded as much more than just educating pupils about other people's religions and worldviews but where the school is intentionally inducting children into a particular faith and practice.

By the end of this chapter, you should be able to:

- Explain to a beginning RE teacher the range and variety of faith schools in England.
- Help a beginning RE teacher understand why faith schools exist and how they might contrast with other secular institutions.

DOI: 10.4324/9781003191087-10

- Recognise how mentoring a beginning RE teacher in a faith school might potentially require more, or different kinds of, support from that required in mentoring beginning RE teachers in other educational institutions.
- Be alert to the levels of awareness and sensitivity that might be required of a mentor in some faith schools.

Understanding education and faith in a variety of cultural contexts

The UN Declaration of Human Rights states:

> Article 18: *Everyone has the right to freedom of thought, conscience and religion; this right includes freedom to change his religion or belief, and freedom, either alone or in community with others and in public or private, to manifest his religion or belief in teaching, practice, worship and observance.*
>
> Article 26: 3 *Parents have a prior right to choose the kind of education that shall be given to their children.*
>
> (United Nations, 1948)

Some countries (e.g. France and the US) interpret this by making a clear distinction between religion and state in their constitution and so offer a state-run education system that excludes religion from the curriculum, allowing families to provide their own RE outside of school. In such systems, the only reference to religion will be included in the study of school subjects like art, literature and history. Other countries (e.g. much of Europe) provide some form of denominational RE within mainstream education, where pupils are separated off into segregated classes for RE so that they can receive teaching from the perspective of their own faith or denomination. In England, the state provides a 'dual system' in which faith schools are funded alongside non-faith schools, although RE and the daily practice of religion (i.e. Collective Worship) are provided in all schools but with provision for parents to remove their children where they feel that this is in conflict with the faith perspective they wish to provide for their children (the 'conscience clause'). This withdrawal clause is considered particularly important for parents who allow their children to attend denominational faith schools which do not reflect their own particular faith perspective, allowing them to avoid their children being confused between a difference in teaching provided at school and home.

If we take the example of England, it has a complex history in respect of its faith schools. Prior to the 1870 Education Act, there was no organised national educational system, but thousands of private and charity schools run by churches, employers and even individual benefactors. The government did not fully engage with the field of education until the 1902 'Balfour' Act, when local authorities were created to take control of and manage the education provision within their jurisdiction. During World War II, when the major education act of 1944 was being considered in parliament, a decision had to be made about whether to take control of all these schools within a single educational system or whether to maintain a dual system of state and churches working together. In the end, the latter structure was agreed, with some faith schools seceding 'control' to the state and others being 'aided' by the state (for full details on the differences between these various groups, see www.gov.uk/types-of-school/faith-schools). Later education acts have retained this dual system, maintaining the framework for a variety of different kinds of faith schools and with various different requirements in respect of their RE and Collective Worship provision.

As has been shown, there is no internationally agreed formula on how religion should be handled within education as a key component of public life. Task 8.1 invites you to discuss this landscape with your beginning teacher. This may be particularly important if they are not familiar with faith schools.

Task 8.1 Supporting a beginning RE teacher to consider differences

If you are working with a beginning teacher who is not familiar with faith schools, it may help them develop an awareness of the complexity of provision for RE in different countries so that they can situate their new experiences in this context.

In one of your early mentoring sessions, discuss with the beginning teacher what the benefits and limitations of each of the different provisions are for RE, considering all the named different state-sponsored education systems as well as the one in which you are working.

Faith schools in England

The remainder of this section focuses on England where there are faith schools in both the state and private sectors. Today, almost a third of English state-run schools are categorised as faith schools (Long and Danechi, 2019). Table 8.1 outlines the number and percentages of

Table 8.1 Faith Schools in England

Type of faith school	State primary schools	State secondary schools	Private schools+ (primary & secondary)
No religious character	10,609 (63.2%)	2,771 (81.3%)	1,305 (55.2%)
Church of England (CE)	4,377 (26.1%)	209 (6.1%)	500*
Roman Catholic (RC)	1,645 (9.8%)	322 (9.4%)	150*
Methodist	25 (0.1%)	0	15*
Other Christian	72 (0.4%)	73 (2.1%)	100*
Hindu	0	1 (less than 0.1%)	7
Jewish	36 (0.2%)	12 (0.4%)	120 (Eng+Scot)
Muslim	13 (0.1%)	4 (0.1%)	155
Sikh	5 (less than 0.1)	6 (0.2%)	14
TOTAL	6,177 (36.8%)	627 (18.4%)	1,601 (44.8%)

Main Source: https://religionmediacentre.org.uk/factsheets/faith-schools-in-the-uk/
Note: 2017 statistics on state-maintained and independent (private) English faith schools. Numbers marked with a * indicate estimates only. Other figures are based on listed schools
+ Details from Independent Schools Directory: www.ukindependentschoolsdirectory.co.uk/ and from www. catholicindependentschools.com/, www.methodistschools.org.uk/about-us/about-us, and https://newchristian schools.org/

the different faith schools in England (if you are mentoring a beginning teacher in another country you will need to collect the relevant data). Task 8.2 presents an opportunity for you and your beginning teacher to reflect on the implications of the data. This will allow the beginning teacher to think about the range of schools and the choices and opportunities that they might have as they go forward in their career.

Task 8.2 Considering the data

Using the data as a stimulus, discuss with the beginning teacher the following questions:

- What surprises you most from the data in Table 8.1?
- Are there any implications from the primary school data for RE teachers working in secondary schools?
- Which of these schools might you be willing to work in?
- Are there any that you feel you could not work in? Why?

However, it is not enough just to focus on the number of faith schools as *not all faith schools are the same*. Within both the state and private sectors, there are different catego-ries of faith school, as illustrated in Figure 8.1. Here 'establishment' religion refers to schools

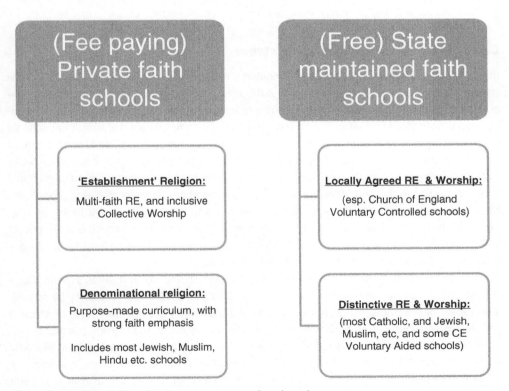

Figure 8.1 English faith schools – a summary of various types

where civic/civil religion is foundational (or where the national mainstream religion provides the foundation but is not the driving energy of the institution); this contrasts with 'denominational' religion, which refers to schools which represent minority religious groups or specific denominational perspectives. Within the state-maintained sector, the diagram distinguishes between those which follow the same RE syllabus as non-faith schools and those which are free to devise their own RE curriculum.

Task 8.3 gives you an opportunity to discuss with a beginning teacher where your school sits within this landscape.

Task 8.3 Your school

Discuss with the beginning teacher where your school 'fits' in the framework in Figure 8.1 and what difference this makes in terms of the ethos and RE curriculum within the school.

The different types of schools in Table 8.1 include those with distinctive faith traditions and those which are more establishment or mainstream. These two different types of schools may have very different theological stances, and they are also likely to offer very different kinds of RE. We will therefore now consider these issues in further detail.

Categories of school by theological stance

In a Christian context, the Church of England's report *The Church School of the Future* (National Society & Archbishop's Council, 2012) identified its schools as expressing two core purposes: *mission* and *service*. These terms represent two distinct theological and missiological emphases: *incarnational* and *transformational* communities. Incarnational schools emphasise the 'living among' element of Christ's ministry, the fact that He becomes 'one of us'. This might be categorised as the 'service' form of mission, one in which the church seeks to be a reforming presence in society, rather than seeking to proselytise, or to specifically focus on nurturing the faith development of its own members. Transformational schools, on the other hand, emphasise Christ's call to His followers to live life differently, to live according to the norms and assumptions of the Kingdom of God. Such an approach is more proactive in seeking to create a church within the school, a community shaped in order to live out and nurture the message and mission of Jesus Himself.

It would be unwise to use the same language for Jewish, Muslim and Hindu schools, but a similar distinction can be made between faith schools that seek to serve society by emphasising a set of specific spiritual/human values and those that seek to transform or shape a community by emphasising particular religious norms, language and cultural practices.

For schools of any religious faith, those with an incarnational emphasis might welcome and accept pupils from all faiths and none, whereas those with a transformational emphasis are more likely to attract children from committed religious families of that particular faith.

Reflect on the different theological approaches that might be taken by schools by considering the questions in Task 8.4.

Task 8.4 Theological stance

Before reading on, spend a few minutes thinking about the question, *How would you describe to a beginning teacher the kind of faith school they are working in?*

Jot down as many words or phrases that you can think of to describe how your school is distinctive, particularly in terms of its faith dimension. Then consider the following questions:

- Do you find the distinction between incarnational and transformational (or values and religion-based) schools a helpful distinction?
- What other terms might be used to distinguish between faith schools that are highly focused on nurturing faith and those that are less focused on faith-formation?
- How helpful might such terms be for explaining the purpose and intention of RE in your school to other staff and, indeed, to a beginning teacher?

The place of RE in the curriculum

Faith schools can also be differentiated by how they place RE within the taught curriculum. In some, the subject of RE will be regarded as a distinct, academic subject in its own right, quite separate from any religious practice that takes place in the school. Here, the curriculum is likely to be comprehensive and inclusive of all religions and outlooks. Thus, the teaching of RE will be separate from, and distinctive to, the work of chaplaincy and school Collective Worship. In other schools, the two will be intertwined, and the head of RE might well be responsible for planning, delivering and monitoring of worship events and spiritual development as well as of the classroom RE programme.

To give some examples:

- An Orthodox Jewish school may consider that all aspects of the curriculum (learning Hebrew, learning about and practising cultural norms, dressing and behaving in particular ways, etc.) are part of the school's 'RE' such that the teacher is as much a model of right religion as a teacher of it.
- A Church of England primary school in an English village may consider itself to be the community school for all the local children rather than a school which exists specifically to shape and direct the religious life of its Anglican pupils. Such a school will include RE in the curriculum, but it may be that this will be taught as a study of the phenomenon of religion within the community rather than as an induction into 'our' religion.

Clearly the expectations, and therefore the mentoring, of a beginning RE teacher will be quite different in the former compared with the latter. Task 8.5 asks you to reflect on how you might articulate the place of RE in the curriculum in your own school setting for a beginning teacher.

Task 8.5 RE, spirituality and Collective Worship in your school

Consider the following questions and discuss the following with your beginning teacher:

- How do RE, religious lifestyle/spirituality and Collective Worship feature in your school?
- In what ways are they all integrated or all distinct from each other?
- Is the planning, and responsibility for them, dealt with as a whole or independently?
- What is the impact of the above on the teaching of RE in your school? As a mentor, how would you explain the rationale for this to a beginning teacher at your school?

Mentoring in faith schools

The second section of this chapter focuses explicitly on mentoring in a faith school. It starts by looking at mentoring a beginning teacher of any subject in a faith school, before focusing on mentoring a beginning RE teacher.

Most faith schools will have a clause in a staff member's contract which requires that they do nothing that will damage or undermine the ethos and foundation of the school. Such a clause binds the staff member to a public lifestyle and defence of the officially sanctioned position that the school might hold on, say, dress code or moral conduct. Any beginning teacher in such a context – with or without a legal contract – will need to ensure that they both understand and are willing to comply with such requirements. They need to clearly understand that it is likely that the faith school will hold values or practices which are distinctive from the norms of the surrounding culture and that these values and practices will be strongly defended, since they are core to what is distinctive about this particular educational context. Clearly, the mentor of a beginning RE teacher has a responsibility to ensure that they have been made aware of such matters as early as possible in their tenure at the school.

When beginning teachers either wittingly or unwittingly speak or act in ways that do not comply with expectations, then the mentor will be faced with the challenge of pointing out the error and perhaps even explaining and defending the position of the school so that this can be understood and appreciated by the beginning teacher. Task 8.6 presents an opportunity to reflect on this in relation to your own school setting.

Task 8.6 School values

In one of your early mentoring sessions explain to and discuss with your beginning teacher the values or practices which are a focus in your school, but which might vary from – or even clash with – those of the surrounding community. Does this present any challenges for your beginning teacher?

Talking to a beginning teacher about these issues is a fundamental aspect in mentoring beginning teachers in faith schools. However, managing conversations on issues such as these can be fraught with difficulty, especially when beginning teachers are not cognisant of the traditions of the school community or may feel a personal disconnection or disagreement with such traditions. Here we may perhaps draw a distinction between someone who has specifically chosen to teach in such a school and a trainee who has been placed there by their training provider. In the case of the latter, it is very important that such conversations are held very early on to make clear that some school values may be quite different to those that the trainee has previously encountered.

Great tact may be required to make clear the concern of the school but to do so in such a way as also to protect the beginning teacher's sense of self-worth. For instance, a female beginning teacher might need to be challenged about the length of her skirt or her overuse of make-up. Another example might be an over-enthusiastic beginning teacher who is unsympathetic to the fragility and sensitivities of pupils during the Ramadan fasting period. The mentor needs to know: Is this a case of ignorance or misunderstanding of expectations, or is it a deliberate challenge to the system? Also, is this a sensitive person who is likely to be mortified that they have transgressed school expectations or someone used to accepting correction and easily responsive to making changes in such matters? Getting it right may be paramount in both developing and maintaining the mentor–mentee relationship and enabling the beginning teacher to offer their best, feeling supported and encouraged in the learning process. Task 8.7 asks you to reflect on this in relation to your experience of your own school setting.

Task 8.7 School values in practice

Consider:

- What kinds of values/behavioural issues of this type have surfaced for beginning teachers in your experience, either in your school or elsewhere? How were they dealt with?
- How might you use such examples as illustrations to talk with beginning teachers about professional expectations in your school?

The kind of issues that might typically make the faith school distinctive in this sense could include the following:

- Dress code issues
- Specific religious practices (e.g. prayers at the start of lessons, meditation periods, etc.)
- Use of specific language (e.g. biblical phrases or Qur'anic/Arabic terms)
- Food rules or norms (e.g. no pork or kosher-only foods)
- Lifestyle norms (e.g. no tobacco or alcohol)
- Curriculum and timetable structure and content (e.g. heavy weighting on religious or denominational teaching)

Task 8.8 asks you to reflect on these examples and consider a case study to help you reflect on how issues might be tackled when working with a beginning teacher.

Task 8.8 Dealing with difficult situations

Look at the earlier list of potential faith-school-distinctive issues. Which are relevant to your school? Are there any others that you would add based on your context?

Now consider how, as the mentor, you would respond to each of the following scenarios.

Scenario 1

The beginning teacher is having lunch in the dining hall with other staff and pupils at Medina Islamic Academy. He removes a scotch egg (probably containing pork sausage meat) from his lunchbox and begins to eat it in front of surrounding staff and pupils.

Scenario 2

An initial teacher education (ITE) student is placed in a Catholic school where the teachers lead the pupils in a short prayer at the start of every lesson. The trainee is enjoying the placement, is supportive of the Catholic ethos of the school and happy to teach the RE curriculum. However, they have expressed their discomfort at the idea of leading prayers.

Think about the following:

- How could the mentors in each of these scenarios deal with the situation they are facing?
- What points need to be made in the conversations they will have?
- What possible solutions might there be in in scenario 2?

Varying expectations of mentoring

Furthermore, the esteem with which mentoring is itself held as a nurturing practice may be quite distinctive within certain types of faith schools. For instance, where the school holds personal spirituality to be of the highest order, attention to this dimension may be given particular priority, with time spent in studying scriptures and praying together, as well as sharing of personal life stories and experiences, all seen as part of the mentoring process. For a beginning teacher keen to develop in this way, the experience could be remarkably supportive, offering both personal and professional support in a single, comprehensive package. For another beginning teacher the experience might be both intrusive and overbearing! The mentor therefore needs to be in a constant state of awareness and constantly checking how the beginning teacher is responding to the process: Do they *appear* to be comfortable with the process, and when asked, do they *confirm* that they are finding this helpful? And the relationship needs to be such that they really do feel comfortable to say 'no'. Ideally within such a system, there ought to be an arrangement whereby someone else, who is less immediate than the mentor, is tasked with checking on the beginning teacher to see how they are experiencing such a high-intensity mentoring experience. I would suggest that the pressure in these kinds of mentoring contexts – that is where they emphasise personal and spiritual development in addition to the slightly more detached 'professional' development – is for the beginning teacher to feel compelled towards conformity and wanting to please. It takes a very skilled and self-aware mentor to be fully cognisant of this fact and recognise that honesty and integrity may be compromised where such forces are at work.

Why and how might the mentoring of RE teachers in faith schools be distinctive?

All faith schools exist with the intention of providing an education which is distinctive. This is usually spelled out in detail within the foundational documents of the school. For example, in the case of Catholic schools, all Catholic teachers are there to establish a 'unique Christian school climate' (Sacred Congregation for Catholic Education, 1998. #19) which nurtures faith and guides young people in life regardless of the subject being taught. Mentoring all teachers within such a school is therefore of vital importance to ensure that this distinctiveness is upheld. Such mentoring is clearly about much more than simply ensuring that teachers can plan and deliver classroom units of work effectively. Rather, each member of staff is contributing to the wider values and ethos of the school and is involved in the faith formation of pupils. Each therefore plays a significant part in furthering the school's overall faith identity.

In some faith schools, however, where key to the founding purpose was the provision of distinctive teaching within a particular religious tradition, RE is likely to be deemed, and given the status of, a core subject, alongside, or perhaps even ahead of, English, maths and science. In a document by the *Catholic Education Service of England and Wales* (2020) for instance, RE is described as 'core of the core curriculum' (although not all Catholic educators would agree that RE should be so distinctive in Catholic schools: see Whittle [2021] for instance). For such a school, how the subject is taught will be of vital importance, and the institution will be keen to ensure that accurate pupil instruction is provided and that this is delivered in an appropriate style so that the faith – the raison d'être for the school – is upheld and defended. Mentors in all faith schools therefore need to share with beginning teachers the specific approach taken to RE within their own context so that, from the outset, beginning teachers precisely understand the aims of the subject in that particular setting and that they approach lesson planning with an informed interpretation of exactly what it is that is required or expected of them.

Mentoring beginning RE teachers in faith schools

We now turn to consider the key question, *What mentoring support is required for a beginning RE teacher in a faith school?* The first point to note is that, like any beginning teacher, they will need help to develop skills and understanding across all aspects of the profession which may be broken down into focus categories, such as behaviour management, pedagogy, the RE curriculum, assessment and professionalism. However, beyond that, what might be different about mentoring support for an RE teacher in a faith school, first, because it is a faith school and, second, because they are teaching about religion in a faith school? We have previously noted that religious education may hold a range of different 'positions' within a faith school. Where it is treated as a distinctive academic subject in its own right, there may be hardly any features that make mentoring an RE teacher in a faith school different from doing the same in any other school or mentoring any other subject teacher in a faith school. However, where the subject is given high status as being core to the purpose and intention of the institution, this may be quite different.

First, especially where faith formation through RE is a core purpose of the school, there may be a uniquely robust emphasis on teaching certain 'right' beliefs and doctrines. Mentoring in this context is clearly more than just a professional practice. In describing his version of 'Christian mentoring' for instance, Wakeman (2012) argues for a 'transformation of the mind' so that the mentoring practice both proceeds from, and nurtures, a Christian worldview. This form of mentoring might more accurately be described as 'discipling' and could only be carried out by a member of the faith community itself. In such a context, beginning teachers might need particular help in responding to unexpected pupil questions and providing examples which help make the case for the preferred denominational stance. For instance, in a strongly evangelical Christian school, the RE teacher might be encouraged to avoid questions which challenge a literalist interpretation of scripture or which imply that the Bible is anything other than the verbally inspired Word of God. In this context, they might be expected to be able to offer scriptural and other 'evidence' to support a preferred position and fend off other perspectives. When a beginning teacher does not themselves hold to such a perspective or when they have not previously been schooled in this theological standpoint, it is unlikely that a placement or early-career teaching post would be offered in the first place. However, if they have been, and yet still are perceived as unable to effectively teach the school's curriculum, then the mentor will find themselves with a more challenging task in hand, requiring them to offer exceptional levels of support in order to enable the beginning teacher to cope.

A second, related problem with regard to specific denominational knowledge, also exists where a school might be open to a wider range of perspectives, but still teaches a specific curriculum, focused on its own particular beliefs and practices. In an example of this, a very committed evangelical Christian trainee went to complete an ITE placement in a Catholic school. The trainee's upbringing was in the Protestant tradition, which included wide knowledge and experience of the Bible and of various aspects of the Protestant faith. Prior to this school placement, they considered themselves very knowledgeable about Christianity but, in teaching a specifically Catholic syllabus, realised that their own understanding was limited to a particular perspective. Fortunately, the mentor was very supportive and understanding and made a wide range of school textbooks and other resources available so that the trainee could fill the gaps in their knowledge. A less understanding and supportive mentor might have unhelpfully confronted the trainee or even suggested that they might not have been suitable for the school in the first place. However, with appropriate support, in this instance, the school benefitted from a good classroom practitioner, and the trainee was able to expand their understanding of Christian faith and practice into a wider sphere.

A third context in which difficulties might potentially exist for a beginning RE teacher is when the school's RE classes are considered part of the faith formation, or induction of pupils into faith, and when, therefore, the RE teacher is perceived to be as much a religious leader as classroom teacher. Paul Hirst (1972) classifies this as 'tribal education', in which education exists in order to maintain the survival and continuation of the tribe. In RE parlance (Grimmitt, 2000), it has often been described as *confessional* RE to distinguish it from RE which is more interested in the *study* of religion rather than induction into a particular way of seeing the world. In this tribal or confessional scenario, the RE syllabus covers not just information about the faith but also an actual induction into the faith. In an Orthodox Jewish school for instance, this might be a bar/bat mitzvah class or, for an Islamic school, a sunnah class, wherein pupils learn the social and legal practices and customs of the faith. Clearly, in this context, the teacher is not just a teacher but also a model or example of faith. It is unlikely therefore that the school would intentionally offer an ITE placement or early-career post to someone who did not fit the bill for such a role, but even if the beginning teacher was in all respects suitable, there might still be all kinds of reasons why the mentor might need to provide additional support and challenge that goes well beyond academic and pedagogical knowledge. Task 8.9 offers some case studies to help you reflect on how you might respond in such situations.

Task 8.9 Dealing with challenges

Consider the following scenarios:

Scenario 1

In a Church of England voluntary-aided school, it comes to light that the new RE teacher's social media site shows her clubbing and joking about being drunk. The fact is drawn to the school's attention by a parent.

Scenario 2

In an Orthodox Jewish school, the beginning RE teacher has been observed to teach using neutral pronouns ('they', 'them') rather than first person plural pronouns ('we', 'our').

How might you address these issues with the beginning teacher?

Mentor as coach, counsellor, fellow traveller, guru and guide

As outlined earlier, the mentor in a faith school might offer much more than just professional support for a beginning RE teacher, especially in the context where the school is involved in faith formation. The RE mentor role will always be like that of any school subject mentor – a specialist support for helping the beginning teacher grasp the technical skills of classroom organisation, behaviour management, pupil assessment and so on – but they may also need to take on a number of further roles. Sometimes they may be a counsellor to help the beginning teacher work through the emotional journey of personal growth through failure; sometimes a guide to help the beginning teacher understand the different and distinctive focus and emphasis of RE within this particular educational context; and, sometimes, a spiritual adviser, helping and enabling the beginning teacher to grow in their own religious journey so that they are better equipped to share examples from their own faith and thus nurture the faith of those entrusted to their care. A case might be made that such support provisions could be expected of any mentor and within any type of school, but I hope that we have been able to show that there are particular reasons why this might uniquely be expected of the faith school mentor.

Mentoring then, from a faith perspective, may be seen as a form of servant leadership, or as a pilgrimage, in which both mentor and mentee are on a faith journey together, and both participants will be shaped and changed by the process. Task 8.10 invites you to consider how you see yourself and your role in relation to this.

Task 8.10 Metaphors for mentoring

How does changing the language to a more faith-based form of metaphor change your perspective on what mentoring is?

How might each of the following metaphors shape your perspective on the role of the mentor and the process of mentoring?

Discipling
Shepherding
A shared pilgrimage
Servant leadership

Can you suggest other metaphors which, for you, help conceptualise the task of mentoring?

Dangerous quicksands in faith school mentoring

It is a great privilege to be able to pass on expertise and experience to the next generation. Indeed, JoAnn Looney (2008) argues that mentoring is such a vital feature of Christian schools that it is likely to determine the outcome of a beginning teacher's career and is vital for maintaining ongoing staff loyalty. Noting the attrition rate of teachers from the profession, Looney makes a case that mentoring is perhaps one of the most important tasks that faith schools can undertake.

Mentoring also gives an opportunity to reflect on your own practice and offers wider windows for personal and professional development across the school. However, one must also beware of those who are too keen to pass on their own entrenched ideas and attitudes regardless of the relevance or benefit to those on the receiving end. Our task is not to impose ourselves on others but to enable others to grow and, ultimately, even to surpass us. The ultimate aim of the process must be self-direction and autonomy, not cloning or dependence. Mentoring is thus a collaborative process (English, 1998), embodying a circular rather than triangular model of leadership and guidance.

Mentorship also has the potential for interpersonal conflict (Cohen, 1995) as well as personal and professional benefits. Confrontations such as those outlined earlier are by their very nature pastorally delicate and potentially inflammatory, and the mentor is always advised to approach such situations with great compassion and sensitivity. Here we might learn from therapeutic practice: repeating and restating 'facts' to check that this is also how the mentee understands the context, reflecting back the mentor's observations or experiences to check that this is actually what was intended by the trainee, asking the beginning teacher how they think that their behaviour is likely to be perceived and interpreted by the faith community rather than simply telling them how to improve and so on. In all these contexts, the mentor is seeking to maintain a balance between confrontation and relationship, holding the mentee to account, while ensuring that the dignity of both parties is not diminished or undermined.

All of this requires time and energy, and without structural support, neither mentor nor mentee is likely to have the space and freedom required to develop the process effectively.

Summary and key points

This chapter has explored the mentoring of RE teachers in faith schools, recognising both the variety of what we might mean by 'faith' school and the potential complexity of the role when it is overlaid with additional assumptions of faith formation. In summary, we might note the following:

- There are many different kinds of faith schools, and RE teaching will vary in its focus and emphasis between these schools.
- The degree of profile and denominational emphasis given to RE in any school will determine the level of scrutiny that the beginning teacher will face in providing a form of RE that is specific to the needs of the given institution.
- When RE is offered for the development of personal faith in pupils rather than merely for academic understanding, the beginning teacher will be monitored as a role model for faith in addition to their classroom teaching expertise.
- Depending on the level of faith nurturing expected of the RE teacher at a given school, the mentor may be required to provide spiritual and lifestyle direction as well as professional monitoring and guidance.

Further resources

English, L. M. (1999). *Mentorship: Adult Formation for Educators in Catholic Schools*. https://digitalcommons.lmu.edu/cgi/viewcontent.cgi?article=1120&context=ce

This particularly focuses on mentoring in a Catholic school context.

The House of Commons Briefing Paper Number 06972, 20 December 2019. *Faith Schools in England: FAQs*, by Robert Long and Shadi Danechi. https://researchbriefings.files.parliament.uk/documents/SN06972/SN06972.pdf

This is an excellent summary of the variety and nature of faith schools in England.

Zeldin, M. and Lee, S. S. (eds.) (1995). *Touching the Future: Mentoring and the Jewish Professional* (pp 66–73). Los Angeles: Hebrew Union College- Jewish Institute of Religion.

This particularly focuses on mentoring in a Jewish school context.

References

Catholic Education Service of England and Wales. (2020). *Why Is Religious Education in Catholic Schools Important?* https://www.catholiceducation.org.uk/schools/religious-education/item/1002967-about-religious-education-in-catholic-schools

Cohen, N. H. (1995). *Mentoring Adult Learners: A Guide for Educators and Trainers*. Krieger.

Department for Education (DfE). (2022). *Faith Schools*. https://www.gov.uk/types-of-school/faith-schools

Education Reform Act *1988*, c. 1. (n.d.) https://www.legislation.gov.uk/ukpga/1988/40/contents/enacted

English, L. M. (1999). *Mentoring in Religious Education*. Religious Education Press.

Grimmitt, M. (Ed.). (2000). *Pedagogies of Religious Education: Case Studies in the Research and Development of Good Pedagogic Practice in RE*. McCrimmon.

Hirst, P. H. (1972). Christian education: A contradiction in terms? *Learning for Living*, 11(4), 6–11.

Long, R. and Danechi, S. (2019). *Faith Schools in England: FAQs. House of Commons Briefing Paper 06972*. https://researchbriefings.files.parliament.uk/documents/SN06972/SN06972.pdf

Looney, J. (2008). Developing comprehensive induction programs at Christian schools. *International Community of Christian Educators*, 3(2), 1–9. https://digitalcommons.georgefox.edu/cgi/viewcontent.cgi?article=1040&context=icctej&httpsredir=1&referer=

National Society & Archbishops Council. (2012). *The Church School of the Future Review, March 2021*. https://www.churchofengland.org/sites/default/files/2017-10/2012_the_church_school_of_the_future_review_web_final.pdf

Sacred Congregation for Catholic Education. (1998). *The Catholic School on the Threshold of the New Millennium*. https://www.vatican.va/roman_curia/congregations/ccatheduc/documents/rc_con_ccatheduc_doc_27041998_school2000_en.html

United Nations. (1948). *Universal Declaration of Human Rights*. https://www.un.org/en/about-us/universal-declaration-of-human-rights

Wakeman, B. E. (2012). A Christian perspective on mentoring. *Transformation (Exeter)*, 29(4), 277–292. https://doi.org/10.1177/0265378812457752

Whittle, S. (2021). Why is it time to stop referring to 'Catholic Religious Education'? *Journal of Religious Education*, 69(3), 401–410. https://doi.org/10.1007/s40839-021-00145-7

9 Developing beginning teachers' understanding of knowledge and skills in the RE curriculum

James Holt

Introduction

This chapter is intended to support mentors as they help beginning teachers explore the place of knowledge and skills within the religious education (RE) classroom. The approach taken is to describe different types of knowledge and skills to enable the mentor to reflect on these. This will provide the background to support beginning teachers as they seek to develop their own substantive knowledge to inform their lesson planning and identify the skills their pupils will need to engage with religion and worldviews in the RE classroom. Two models of progression, one of knowledge and the other of skills, have been utilised within the teaching of RE, both of which should be developed. Beginning teachers need to explore how progression is made in terms of both knowledge and skills.

By the end of the chapter, you should be able to:

- Identify the knowledge and skills secondary pupils need to learn and develop in RE.
- Articulate the complex nature of knowledge in RE, including the 'messiness' of religion that should be explored as substantive knowledge is developed.
- Identify the types of knowledge developed in the RE classroom, including conceptual knowledge.
- Identify the skills developed by pupils in RE and how these can be explored in different classroom pedagogies and activities.
- Identify the ways in which you can help develop a beginning teacher's understanding of wider RE subject knowledge, practice and pedagogical philosophy.

Knowledge

Teachers go through a process of knowledge selection when designing the curriculum, but elements of this will also have happened at the design stage of the agreed syllabus, or the exam specification. At one time, knowledge was the accepted range of information used to help pupils develop their understanding of religion and belief and meet the wider aims of RE. It has become evident that knowledge serves a much greater function than developing the religious literacy and understanding of pupils. Knowledge is also a reflection of the concerns

DOI: 10.4324/9781003191087-11

of the person, people or group who are establishing it as the focus of the curriculum. This is not a new observation, and in your role as a mentor, it would be useful for you to reflect on and recognise what has influenced the content and organisation of your curriculum. Your department may have chosen the material, but it is important to step back and consider the nature of the knowledge being taught so that you can articulate this for a beginning teacher. The educationalist Michael Apple has suggested that, when faced with what to teach, certain questions should be asked: "Whose knowledge is it? Who selected it? Why is it organized and taught in this way? To this particular group?" and he highlighted that the answers to these questions are informed by "competing conceptions of social and economic power and ideologies" (Apple, 2019, p. 6). This recognition of a teacher's background and experiences providing unconscious bias in the selection of knowledge and interpretation of knowledge has, perhaps, become more obvious in society as phrases such as 'alternative facts' and 'post-truth world' are heard. Teachers, at any stage of their career, must recognise how their background influences their view the of world, but a beginning teacher may need your support to do this.

Task 9.1 is designed to help you think your own conception of knowledge before you start to discuss this with a beginning teacher.

Task 9.1 How do you view knowledge in RE?

Reflect on your own teaching career to date. Consider the following:

- Has the way that you think about knowledge in RE changed at all over that time?
- Are you conscious of your own background and experiences influencing the knowledge you include in your curriculum? Can you articulate this for a beginning teacher?

The *Research Review Series: Religious Education* (Ofsted, 2021) has drawn together some of the narratives surrounding knowledge in RE and suggests three types of knowledge are found in the curriculum:

- "First, 'substantive' knowledge: knowledge about various religious and non-religious traditions
- Second, 'ways of knowing': pupils learn 'how to know' about religion and non-religion
- Third, 'personal knowledge': pupils build an awareness of their own presuppositions and values about the religious and non-religious traditions they study"

Although each of these should be woven together in the classroom and in the curriculum, this chapter considers each in turn, reflecting on how mentors can work with beginning teachers to ensure they understand the nature of the knowledge and skills that underpin the RE curriculum. Task 9.2 encourages you to reflect on your own understanding of these three types of knowledge.

Task 9.2 Three types of knowledge

Write down your initial thoughts on the definitions of the three types of knowledge identified earlier: substantive knowledge, ways of knowing and personal knowledge. Are you clear about the differences between them?

In a mentor meeting, ask your beginning teacher to reflect on the three types of knowledge. Discuss their understanding of each with them, and encourage them to think about the kind of classroom activities that might be used to develop each type of knowledge.

Substantive knowledge

Substantive knowledge is the 'stuff' that is taught in the classroom and is the basis for every other aspect of the curriculum. Over the years, there seems to have been a pendulum swing regarding the desirability of this knowledge as a focus of the curriculum; sometimes, it has been pre-eminent in the focus of the curriculum, while at other times, it seems to have been sidelined in favour of skills. As is evident from the different sections of this chapter, substantive knowledge is central to classroom practice, progression and curriculum design, but it cannot, and should not, be separated from other aspects of the curriculum.

RE teachers today are very much the inheritors of the world religions approach to the teaching of RE, and it may be that this is the style of RE many beginning teachers experienced as a school pupil. In this approach, preference is given to what are considered to be the six 'main' religions in the UK and, to some extent, the wider world: Buddhism, Christianity, Hinduism, Islam, Judaism and Sikhism. Although there are many merits to this approach, there are also issues with it, including the exclusion of minority expressions of these religions or religions and worldviews lying outside of the 'big six' (see Holt, 2019). Therefore, beginning teachers should be encouraged to acknowledge the 'messiness' of religion and worldviews, and this should have an impact on the way they engage with subject and pedagogical knowledge. It is important that, in your discussions with them, you problematise and challenge the accepted corpus of knowledge that they may have developed. This problematisation will help the beginning teacher understand that religion is not fixed and that the codification of religions and worldviews can cause teachers to reinforce stereotypes and not recognise the rich diversity that can be found through its study. Unfortunately, this messiness may not even be recognised by members of faith communities who contribute to the design of agreed syllabi or specifications. A concrete and static understanding of religion is easy and comfortable, and some leaders and believers of traditions may be concerned to establish boundaries of orthodoxy which lead to a rejection of the lived reality of religion.

There are two dangers in the RE classroom when a teacher only recognises religions as monoliths. Both relate to the question of diversity within the religion in terms of orthodoxy and orthopraxy. The first surrounds the possibility of personal interpretation of faith. If the diversity in the day-to-day lived experience of a religion is not acknowledged, RE can become less valid in the eyes of pupils because it is out of step with their own experiences. Second, there is a danger surrounding the question of which groups can be considered part of the worldview being studied. This is exemplified by the Latter-day Saints, Jehovah's Witnesses, and others within Christianity (see Holt, 2019) or perhaps Shi'a and Ahmadiyya within Islam (see Holt, 2019); further examples may surround the inclusion of Namdharis and Guru Nanak Nishkam Sewak Jatha in the Sikh Panth (see Kaur Takhar, 2005). It is essential that teachers of RE recognise the debate, but they are not the arbiters of the boundaries of religions and therefore should not dismiss, for example, the 'Sikhness' of a group. This means that teachers need to teach 'Big Tent' religions, exploring how groups differ but share core values/ concepts that mean they would place themselves within the wider tent of the tradition. Whatever a teacher's personal views about Christianness or Muslimness (or the shape and boundaries of any other religious or non-religious worldview), teachers of RE must respect the self-identification of a group or individual. It is important to help beginning RE teachers recognise the limits of a teacher's knowledge when faced with a difficult question and why 'many', 'most' or 'some' are used in describing and explaining beliefs and practices associated with religions and worldviews.

This debate may seem to have diverged from a discussion of the substantive knowledge within RE, but it is important to frame the knowledge that is being taught rather than perpetuating an accepted narrative. Having established this frame, it is possible to explore the nature of substantive knowledge within RE. Ninian Smart's (1989) seven dimensions of religion have generally been used to organise knowledge about religion in the RE classroom:

- The doctrinal
- The mythological (narrative)
- The ethical
- The ritual
- The experiential
- The social
- The material (aesthetic)

These dimensions have an advantage over perhaps more popular categorisations of religious belief and practice such as 'deities', 'places of worship', 'founders', 'sacred texts' and so on because these are reductive and not inclusive of all religions and worldviews. For example, can the Guru Granth Sahib really be considered a sacred text when it is better described as a living Guru? Or, perhaps the lack of a founder within Hinduism places it outside of the discussion. Beginning teachers need to be aware that these oversimplifications can often lead to the static knowledge that this chapter has warned against. How each of the religions and worldviews, as well as its adherents, engage with the different aspects of Smart's seven dimensions is a useful starting point but is only one possible approach, and it should be approached against the background of messiness. Smart's dimensions may be seen to support or be at odds with Ofsted's (2021) idea of a curriculum that is "collectively enough"; indeed, they suggest that substantive knowledge would incorporate "representations of religious and non-religious traditions that would, over the span of the curriculum, enable pupils to grasp 'big ideas' about religious and non-religious traditions" rather than focussing on all the dimensions for all religions. Task 9.3 suggests a way that you can work with your beginning teacher to explore how the 'messiness' of religion can be acknowledged and explored in schemes of work.

Task 9.3 Working with the 'messiness' of religion

Select one scheme of work from your curriculum to examine with your beginning teacher. In your discussion with them consider the following questions:

- How would you incorporate acknowledgement of diversity within/between religions into the topic?
- Is there a way to recognise the messiness of religion in teaching the beliefs and practices of one religion?
- Is there anything that should be added to the unit of work to help pupils understand the diversity within or between religions?

Developing concepts

As Smart's seven dimensions indicate, there are commonalities that are evident within, and between, religions and worldviews. This has led to another way in which knowledge is developed in the RE curriculum; through the threads of conceptual development. Conceptual development lies at the heart of the various iterations of the *Living Difference* Agreed Syllabus (Hampshire County Council et al., 2016). It has been further discussed by Lowndes (2012), Holt (2015) and Hutton and Cox (2021). In a conceptual knowledge development curriculum, there are four different levels of concepts that can be used:

- Concepts in the pupil's own experience
- Concepts common to human experience
- Concepts common to different religions
- Concepts specific to individual religions

Beginning teachers need to understand that, to develop pupils' conceptual knowledge, curricula are designed to build on previous knowledge, and as such, the concepts used become the driver of the curriculum and tie all learning together. For example, in England, this approach has been highlighted by the *ITE Core Content Framework* (Department for Education, 2019):

> Prior knowledge plays an important role in how pupils learn; committing some key facts to their long-term memory is likely to help pupils learn more complex ideas.
>
> (p. 11)

> Ensuring pupils master foundational concepts and knowledge before moving on is likely to build pupils' confidence and help them succeed.
>
> (p. 13)

It should be noted that here there is a distinction between concepts and knowledge which, in this chapter, are drawn together. This builds on the work of people such as Piaget and his work on schemata, where existing knowledge and concepts are used to develop new schema and bodies of knowledge. You will be conscious of the fact that it is impossible to teach everything about one religion, let alone all religions. As such concepts provide a way of ensuring progression in the curriculum as they find their expression in different religions and worldviews.

Table 9.1 offers an example of how the concept of sacrifice might be developed across the curriculum and in the context of different religions. You may wish to use this example in discussions with your beginning teacher to help them understand how conceptual understanding can be developed.

Table 9.1 An example of conceptual development in the classroom

---

Concept: Sacrifice

Level 1 conceptual development questions: Have you sacrificed anything in your life? Can you think of specific examples? How did you feel? Why did you sacrifice *x* for *y*? Was the sacrifice worth it?

Level 2 conceptual development questions: Can you think of any examples when someone has sacrificed something? Why do you think they sacrificed *x* for *y*? Was the sacrifice worth it?
You will notice that the second level moves from the personal in level 1 to the more 'outside' and 'theoretical'. It may be, dependent on the age and experiences of pupils, that the teacher might want to begin with level 2 questions. Sometimes the levels do not have to be linear and are interchangeable.

Level 3 conceptual development questions: Can you think of examples from the religions that we have studied of sacrifice? Why is that sacrifice important? What do believers learn from that example of sacrifice? How do believers sacrifice in their lives?
These are 'general' religious questions but can be adapted to be specific religions that pupils have already studied.

Level 4 conceptual development questions: What were the events surrounding Jesus' sacrifice? Why did he allow himself to be killed? How is Jesus' sacrifice remembered today? What impact does Jesus' sacrifice have on Christians today?
The curriculum plan that follows illustrates how certain lessons in different year groups can pick up on this thread of conceptual development as religions are explore in a systematic way.

Year 7: Buddhism
Short discussion: Have you sacrificed anything in your life? Can you think of specific examples? How did you feel? Why did you sacrifice *x* for *y*? Was the sacrifice worth it?
Life of the Buddha: What did the Siddhartha sacrifice on leaving the palace? Why might some people see this sacrifice as too much? What does the leaving of his family and life of wealth show to Buddhists today?

Year 8: Judaism
Short discussion: Can you think of examples from our discussion of Buddhism in Year 7 where someone made a sacrifice? Why is that sacrifice important? What do Buddhists learn from that example of sacrifice? *Sometimes teachers can see building on prior knowledge to be the immediate context of the previous lesson; this example shows that a well-designed curriculum can build on conceptual knowledge from previous units and years.*
Life of Abraham: What did Abraham sacrifice for the covenant? Why was he prepared to sacrifice his wealth and security? What can Jews learn from Abraham and his sacrifice for the covenant? Why was he willing to sacrifice Isaac? What does this teach Jews today?

Year 9: Islam
Short discussion: What can you remember about the sacrifice expected of Abraham and Isaac? Why is this event important for Jews today?
Ibrahim and Id-ul-Adha: What is the difference between the two stories of Abraham's sacrifice? Is there anything different that Muslims learn from the potential sacrifice of Ishmael? How is this sacrifice remembered today? What does this mean for Muslim identity today?
Hussein: Why is the sacrifice of Hussein different to that of Ishmael? Why is this sacrifice/martyrdom important for Muslims today? Why is the Shi'a remembrance of Ashura so solemn? What does this sacrifice mean for Islam?

The example in Table 9.1 illustrates the concepts with reference to aspects of three larger schemes of work; there is scope to explore sacrifice in other religions and worldviews and develop this example further. However, it highlights the way that concepts and the understanding of them can be developed through the use of different knowledge. In each case, existing conceptual knowledge is being used to develop pupils' understanding, with the cautionary note that the understanding of the concepts may vary considerably between religions. Task 9.4 offers a way that you could develop a conversation around this with your beginning teacher.

Task 9.4 Supporting beginning teachers to develop pupils' conceptual knowledge over time

- In one of your mentor meetings, highlight for your beginning teacher how concepts underpin your curriculum.
- Can the beginning teacher identify how concepts are developed?
- Are concepts developed with reference to more than one religion or worldview?
- Is the beginning teacher aware of how understanding of the concepts being discussed may vary between religions?
- Ask the beginning teacher to reflect on ways that they could make this more explicit in their planning and teaching.

Ways of knowing

Ways of knowing is often termed disciplinary knowledge. RE is interesting when considered in disciplinary terms as it is generally deemed to be a multidisciplinary study, which includes anthropology, sociology, theology, philosophy, psychology and history; the list could go on. Within RE, all these coalesce into a subject which is grounded in academic disciplines but which, at the same time, reflects peoples' experiences and most deeply held beliefs. What this means is that, in the RE classroom, there is scope for the exploration of knowledge through a variety of approaches and disciplinary methods. To help understand how this works in practice a question from outside RE might help: 'Why did the fire of London spread so quickly?' It is possible to explore this question from the perspective of a historian or a scientist; each would be looking at the same question but utilising very different tools and coming to different but complementary conclusions. It is important to recognise that the two disciplines or ways of knowing are not competing but rather helping build a complete picture.

This also the case with RE; in using different disciplines to approach the knowledge, a more complete picture of what religions and worldviews are and how they are practised can be developed. This may present a challenge for beginning RE teachers who, due to their own previous study, feel more confident with some disciplinary approaches than others or who are starting to understand the complex challenge of incorporating a variety of disciplinary approaches into one subject. In RE, there have been a number of different suggested approaches that can be used to develop this aspect of 'ways of knowing'. For example, the Norfolk Agreed Syllabus (Norfolk County Council, 2019) provides a worked example of how disciplinary lenses might be used. Its approach is rooted in a multidisciplinary understanding of the subject to ensure that pupils see religion and worldviews through a number of "different lenses" (2019, p. 9). The lenses that this syllabus suggests are:

- Theology: asking questions that believers would ask.
- Philosophy: asking questions that thinkers would ask.
- Human/ Social Sciences: asking questions that people who study lived reality or phenomena would ask.

(Norfolk County Council, 2019, p. 14; see also Hutton and Cox, 2021)

This approach (which is explored in more detail in Chapter 6) dovetails with the approach Ofsted seem to be taking to disciplinary knowledge; it also links with other approaches that have developed over time. For example, the *REsearchers* model also suggested a disciplinary approach to teaching:

This does not mean acquiring more and more knowledge about religions, but instead learning how to participate in the sort of academic enquiry which gives rise to such knowledge and the intellectual discourses which seek to understand and critique it.

(Freathy and Freathy, 2014, p. 159)

Wintersgill et al. (2019) also suggested that "[d]isciplinary knowledge applied to substantive knowledge brings it to life, raising it from 'facts' to 'understanding'" (p. 7). Therefore, it is important that beginning RE teachers understand how this lenses approach could be applied to the substantive knowledge being taught in the RE classroom. The fact that there are alternative approaches to the three lenses suggested by the Norfolk Agreed Syllabus highlights that this approach is still being developed. There is scope in RE to recognise and apply different lenses to the material being taught and design the curriculum in different ways. For example, one resource that combines elements of distinctive disciplinary lenses and the *REsearchers* and Big Ideas approaches is *Who is Jesus?* (Freathy et al., 2018), which explores, in a series of lessons, the person of Jesus from different perspectives. The lessons focus on "who is Jesus" for historians, the Gospel writers, Muslims, feminists, the visually impaired, people from different cultures, Christians today, and for an artist? Further examples that exemplify different disciplinary approaches can be found in the *Challenging knowledge in RE* series from RE Today. Beginning teachers need to spend time exploring resources such as these, and the ideas that underpin them, so that they understand how different lenses can be used in a sequence of lessons or scheme of work. Task 9.5 suggests how you might support them in this.

Task 9.5 Developing schemes of work

Select one scheme of work that doesn't utilise different ways of knowing that you can work to develop with your beginning teacher.

- Consider together how could you incorporate different ways of knowing into this unit.
- Work together to co-plan two or three lessons that use different disciplinary lenses to help pupils understand religions and worldviews.

In some ways, implementing the language of 'ways of knowing' or 'disciplinary knowledge' has superseded that of skills. However, it is impossible to implement these ways of knowing or lenses without the utilisation of skills. It could be argued that each lens brings its own set of skills, and it is important that beginning teachers spend time considering the nature of these skills and how they are built into the curriculum.

Skills

As noted earlier, there can tension in discourse between knowledge and skills. Ofsted (2021) recognise that both are a part of a good curriculum but cautions against the development/ use of skills in a linear way. The research review (Ofsted, 2021) highlights that pupils need lots of opportunities to develop skills over their school career but note that although pupils in both reception and Key Stage 4 might be asked to, for example, analyse something, what you would expect from pupils at each stage would be very different. This research review is not rejecting the use of skills, but the idea that they can be developed in age-specific incremental steps to show progression. However, this is how they have sometimes been used over the past 30 years, and some agreed syllabi suggest that skills progression is a way of pitching the content and the lesson. However, with any skill, there is an ability to become more proficient through practice, and some skills are harder than others. It is possible to see a pupil at all levels analysing and evaluating, but that is not to suggest that it is not more of an intentional and nuanced process in the higher key stages. Similarly, it is necessary at all levels of education to engage in using narrative and the ability to retell the story. This is a skill that should be developed by pupils of all ages and not left behind because it forms an important part of a Key Stage 1 curriculum. Beginning teachers need to understand that knowledge and skills are developed throughout the curriculum and that particular skills should not be assigned to specific key stages (Ofsted, 2021).

Therefore, beginning teachers must recognise the skills that are important for the study of RE. These might include developing pupils' ability to the following:

- ask pertinent and challenging questions
- gather, interpret and analyse information about religions and worldviews
- evaluate issues using reasoning
- express opinions, based on critical evaluation
- reflect on and express their own ideas and the ideas of others
- respond to religions and worldviews in an informed, rational and insightful way
- articulate beliefs, values and commitments clearly

(Ofsted, 2013; RE Council, 2013)

These skills, which can be seen as part of the disciplinary knowledge explored earlier, provide the vehicle for the knowledge to be studied and, if the beginning teacher is aware of them, enables the curriculum to be richer and more engaging. Georgiou (2021) identifies a number of activities that could support the development of skills:

- Source Interpretation. This can utilise different types of sources and has links with a theological, as well as a philosophical and historical lens.

- Written activities enable skills of analysis, evaluation, and reflection to be developed. These lie at the heart of all disciplinary lenses.
- Analysis of different sets of data that provide information about different worldviews could be seen to be an integral part of the social science lens.
- Discussion-based activities allow pupils to gather, interpret and analyse information, in addition to reflecting on and clarifying their own ideas in light of the beliefs of religion and worldviews. This crosses into personal knowledge (see below) but can be found in each disciplinary lens.

The use of ways of knowing does not downplay the role of skills but enhances their importance. Skills, whether as a part of a lens or more generally interpreted, enhance the curriculum that draws on substantive knowledge.

Consider the following example. Martha is in Year 9 and doesn't see the point of RE. She quite enjoys the lessons because not much is expected of her. In one lesson, she is asked to design a prayer mat; in another, she designs a storyboard about the life of Moses; and the next week, the class is watching a video about the life of the Buddha. All the activities are designed to stop her getting bored, but they don't seem to engage or stretch her. She knows that she will have to do RE in Years 10 and 11 but isn't looking forward to it, as she's not sure what relevance all these activities and people have to her life.

It is possible to use skills to begin to redesign the experience of Martha in the lesson about the prayer mat. If the lesson is framed around the question, 'Why does a Muslim need a clean place to pray?' the design of the prayer mat becomes an ancillary part of the discussion. This raises questions about the symbolism of cleanliness and what types of things might make a Muslim physically or spiritually unclean. It could lead to a further question of "Does a Muslim need a clean place to pray?" discussing all the issues surrounding intent and purpose rather than outward observance. The disciplinary knowledge/skills can be developed when the teacher introduces a passage from the Qur'an or hadith and skills of textual interpretation are used to identify what sources of authority underpin this practice, demonstrating specialised knowledge/skills for theology. The skills of analysis are used to identify that this practice might look slightly different for different Muslims (e.g. Shi'a Muslims using the tablet of clay), thus helping pupils understand the impact of context on practice which might develop specialised knowledge/skills for human/social sciences. The pupils' skill of constructing a well-reasoned response to the question, 'Does a Muslim need a clean place to pray?' and developing a specialised skill for philosophy might then be developed.

For this approach to be successful, it is important that beginning teachers have good understanding of the disciplinary skills required, as well as the substantive knowledge covered in the lesson. It is likely that, initially at least, they will need guidance to ensure that, when lesson planning, they frame the substantive knowledge in a way that draws on disciplinary skills that will enhance pupils' understanding of the subject knowledge. Task 9.6 draws on Martha's experience and presents a task you can work on with your beginning teacher to help model thinking that underpins this process.

Task 9.6 Developing skills to support the development knowledge

Talk through the example of Martha's experience with your beginning teacher to ensure they understand how disciplinary knowledge and skills can be used to transform her experience.

Take one of the other activities Martha has been asked to complete – the storyboard or watching the video – and work together with the beginning teacher to identify how disciplinary knowledge and skills could be used to frame this lesson differently.

For example, the storyboard of the life of Moses could be extended to include questions surrounding the importance of Moses to Jews today or reasons why he is an inspirational figure. It could also be linked to the festival of Pesach and the reasons that is still remembered today. Encourage the beginning teacher to think beyond the purely factual, to develop RE that questions and explores the impact on the life of a believer today. Pupils should be given opportunities to investigate religions and worldviews and develop their skills through varied experiences, approaches and disciplines.

In terms of challenge and the skills utilised, whilst the skills 'ladders' in some agreed syllabi might criticised, they are still useful for illustrating how skills can be applied in different ways. For example, consider the skills used to engage with story:

• Retell some religious and moral stories.
• Suggest meanings to some religious and moral stories.
• Describe links between stories and other aspects of the communities they are investigating.
• Respond thoughtfully to a range of sources of wisdom and to beliefs and teaching.
• Understand links between stories and other aspects of the communities they are investigating maybe by offering opinions.
• Explain range of beliefs, teachings and sources of wisdom and authority.
• Interpret and analyse the influence of religions and worldviews on individuals and communities.

The skills indicated by the words at the start of each sentence can help beginning teachers reflect on the way that pupils engage might engage with stories and may support the framing of enquiry questions. This is too far away from the earlier reference to the story for this to make sense. Consider the story of the sacrifice of his son by Abraham/Ibrahim:

• What are the main events in the story of Ibrahim and Ismail?
• What lessons might a Muslim take from the story of Ibrahim and Ismail today?
• What ways do Muslims remember this story today?
• What are the differences between Jews and Muslims in the way that they tell the stories?
• What links are there between the story of Ibrahim and the observance of Hajj and Eid-ul-Adha?

- Why do Muslims believe that the story is about Ismail, while Jews believe it is Isaac?
- What consequences do these different interpretations have for Jews and Muslims today?

Whilst the depth of exploration will vary between different year groups, pupils at any age can develop skills that enable them to engage with stories in a meaningful way.

Task 9.7 Developing pupils' skills

In a meeting with your beginning teacher, review a week's worth of their lessons to identify the skills that pupils are being asked to develop/employ. Consider the following:

- Is there variety in the skills used?
- Are there opportunities to develop additional skills?

Personal knowledge

"'Personal knowledge' has been described by various educators as 'knower-knowledge', 'personal worldview', 'reflexivity' and 'positionality'" (Ofsted, 2021). To some extent, personal knowledge is the recognition that everyone has a worldview. Pupils come to the classroom with prior knowledge, experiences, prejudices and their own sense of identity which, together, make up their "position" or "perspective on the world" (Ofsted, 2021). This personal knowledge is developed in every aspect of a person's life, and it is useful for the teacher, and the pupil, to understand the personal knowledge they have as it will influence how they approach, view and respond to aspects of that which is taught and learned.

This approach to personal knowledge seems to have links with the pedagogy of critical realism/ critical religious education (see Wright (2000) and Easton et al. (2019)). In this approach learning in RE goes through three phases:

- The Horizon of the Pupil
- The Horizons of Religion
- The Engagement of Horizons

(Wright, 2000, p. 181)

This is developed further in *Critical Religious Education in Practice* which recognises the realm and importance of personal knowledge in that "it has to do with students'

- reason and comprehension
- feelings and emotions
- actions and behaviour
- judgments and commitments".

(Easton et al., 2019, p. 4)

The first and third horizons enable pupils to recognise their personal knowledge and integrate it into their learning.

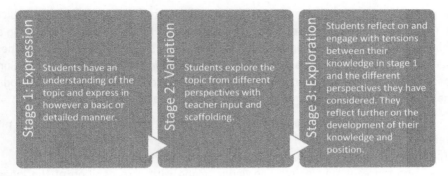

Figure 9.1 Three Stages of Critical Religious Education

(adapted from Easton et al., 2019)

It is possible to see the links between this approach to personal knowledge and the disciplinary knowledge discussed earlier. In considering different approaches to the subject matter in stage 2 (see figure 9.1) the teacher and pupils are able to use, not just different views but also different disciplines in developing their personal knowledge and skills in the application of the different lenses outlined earlier. For example, they might become better at interpreting data and become more critical as individuals.

It is also possible to view this as the 'learning from' approach that was popular for so long in RE. This, however, is a much more robust and concrete way of incorporating the personal knowledge and response than the approach in which 'learning from' sometimes became a bolt-on rather than an integral part of the pedagogy which Grimmitt articulated (2000). What beginning teachers must never lose sight of is the fact that all knowledge should be framed by the engagement of the person, and in the classroom, this will enable them to reflect more deeply on the learning that the pupil is undertaking. Task 9.8 offers an opportunity to explore this further with your beginning teacher.

Task 9.8 The impact of personal worldviews on teaching

In striving to understand pupils' own worldviews a beginning teacher should start by articulating their own. Ask your beginning teacher to consider the following questions and then discuss their answers with them.

- How do you make sense of the world?
- What are the various cultural, religious, non-religious, moral influences that form part of your worldview and the way that you understand the world?
- How might this affect the way you approach a specific religious topic?

Summary and key points

This chapter has explored what is meant by knowledge and skills in the context of RE and how you can support a beginning teacher to develop their understanding of this. In some ways, the accepted corpus of knowledge about religion and religions has been problematised. This should be seen as an opportunity to develop an RE that is robust, engaging and, most importantly, real. The recognition of this messiness and the different approaches to the material and people studied are most crucial in developing your own, and your beginning teachers, understanding of the practice and importance of religions and worldviews today.

The key points that have been made throughout this chapter include the following:

- The importance of recognising the knowledge that is taught and the bias that it might reflect
- The three types of knowledge: substantive, disciplinary and personal
- The importance of substantive knowledge, along with a recognition of the inherent messiness of religion and the attendant limits of knowledge for teachers when designing the curriculum and teaching
- Concepts are central to the development of conceptual knowledge within and between religions
- Ways of knowing and disciplinary knowledge as a way of understanding approaches to teaching and the integration of skills
- Personal knowledge and how it can be used to frame the other types of knowledge

Further resources

Ofsted (2021). Research *review series: religious education*. www.gov.uk/government/publications/research-review-series-religious-education/research-review-series-religious-education

This document, which is referred to throughout the chapter, serves as a summary of all the research surrounding RE in the classroom and how this can be effectively taught.

Pett, S. (Ed.). *Challenging knowledge in RE series*. RE Today Services.

A series of books that seeks to apply disciplinary lenses to aspects of RE. These help teachers understand what a disciplinary approach may look like in practice.

RE:ONLINE - www.reonline.org.uk/

This website is an invaluable resource that collects together introductions to religions and worldviews, as well as case studies of research. There are many classroom-ready resources that reflect the 'essential' aspects necessary for a religion and worldviews approach.

TrueTube - www.truetube.co.uk/

This website brings together films for immediate use in the classroom. Whatever age group being taught TrueTube has videos that will engage students and do so in a pedagogically effective way.

References

Apple, M. W. (2019). *Ideology and Curriculum* (4th ed.). Taylor and Francis.
Department for Education. (2019). *ITE Core Content Framework*. https://assets.publishing.service.gov.uk/government/uploads/system/uploads/attachment_data/file/974307/ITT_core_content_framework_.pdf

Easton, C., Wright, A., Goodman, A., Hibberd, T., & Wright, A. (2019). *A Practical Guide to Critical Religious Education: Resources for the Secondary Classroom*. Routledge.

Freathy, R., & Freathy, G. (2014). Initiating children into hermeneutical discourses in Religious Education: A response to Rachel Cope and Julian Stern. *Journal for the Study of Spirituality*, 3(2), 156–167.

Freathy, R., Doney, J., Freathy, G., Walshe, K., & Teece, G. (2017). Pedagogical bricoleurs and bricolage researchers: The case of religious education. *British Journal of Educational Studies*, 65(4), 425–443.

Freathy, R., Reed, E., Davis, A., John, H., & Schmidt, A. (2018). *Who Is Jesus? Supplementary Materials for Religious Education in the Upper Secondary School*. University of Exeter.

Georgiou, G. (2021). *Assessing Progress in RE Guidance*. Diocese of Lincoln, Board of Education.

Grimmitt, M. (Ed.). (2000). *Pedagogies of Religious Education. Case Studies in the Research and Development of Good Pedagogic Practice in RE*. McCrimmons.

Hampshire County Council/Portsmouth City Council/Southampton City Council/Isle of Wight Council. (2016). *Living Difference III The Agreed Syllabus for Hampshire, Portsmouth, Southampton and the Isle of Wight*. Hampshire County Council/Portsmouth City Council/ Southampton City Council/Isle of Wight Council.

Holt, J. D. (2015). *Religious Education in the Secondary School: An Introduction to Teaching, Learning and the World Religions*. Taylor & Francis.

Holt, J. D. (2019). *Beyond the Big Six Religions: Expanding the Boundaries in the Teaching of Religions and Worldviews*. University of Chester Press.

Hutton, L., & Cox, D. (2021). *Making Every RE Lesson Count: Six Principles to Support Religious Education Teaching*. Crown House Publishing.

Lowndes, J. (2012). *The Complete Multifaith Resource for Primary Religious Education: Ages 4–7*. Routledge.

Norfolk County Council. (2019). *Norfolk Agreed Syllabus for Religious Education*. https:// www.schools.norfolk.gov.uk/teaching-and-learning/religious-education-agreed-syllabus

Ofsted. (2013). *Religious education: realising the potential*. https://assets.publishing.service. gov.uk/government/uploads/system/uploads/attachment_data/file/413157/Religious_ education_-_realising_the_potential.pdf

Ofsted. (2021). *Research review series: religious education*. https://www.gov.uk/government/ publications/research-review-series-religious-education

RE Council of England and Wales (2013). *A Review of Religious Education in England*. RE Council of England and Wales.

Smart, N. (1989). *The World's Religions: Old Traditions and Modern Transformations*. Cambridge University Press.

Takhar, O. K. (2016). *Sikh Identity: An Exploration of Groups Among Sikhs*. Routledge.

Wintersgill, B. (Ed.). (2017). *Big Ideas in Religious Education*. University of Exeter.

Wintersgill, B., Cush, D., & Francis D. (2019). *Putting Big Ideas into Practice in Religious Education*. University of Exeter.

Wright, A. (2000). The Spiritual Education project: Cultivating Spiritual and Religious Literacy through a Critical Pedagogy of Religious Education. In Grimmitt, M. (Ed.), *Pedagogies of Religious Education. Case Studies in the Research and Development of Good Pedagogic Practice in RE* (pp. 170–187). McCrimmons.

10 Supporting beginning teachers to audit and develop their knowledge, skills and understanding in religious education

James Holt, Lara Harris and Lucy Rushforth

Introduction

This chapter suggests a way forward in supporting beginning teachers to develop their subject knowledge in the early years of their careers. When exploring this, it is important to be aware of the debate around knowledge and skills and the ongoing discussion around the implementation of a religion and worldviews paradigm. It is also important to reflect on the implications of this for classroom teaching; this can be done by recognising and articulating the importance of an individual worldview and the diversity within institutional worldviews and religions. It is, however, necessary to see the wood for the trees; in all approaches to knowledge in religious education (RE), there has to be a recognition of essentialism. This does not dilute the rich diversity but recognises the 'essential' aspects of religion against which religions are constructed and worldviews can find their expression. This approach to the messy world of religion and worldviews will enable beginning teachers to develop their subject knowledge in a way that means they are prepared to teach the lived reality of religion in the classroom.

The chapter includes the framework for a subject knowledge audit document. It is acknowledged that you may be working with a beginning teacher who has been asked to audit their knowledge using a different pro forma. However, it is intended that the ideas and strategies suggested here will be useful, whatever the format in which they are to be recorded, and highlight ways that you can support a beginning teacher as they develop their subject knowledge.

By the end of this chapter, you should:

- Be able to support a beginning teacher as they subject audit their knowledge and skills.
- Have knowledge of practical ways in which you can support a beginning teacher to analyse, reflect and develop their knowledge and skills.

Subject knowledge audit

In England, it is common for beginning teachers on teacher education courses to complete a subject knowledge audit based on the Department for Education (DfE) document that

DOI: 10.4324/9781003191087-12

outlined their expectations for the construction of the General Certificate of Secondary Education (GCSE) specifications (DfE, 2015). This had been pulled together by representatives of faith communities and seemed to provide a good starting point for beginning teachers and their mentors. Indeed, the document has much to recommend it; it developed the religious aspects of religious studies (RS) qualifications and broadened some understandings of religion (e.g. the expansion of GCSE Islam to cover Shi'a and Sufi expressions). However, it is rather unwieldy, and it has reinforced the idea of religions as static and somewhat monolithic, despite its repeated reference to 'divergence' which seems to have been understood as tokenistic difference in 'mainstream' expressions. For example, the Christian material in the document has led one awarding board to establish a definition of Christianity that is very narrow and excludes understandings outside of the 'mainstream'. Meanwhile, the GCSE textbook developed by the Board of Deputies outlines aspects of Judaism that have been given too much attention and others that are more important receiving cursory attention.

Therefore, a subject knowledge audit that takes into account aspects of essentialism and also the broadening nature of RE in schools is needed. This should be a living document that can be started in initial teacher education and returned to throughout the early years of an RE teacher's career. It should go beyond identifying what the beginning teacher can already do. Rather, the first step in developing subject knowledge is to identify what isn't known. Before they will be able to plan and implement a successful lesson, it is essential that beginning teachers identify the gaps in their subject knowledge. There are many ways in which the gaps might become apparent; when looking at a school's curriculum, when completing a subject knowledge audit, in a taught initial teacher education or continuing professional development session with a subject specialist or even when observing a lesson. However, it is likely gaps in subject knowledge will also become apparent when the beginning teacher sits down to plan a lesson.

One of the great dangers for the beginning teacher is being overly confident in their own subject knowledge. Confidence is great, but a person who recognises the gaps in their knowledge and therefore approaches their teaching with an intellectual humility is far more effective and easier to work with than someone who thinks they know it all. Consider Lara's experience from when she was a beginning teacher:

> Do not assume you are all-knowing when going into teaching. I left University after 4 years of studying Theology and Religion, and whilst there were definite areas of strength in my subject knowledge, there was also areas I had never even explored until I first started teaching.

An over-confidence in knowledge can lead to errors being passed on to pupils themselves. For example, one beginning teacher was asked to prepare a lesson to deliver to Year 7 on "Poverty and Social Justice". Whilst he had planned some activities and had basic transitions between tasks, his lack of subject knowledge was severe. The reason he was so unprepared? He had assumed he knew more than he did. He knew the definition of *poverty*, and he remembered his own learning about the "Brandt line" in his own Year 7 Geography lessons. However, he did not know that the Brandt line was from 1980s and has since been revised due to the growing number of industrialised countries. Therefore, the north and south divide of rich versus poor countries is no longer the same map he would have studied back when he was in Year 7. He had not truly considered what poverty and the Brandt line really had to do with social justice or how it fitted within an RE lesson.

A further example involves one beginning teacher responding to a pupil asking, "Why don't I get to go up and take the Eucharist?" The answer is to do with whether a person has been baptised into the Catholic faith. Whilst the beginning teacher might not know all the details or give the exact same answer as the mentor, there is the expectation they have some understanding of the basic fact that "Only Catholics take the Eucharist". The actual answer that was given was "It's probably because of COVID, people aren't going to church anymore". Now you will be aware that there are many things wrong with this statement; first, the student teacher has totally misunderstood the heart of the question asked by the pupil. This is not a generic "Why aren't we going to holy communion anymore?" but, rather, a very specific and personal question, "Why can't I go?" Second, the student teacher uses the term "people", rather than identifying the specific faith, such as Catholic, Protestant and Methodist, thus giving pupils a very limited understanding of the issue. Third, it is not a question about going to church, nor is this a lesson about going to church; it is about the sacrament of the Eucharist. As you might imagine, this is one example of a lesson in which intervention was necessary. A humility in knowledge is crucial if teachers are to exhibit an approach to religions and worldviews that they would be happy for their pupils to replicate. An effective subject knowledge audit is one tool that can be used to accomplish this.

In designing a subject knowledge audit, it is important to consider the why, the how and the what. In this way, three elements of the audit are constructed. There are different ways that this can, and has, been done: first, a tick-box exercise of self-reflection and, second, writing short reflections on aspects of subject knowledge. The audit suggested in this chapter utilises aspects of both approaches so that the beginning teacher and their mentor can truly reflect on where the beginning teacher is at different points in their development as a teacher, supported by wider reading and personal experience. This will become evident as each section of the audit is explored.

Part 1: The nature and purpose of RE

Part 1 of the proposed audit focuses on 'the why'. Topics in this area of the audit would include the following:

- The nature and aims of RE
- Issues of teacher identity and neutrality
- RE in a faith school
- The legal position of RE
- The assessment of RE

In considering the nature, purpose and aims of RE the beginning teacher should reflect on their own experiences up to this point and what other people have said.

The importance of this overarching understanding of the nature and purpose of RE for ensuring that teachers can plan well-structured and sequenced lessons has been highlighted by Ofsted (2010, p. 6). At the immediate classroom level, teachers may understand what they are trying to achieve, for example to be able to describe the features of a mosque and why the mosque is important to Muslims. However, the telos, or overall purpose of the subject, gets lost in the immediacy of the classroom. It is important for beginning teachers to have the purposes of RE clear in their minds and retain them throughout the course of their teaching career. This will affect how RE is taught and will enable the teacher to navigate the various demands that might be faced in the school while maintaining the integrity of the RE that is offered (Task 6.3 in Chapter 6 may help you engage in discussion about this with your beginning teacher).

To borrow an aspect of Ofsted's (2021) approach to knowledge this is the recognition of personal knowledge of the RE teacher. Where does the teacher stand in relation to the content that they teach? It is important for a beginning RE teacher's practice that they reflect on how much of themselves they are willing to share in their teaching. This is a contested area; the authors of this chapter have differing standpoints and experiences, not least because Lucy and Lara teach in the Catholic school sector and James is from a faith that can be seen to be fairly proselytising and so began his teaching career very conscious not to talk about his beliefs for fear of complaint. There may not be a correct answer to this question, but it is one that needs to be considered by any RE teacher. One example that comes to mind is of the teacher who stood in front of the class and asked the question:

I am an atheist; why does that make me a better RE teacher?

Essentially, the answer was that because he did not believe in any religion; he was unbiased. The conversation that ensued after the lesson surrounded the fact that he had biases like anyone, but he didn't recognise them. Noting the contested nature of the sharing of one's beliefs with classes, beginning teachers could be asked to read an article by Dawn Cox (2016) and another by Neil McKain (2016) that are seemingly in opposition. In so doing, they are then asked to reflect on their own standpoint and why they need to be aware of that in the classroom. Task 10.1 suggests how you might prepare to discuss this with your beginning teacher.

Task 10.1 Audit – The nature and purpose of RE

The first part of the proposed audit (Table 10.1) focuses on the nature and purpose of RE. Review this section of the audit before discussing it with your beginning teacher. Consider the following:

- Are there any areas where you want to reflect on your own position before you engage in discussion with your beginning teacher (earlier chapters of this book may support this reflection)?
- Is there any of the suggested reading that you would like to or feel you need to read for yourself?
- Are there any areas of the audit that you think may raise any issues for your beginning teacher?

Table 10.1 Audit part 1: The nature and purpose of RE

Religious education – Subject Knowledge Audit
This is a working document that should be returned to regularly

---

Part 1: The nature and purpose of RE

---

a) The nature and aims of RE

Based on your observations, conversations with others and reading, write a paragraph explaining your
   thoughts about the aims of RE.
Suggested reading:

- Holt (2022) – Chapter 1
- hooks (1994)
- Teece (2018)

How will this impact on your practice?

Examples from your teaching that show how the aims of RE are integrated into lessons.

---

b) Religion and worldviews

Based on your observation, conversations with others and reading, write a paragraph explaining your
   thoughts about religion and worldviews.
Suggested reading:

- Chater, M. and Donnellan, L. (2020)
- Commission on Religious Education. (2018)
- Cooling, Bowie and Panjwani (2020)
- Holt (2022) – Chapter 2

How will this impact on your practice?

---

c) Issues of teacher identify and neutrality

Based on your observation, conversations with others and reading, write a paragraph explaining your
   thoughts about whether you will share your beliefs in the classroom and why.
Suggested reading:

- Cox (2016)
- McKain (2016)

How will this impact on your practice?

---

d) RE in a faith school

Based on your observations, conversations with others and reading, write a paragraph explaining how RE in
   faith and non-faith schools is similar and different.
Suggested reading:

- Cush (2005)
- Humanists UK (2006)

(Continued)

Table 10.1 Cont.

e) The legal position of RE

Based on your observations, conversations with others and reading, write a paragraph explaining the legal position of RE.

Suggested reading:

- Holt (2022) – Chapter 1
- Lundie (2018)

How will this impact your practice?

f) The assessment of RE

Based on your observations, conversations with others and reading, write a paragraph explaining your thoughts about assessment and RE.

Suggested reading:

- Fancourt (2018)
- Holt (2022) – Chapter 4
- Ofsted (2021)

How will this impact your practice?

Examples from your teaching of the use of assessment.

For this aspect of the audit (along with the two sections that follow), there are a number of ways in which mentors can support beginning teachers. One example is of a mentor who drew up a list of continuing professional development (CPD) opportunities (e.g. online courses or seminars, web-based resources, suggested reading, etc.) for a beginning teacher to dip in and out of where necessary for their own development. This could provide the opportunity to listen to a variety of speakers and institutions to begin to build links in their early career, which can also be beneficial in interviews. This could give beginning teachers an opportunity to explore subject knowledge that either they haven't come across in teaching or they had not thought they could use within lessons.

This is developed further by engagement with social media – this is where a considerable amount of communication can happen. Engagement with online communities, such as #ReChatUK on Twitter, supports subject knowledge development as, through conversations with charities, institutions and other educators, beginning teachers can draw on others' experiences, articles and the like that can help to support knowledge in lessons to make topics current and so on.

As the beginning teacher and the mentor work together to reflect on this aspect of the audit, they are able to explore important questions and establish a strong base for the teaching of RE. The beginning teacher will not be picking up things as they go or developing approaches in an ad hoc way, but it will be an intentional development of a teaching persona and understanding of the purpose of RE. While this might happen at the beginning of a course, it can be returned to at different points in the early years of their career.

Part 2: Pedagogy and RE

The second section of the audit explores the 'how' of RE teaching to develop an understanding of the underlying pedagogy, or pedagogies, which is essential to ensure that RE is rich, engaging and able to meet the aims of the subject. Whichever pedagogical approach(es) are utilised, it is important that the beginning teacher understands that there are different ways to teach RE and how these may be manifest in the classroom. As such, classroom experience and application are important in helping beginning teachers develop as teachers with a keen understanding of pedagogy. It is possible to meet experienced teachers who are dismissive of pedagogy as detached from classroom practice or a mere fad. Mentors play an important role in enabling beginning teachers to see the links and develop the confidence to try things out and begin to think about research-informed practice. The subject knowledge audit can help the beginning teacher identify and prioritise areas of focus.

Two activities that are crucial to enable beginning teachers to reflect on the suitability of their approach and the underlying pedagogy are shared planning and team teaching:

- **Shared planning** – This is an opportunity to enable beginning teachers to adapt teaching approaches, check knowledge or research further into a topic if they are not confident. It can be as easy as recommending reading or getting in touch with world faith speakers.
- **Team teaching** –This is often an underutilised aspect of a beginning teachers experience. It supports pupil questioning if the beginning teacher is unsure of knowledge when pupils are curious and asking those big questions. It provides security for the beginning teacher that approaches, timings and content can be adapted.

Shared planning can be built into the beginning teacher's experience. The process could include the following:

- The beginning teacher and mentor decide a class, topic and approach for the lesson design.
- The beginning teacher conducts research to inform their understanding of the concepts, pedagogy, current practice and research that informs the sequence of learning for this class.
- A lesson is designed collaboratively with the mentor – this should include looking at pupils' prior knowledge, class data and selecting appropriate strategies to meet the needs of learners.
- The beginning teacher will observe the mentor and, in some cases, may also team teach alongside the mentor, the purpose being to learn from an experienced professional and notice classroom practice as it evolves in response to the pupils needs and progress.
- The observation should include significant comments that demonstrate how learners have responded to specific strategies, as well as assessment information (formative or summative) that has been collated or evidenced and/or photograph or descriptions of anonymised pupils' work.
- In discussion, the mentor and the beginning teacher should review the lesson design and observation considering the impact of the lesson design on the pupils' learning.
- The beginning teacher should then use their findings from the collaborative lesson study to inform the design of the next lesson in the sequence.

- The final part of this process will include further reading and the identification of the significance of the collaborative lesson research on their practice.

This process helps the beginning teacher explore the nuances of planning, pedagogy and subject knowledge. One of the other activities that could be completed with beginning teachers is an action research project in which they identify an aspect of learning in RE that they are interested in and, after research into the area and discussion with you, implement strategies to explore whether this approach is effective in developing pupils' learning and/or engagement. For example, one beginning teacher was encouraged by her mentor to complete her enquiry on retrieval. This was something the mentor was studying herself for a National Professional Qualification for Middle Leadership (NPQML); her passion and enthusiasm were evident throughout the department, and retrieval had been key to the department's improvement plan in response to an Ofsted inspection. Working on an enquiry which focused on this allowed the beginning teacher not only to increase her knowledge of this pedagogy but also to build her knowledge when teaching. Her knowledge increased immensely once she had implemented this enquiry into her lessons as she was constantly revisiting subject knowledge with her pupils.

These activities of discussion, curriculum and lesson design can all be vehicles through which pedagogy can be explored. Engagement with Part 2 of the audit (Table 10.2) will enable beginning teachers to understand the impact that an implementation of intentional pedagogy can have on classroom practice. The section of the audit is, again, a living document that should be returned to regularly over time. Task 10.2 suggests how you might work with your beginning teacher on this section of the audit.

Table 10.2 Audit part 2: Pedagogy and RE

Religious education – Subject Knowledge Audit
This is a working document that should be returned to regularly
Part 2: Pedagogy and RE
a) What is pedagogy?
Based on your observations, conversations with others and reading, write a paragraph explaining what pedagogy is.
Suggested reading:
<ul><li>Grimmitt (2000)</li><li>Holt (2022) – Chapter 3</li><li>Stern (2018)</li></ul>
How will this impact your practice?
Examples from your teaching/observation of the implementation of pedagogy.

(Continued)

Table 10.2 Cont.

b) What are some of the existing pedagogies of RE

Based on your observations, conversations with others, and reading summarise the various pedagogies of RE.

Suggested reading:

- Blaylock (2004)
- Grimmitt (2000)
- Holt (2022) – Chapter 3
- Stern (2018)

How will this impact your practice?

Examples from your teaching/observation of the implementation of different pedagogies

c) Disciplinary knowledge and lenses in RE

Based on your observation, conversations with others and reading, write a paragraph to summarise the place of disciplinary knowledge and lenses in RE.

Suggested reading:

- Freathy, et al. (2017)
- Holt (2022) – Chapters 2 and 4
- Hutton and Cox (2021)
- Norfolk SACRE (2019)
- Ofsted (2021)

How will this impact on your practice?

Examples from your teaching/observation of the implementation of different pedagogies

Task 10.2 Auditing pedagogy and RE

In one of your scheduled mentor meetings, discuss your beginning teacher's responses to this section of the audit with them.

Agree on a schedule for revisiting this section of the audit through the time you are working together (perhaps termly) to encourage your beginning teacher to reflect on how their teaching experiences impact their thinking.

Part 3 – Substantive knowledge in RE

The final section of the subject audit (although it should be noted that the sections will be completed alongside each other rather than one after the other) focuses on substantive knowledge which could be daunting for a beginning teacher. When the amount of knowledge for each religion is listed, and that is without exploring religions beyond the big six or even the immense diversity within each religion, the audit could run for pages. Audits based on the DfE (2015) GCSE content were often lengthy and detailed. There is also the danger that such an audit could simply be a check box exercise where beginning teachers rate themselves and keep a note of any activities with which they engaged to develop their substantive knowledge. However, this approach might also put beginning teachers off and be demoralising as the gaps in knowledge become apparent. Therefore, the following audit offers a different approach to assessing and keeping track of substantive knowledge development.

In this alternative approach, it is intended that beginning teachers would initially take responsibility for identifying for themselves areas of knowledge requiring development, based on a review of the school's curriculum and exam specifications. Mentors would then work with them to review their audit and identify gaps or areas that have not been included that should be added. If you are working with an initial teacher education student, the policies in place may not allow for the responsibility to be given to the beginning teachers in this way. In this case the approach to the following suggested audit could be adapted so that the course leader or mentor populates the content column before giving it to the beginning teacher to reflect on their experience. However, it could be argued that the self-directed task is useful in that it engages the beginning teacher with the substantive content at the beginning of the course and may highlight areas requiring further research for them. Another benefit of a self-directed approach is that it enables new tables to be designed as appropriate for religions and worldviews that they may be asked to teach within the classroom.

Once this 'essential' content is noted, the beginning teacher should reflect on their experiences up to this point and fill in those activities that they have engaged with to enable them to understand the various beliefs and practices. At this point, it is their responsibility to update their experiences and activities at regular intervals as they work with mentors.

An outline of the suggested structure for this section of the audit is given in Table 10.3, with a completed example for Buddhism to exemplify what kind of content and experiences/ activities could be included in Table 10.4. In the Further Resources section at the end of this chapter, suggested introductory reading is given for the 'big six' religions, along with Humanism and Paganism.

Table 10.3 Audit part 3: Substantive knowledge pro forma

Religious education – Subject Knowledge Audit
This is a working document that should be returned to regularly
Part 3: Substantive knowledge
Religion: Buddhism/Christianity/Hinduism/Humanism/Islam/Judaism/Paganism/Sikhism
Introductory reading:

Content identified from reading/ experience/ specifications	**Subject knowledge experiences/activities**

Table 10.4 Audit part 3: Substantive knowledge exemplar – Buddhism

Religious education – Subject Knowledge Audit
This is a working document that should be returned to regularly

Part 3: Substantive Knowledge

Religion: Buddhism

Introductory reading:

Bechert, H. and Gombrich, R. (1991). *The World of Buddhism*. Thames and Hudson.

Chryssides, G. (1988). *Introduction to Buddhism*. Cambridge University Press.

Cush, D. (1990). *Buddhism in Britain Today*. Hodder.

Fowler, M. (1999). *BuddhisM. Beliefs and Practices*. Sussex Academic Press

Hawkins, B. K. (1999). *Buddhism*. Routledge.

Holt, James (2022). *Religious Education in the Secondary School. An introduction to teaching, learning and the World Religions* (2ⁿᵈ Ed.). Routledge. - Chapter 8

Keown, D. (1996). *Buddhism: A Very Short Introduction*. Oxford University Press.

Kulananda. (2001). *Buddhism*. Thorsons.

RE:ONLINE. (2020.) *Buddhist worldview traditions* available at https://www.reonline.org.uk/knowledge/buddhist-worldview-traditions/

Schmidt-Leukel, P. (2006). *Understanding Buddhism*. Dunedin.

Williams, P., Tribe, A., & Wynne, A. (2012). *Buddhist thought: A complete introduction to the Indian tradition*. Taylor and Francis

Content identified from reading/experience/ specifications	Subject knowledge experiences/activities
The Four Noble Truths	Explored as part of second year degree module on issues surrounding suffering and responses from religions of the world. 2020-21.
	Participated in a University Lecture on 'Teaching Buddhism' to explore the importance of the Four Noble Truths (September 2, 2022)
	Preliminary reading prior to teaching (RE:ONLINE, Holt, 2022 and Keown, 1996)
	Taught a Year 7 lesson based on the Four Noble Truths and their importance for many Buddhists today (September 9, 2022).
	Taught a Year 7 lesson on the life of the Buddha and explored how his life might be seen as a metaphor for the Four Noble Truths (October 6, 2022).
Mahayana Buddhism	Participated in a University Lecture on 'Teaching Buddhism' to explore various traditions within Buddhism (September 2, 2022)
	Preliminary reading prior to teaching (REOnline (2020), Karel Werner; Jeffrey Samuels; Bhikkhu Bodhi; Peter Skilling, Bhikkhu Anālayo, David McMahan (2013). *The Bodhisattva Ideal: Essays on the Emergence of Mahayana*. Buddhist Publication Society.)
Triratna Buddhism	Background reading: Vajragupta, (2010) *The Triratna Story; Behind the Scenes of a New Buddhist Movement* Windhorse Publications (see subject knowledge notes)
	Attended Triratna Centre and spent time speaking with a volunteer to explore the place and practice of Triratna (December 2, 2022)
Meditation	Attended University of Chester TRS CPD event 'Is Mindfulness Buddhist?' - Dr Wendy Dossett available at https://vimeo.com/showcase/8411187/video/565526831 Helped crystallise the modern practice of mindfulness with the Buddhist practice in preparation for A level lesson.

It is evident that central to developing beginning teachers' understanding of substantive knowledge it is imperative that they engage with reading, observation, teaching and many other experiences that will enable them to engage with the diversity within religions and worldviews. Two other examples of activities that should be encouraged by mentors are engagement with planning, and utilising and experiencing the authentic voice.

Although planning was referenced earlier, the focus was very much on the development of pedagogy and approach. It is, however, obvious that one of the ways for a teacher to develop knowledge is to prepare to teach a topic and then to teach it in the classroom. The starting point for every teacher before planning a lesson is always to complete research. You should encourage beginning teachers to read as much as they can on the specific subject and topics they will be covering. There are many resources for learning key subject knowledge online that can be accessed.

Then, once the lesson is planned and resourced it is important to review it. The beginning teacher should be encouraged to put themselves in the shoes of a Year 7 pupil, approaching each part of the plan with curiosity and question everything – from the meaning of key terms to the age of the religious figure pupils might be studying. With a bank of possible questions prepared, find an answer to them and, if this leads to more questions, then that lead should be followed. When beginning teaching starts teaching, every element of the lesson may be planned, from the routine of welcoming pupils into the lesson to checking uniform to then moving onto lesson objectives. A beginning teacher might have a piece of paper in front of them as a checklist to help remember everything. They might also have a list of answers to potential questions prepared. It might sound like a lot of work, and it is, but it might feel necessary so that the beginning teacher is never put in a position which could stun or panic. It is not realistic to imagine that a beginning teacher can plan for every single eventuality, but the chances of freezing in front of a classroom of 32 pupils or pretending to have an answer can be reduced.

Another way mentors can work with beginning teachers to ensure that subject knowledge is secure is to give clear guidance regarding the direction of questions in a lesson. This not only gives clarity about what pupils need to know but also supports the beginning teacher in determining the types of questions pupils might ask.

For example, in a Year 10 lesson on "The Sanctity of Life" the beginning teacher could be guided to start with the key question, "What is the sanctity of life?" Their key question for the pupils should be "What does the word *sanctity* mean?" and it should be made clear to the beginning teacher that they should teach pupils the following definition: "That every human life is sacred and belongs to God". After this, the lesson might move onto an activity which explores this further, but before that, pupils may be asked if they know what the word *sacred* means? Or what does "belonging to God" imply for a believer? What about the questions, "Well, when we say every human life, what defines a life? When does life begin?" Whilst these may seem to be big questions, ones that may take hours to fully answer, never mind a few minutes of a lesson, planning them into the body of a lesson can help minimise the chances that pupils will ask unexpected questions.

One of the key elements of any teacher's experience is the ability to utilise the authentic voice within the classroom. This helps with not only recognising the diversity within worldviews but also recognising the individual experience in the UK today. A beginning teacher's exposure to people of different religions and worldviews will depend on their life experiences. Exploring different places of worship and talking to people from different religions is important and the benefits to a beginning teacher's teaching is phenomenal. They are able to use photos they have taken, but they are able to include the individual expression of religion in the classroom as they recall their experiences speaking with people from the community. If visits are not possible, then there are many television programmes and videos available where people talk about their faith.

Summary and key points

Each section of the audit has explored the different activities that can be used to support a beginning teacher in developing their subject knowledge. The various activities will need to be bespoke for each beginning teacher, and the role of the mentor is key in helping the teacher identify gaps and making suggestions for addressing those areas. The use of the subject knowledge audit helps the beginning teacher recognise the progress being made and the areas still to be addressed. In developing a bespoke subject knowledge audit, it is possible to see the completion of such as more than a tick-box exercise. Rather, it becomes a living document that goes with the beginning teacher through their career.

- There are three important elements to an audit: the nature and purpose of RE, pedagogy and RE and substantive knowledge.
- The process should be structured but managed by the beginning teacher with support from their mentor.
- The mentor is there to guide, suggest and ensure progression is being made.
- It is important that a beginning teacher is not overawed but that subject knowledge activities are appropriate and used to support development.
- Opportunities should be sought to help beginning teachers recognise their intellectual humility and begin their journey as RE teachers.
- This development of knowledge will last a lifetime in teaching as new things are added to the audit each year.

Further resources

The 'introductory reading' sections in part 3 of the audit will need to be populated with appropriate texts in the same way as the given Buddhism example. The following resources will offer a useful starting point.

Subject Knowledge Audits – https://jamesdholt.com/subject-knowledge-audits/

This website provides suggestions for introductory reading on individual religions and worldviews that could be used to begin the subject knowledge audits as suggested in Table 10.3.

Holt, J. (2022). *Religious Education in the Secondary School. An introduction to Teaching, Learning and the World Religions* (2nd ed). Routledge.

This text, which supports beginning teachers in all aspects of teaching and learning in RE, includes chapters on each of the religions and worldviews that may be included on the RE curriculum.

Holt, J. (2019). *Beyond the Big Six Religions: Expanding the Boundaries in the Teaching of Religions and Worldviews*. University of Chester Press.

This book explores the desirability and possibility of expanding the breadth of religions and non-religious worldviews in the RE classroom.

RE:ONLINE – www.reonline.org.uk/knowledge/

This website provides detailed essays on a range of religions and worldviews that offer a useful starting point for the development of subject knowledge.

References

Barnes, P. (ed.) (2018). *Learning to Teach Religious Education in the Secondary School: A Companion to School Experience*. (3rd ed). Routledge.

Bechert, H. and Gombrich, R. (1991). *The World of Buddhism*. Thames and Hudson.

Blaylock, L. (2004). Six Schools of Thought in RE. *Resource*, 27(1), 13–16.

Chater, M. and Donnellan, L. (2020). What do we mean by worldviews? In Chater, M. (ed.) *Reforming Religious Education: Power and Knowledge in a Worldviews Curriculum* (pp. 115–130). John Catt Educational Ltd.

Chryssides, G. (1988). *Introduction to Buddhism*. Cambridge University Press.

Commission on Religious Education. (2018). *Religion and Worldviews: The Way Forward. A National Plan for RE*. Religious Education Council of England and Wales.

Cooling, T., Bowie, R., and Panjwani, F. (2020). *Worldviews in Religious Education*. Theos.

Cox, D. (2016, May 9). Why RE teachers should not tell students their religion. *missdcoxblog*. https://missdcoxblog.wordpress.com/2016/05/09/why-re-teachers-should-not-tell-students-their-religion/

Cush, D. (1990). *Buddhism in Britain Today*. Hodder.

Cush, D. (2005). The faith schools debate. *British Journal of Sociology of Education*, 26(3), 435–442. https://doi.org/10.1080/01425690500128957

Department for Education (DfE). (2015). *Religious studies: GCSE subject content*. https://assets.publishing.service.gov.uk/government/uploads/system/uploads/attachment_data/file/403357/GCSE_RS_final_120215.pdf

Fancourt, N. (2018). Assessment in Religious Education. In Philip Barnes (ed.) *Learning to Teach Religious Education in the Secondary School: A Companion to School Experience* (3rd ed., pp. 89–101). Routledge.

Fowler, M. (1999). *Buddhism. Beliefs and Practices*. Sussex Academic Press.

Freathy, R., Doney, J., Freathy, G., Walshe, K., and Teece, G. (2017). Pedagogical bricoleurs and bricolage researchers: The case of religious education. *British Journal of Educational Studies*, 65(4), 425–443. https://doi.org/10.1080/00071005.2017.1343454

Grimmitt, M. (ed.) (2000). *Pedagogies of Religious Education. Case Studies in the Research and Development of Good Pedagogic Practice in RE*. McCrimmons.

Hawkins, B. K. (1999). *Buddhism*. Routledge.

Holt, J. (2019). *Beyond the Big Six Religions: Expanding the Boundaries in the Teaching of Religions and Worldviews*. University of Chester Press.

Holt, J. (2022). *Religious Education in the Secondary School. An introduction to teaching, learning and the World Religions* (2nd ed). Routledge.

hooks, b. (1994). *Teaching to Transgress*. Routledge.

Humanists UK. (2006). *BHA Briefing 2006/4: Faith Schools*. https://humanists.uk/wp-content/uploads/BHA-Briefing-Faith-schools-update.pdf; https://humanists.uk/wp-content/uploads/BHA-Briefing-Faith-schools-update.pdf

Hutton, L. and Cox, D. (2021). *Making Every RE Lesson Count*. Crown Publishing.

Keown, D. (1996). *Buddhism: A Very Short Introduction.* Oxford University Press.

Kulananda. (2001). *Buddhism.* Thorsons.

Lundie, D. (2018). Religious Education policy across the UK. In Philip Barnes (ed.) *Learning to Teach Religious Education in the Secondary School: A Companion to School Experience* (3rd ed., pp. 17–30). Routledge.

McKain, N. (2016, May 9). Reasons why we should tell students our 'religion' (sic). *The Cursed Fig Tree.* https://thecursedfigtree.wordpress.com/2016/05/09/reasons-why-we-should-tell-students-our-religion-sic/

Norfolk County Council. (2019). Norfolk Agreed Syllabus for Religious Education. Available https://www.schools.norfolk.gov.uk/teaching-and-learning/religious-education-agreed-syllabus

Ofsted. (2010). *Transforming Religious Education.* https://dera.ioe.ac.uk/1121/1/Transforming%20religious%20education.pdf

Ofsted. (2021). *Research review series: religious education* available at https://www.gov.uk/government/publications/research-review-series-religious-education/research-review-series-religious-education

Schmidt-Leukel, P. (2006). *Understanding Buddhism.* Dunedin.

Stern, J. (2018). *Teaching Religious Education.* Bloomsbury.

Teece, G. (2018). The aims and purposes of religious education. In Philip Barnes (ed.) *Learning to Teach Religious Education in the Secondary School: A Companion to School Experience* (3rd ed., pp. 3–16). Routledge.

Williams, P., Tribe, A., and Wynne, A. (2012). *Buddhist Thought: A Complete Introduction to the Indian Tradition.* Taylor and Francis.

SECTION 3

The practical picture

Mentoring beginning religious education teachers in practice

11 Helping beginning religious education teachers plan effective and creative lessons

Helen Sheehan and Sally Elton-Chalcraft

Introduction

Effective planning is at the heart of good teaching. Religious Education (RE) teachers are focused on helping pupils learn and progress within the subject and this requires careful planning and preparation. However, careful planning also ensures that beginning RE teachers walk into their classrooms with confidence. They need to know they have planned a lesson which develops pupils' knowledge but in which they have also considered pedagogical approaches, the needs of individual learners and how they will manage pupils' behaviour. If beginning teachers have not thought through these elements, it is more likely that the lesson will not go as they intend. There is much to think about when planning a lesson and, as an experienced teacher, you will do much of this unconsciously. Therefore, supporting a beginning teacher in planning lessons may require consciously identifying things that you do automatically so that you can support them to build up their own knowledge and skills.

Lesson planning is an aspect of teaching where beginning teachers look to their mentors for guidance and where the level of support required may change through the mentoring period. This chapter works through the different stages that you might go through with a beginning teacher – from a novice planning part of a lesson for the first time, to a beginning teacher focused on learning how to construct their own lesson plan and resources, to a teacher in the early years of their career who is looking to develop their skills further as they take on responsibility for developing sequences of learning.

By the end of this chapter, you should be able to:

- Outline the importance of a written lesson plan for a beginning RE teacher.
- Evaluate the key features of an effective and creative lesson plan with a beginning RE teacher.
- Develop strategies for helping a beginning RE teacher engage in the lesson planning process for the first time.
- Support a beginning RE teacher think through each of the key components of a lesson plan including a consideration of their own agency.

DOI: 10.4324/9781003191087-14

- Guide a beginning RE teacher to design their own lessons and draw on pre-existing lesson plans and resources in their own lesson planning in a creative and effective way.
- Understand how theory can inform practice when supporting beginning teachers in lesson planning.

The importance of a written lesson plan

Planning is a time-consuming activity for beginning teachers because they need to consider many different aspects of the lesson and how they all come together to impact teaching and learning. They need to know how to structure the learning and think through what they, and the pupils, will do at each stage of the lesson. For this reason, many initial teacher education (ITE) providers and schools ask beginning teachers to complete a lesson plan proforma as they can help a beginning teacher think through all aspects of the lesson, including things that are easily overlooked. Task 11.1 asks you to review a lesson plan proforma with your beginning teacher. You could focus on the pro forma that is used in your own context, or you can use the one given in Figure 11.1. We are not suggesting the latter is a 'perfect' proforma, but it should act as a springboard for you to discuss what should be considered when planning a lesson.

Task 11.1 Lesson plan proformas

Look at the lesson plan proforma given in Figure 11.1 (or the one that your beginning teacher is being asked to use). Use it to start a conversation with your beginning teacher about the important elements of lesson planning and the value of a proforma. Ask them to consider the following questions:

- Are you clear about how each box should be used? Are any unclear? Are there any you would amend, change or add?
- How does this compare with proformas that you have used before (or the one given by the ITE provider or school)? Is there anything missing or anything you have not seen included before?
- This proforma outlines the activities within the lesson in a linear way. Would you prefer to present this differently (e.g. as a cyclical diagram so that you can link the end-of-lesson assessment activity to the initial learning outcomes)?
- Is there anything on this proforma that is important for you as a beginning teacher that may be unnecessary as you gain more experience?

Some experienced teachers might look at the proforma in Figure 11.1 and conclude that this is an unnecessary amount of detail, but this is from a position where they know their classes and can intuitively gauge how long a particular activity will take or how to scaffold learning for pupils. Initially, a beginning teacher needs to think through every aspect of the lesson in advance; a proforma helps them do this at the planning stage before they are standing in front of the class.

Teacher		Class	
Date		Unit	*Title of the scheme of work*
Class context	*Number of girls/boys/pupil premium/students with particular needs, etc.*		
Bigger Picture	*Where does this lesson sit within the scheme of work? What has been covered and what comes next? What broader concepts will be addressed or developed in this lesson?*		
Aims/Key Question	*What is the purpose of the lesson? What is the question pupils should be able to answer at the end that they could not answer at the start?*		
Objectives/ Outcomes	*Different pro formas may approach or phrase this in different ways, but what are the intended outcomes of this lesson?*		
Keywords	*RE specific vocabulary*	**Potential Misconceptions**	*Is there anything in the lesson content that pupils might misunderstand or misinterpret?*

Lesson Outline		
Time	**Activity**	**Assessing progress**
How long is allocated for each activity?	*The learning activities that will allow pupils to meet the objectives/outcomes listed above.* *This section might include details of each activity that will be undertaken in the lesson and who is involved (e.g., teacher input, group work, individual task).*	*How will you assess the extent to which progress has been made?*
Adaptive Teaching	*What provision will be made for learners who need additional support to achieve the stated objectives/outcomes? How will activities be modelled and scaffolded to ensure success for all pupils?*	
Resources	*It can be useful to have a list of all the resources that will be needed in the lesson.*	
Evaluation	*This may be a separate pro forma, but it is helpful for beginning teachers to consciously reflect on every lesson that they teach.*	

Figure 11.1 Lesson plan proforma

However, many practitioners question the value of completing such documents, particularly if it appears this is being done to fulfil the requirements of ITE courses or professional development programmes rather than to improve a beginning teacher's practice. In 2018, a government review asked ITE providers to reduce the expectation on their trainees to develop individual lesson plans and produce resources for every lesson that they teach (DfE, 2018) and adjustments were made. However, it is true that, particularly at the start of an ITE course, beginning teachers might still be asked to fill in a lesson plan proforma for every lesson. Therefore, it may fall to the mentor to decide the level of detail so that beginning teachers are developing their planning skills but are not overwhelmed by the task. The aim is for beginning teachers to move from a reliance on a proforma to a point at which they intuitively consider all aspects of a lesson as second nature.

First steps in lesson planning

When working with an ITE student who has limited experience of lesson planning one of the first things to consider is establishing a staged approach. For example, the beginning teacher might plan a section of a lesson, or work with you to co-plan a lesson so that you can model how to plan.

Planning part of a lesson

A common first step is to ask a beginning teacher to plan and deliver one activity within a lesson you are teaching. This presents them with a clearly defined task and only requires them to plan for a short period. This may be the start of the lesson where the topic is introduced or part of the central section of the lesson so that they can deliver new content. Alternatively, they could plan the plenary so that you retain responsibility for teaching the new content, and the beginning teacher takes responsibility for assessing progress. Which approach you select will depend on the topic you are teaching, the initial targets of the beginning teacher and what you both feel comfortable with. However, the first step is to identify the lesson into which the beginning teacher will have some input. At an early stage, it may be best if this covers a religion or topic area where the beginning teacher is confident with their subject knowledge so that they can focus on planning the learning rather than the lesson content. Task 11.2 offers a structure for how you might approach this.

Task 11.2 Planning part of a lesson

Having identified an opportunity for your beginning teacher to contribute to the planning and delivery of a lesson, use the following framework to structure your planning meeting.

- Share with the beginning teaching the outline of the lesson, where it fits into the sequence of learning, key concepts that are addressed and the intended outcomes for this lesson.
- Discuss which part of the lesson the beginning teacher is going to plan.
- Be clear with the beginning teacher which of the intended outcomes their planning should address so they understand what they need to achieve and why this is important.

- You may wish to share with them existing resources or explain how you would approach this part of the lesson if you were planning it. Alternatively, this may be an opportunity for them to go away and reflect on how they want to approach this and generate their own ideas.

This discussion should take place in an initial preparation meeting. It is important that a beginning teacher has an opportunity to talk through exactly what is required and share their preliminary thinking with you. After this initial preparation meeting, agree on a deadline for the beginning teacher to share with you their planning and any resources that they intend to use which allows time for you to review the planning with the beginning teacher and gives them an opportunity to make amendments.

Collaborative planning

Working collaboratively with your beginning teacher to co-plan lessons is one of the best ways to support a beginning teacher to deconstruct how and why a particular lesson can bring about effective pupil learning. This strategy offers an opportunity for you to model the planning process and articulate for a beginning teacher the stages you go through and the things you think about when planning a lesson. Task 11.3 provides guidance for working in this way.

Task 11.3 Collaborative planning

Identify a lesson that requires planning (rather than one you have taught before). This may be a lesson for a new scheme of work or one where you feel you need to refresh your approach.

- Ensure the beginning teacher understands the context of the lesson, how it builds on prior learning and/or is essential for later units of work.
- Talk through the substantive subject content. Is the beginning teacher clear about what the pupils are to learn in the lesson, and can they identify pedagogical challenges?
- Together write the aim and intended outcomes for the lesson. Discuss how they are phrased and whether you will be able to easily assess progress. This should also initiate a conversation about what you hope pupils will gain from the lesson and how you are going to ensure that the learning is accessible to all.
- Talk through activities that might help you address each of the objectives. Given your wealth of experience and ideas, this might be part of the conversation when you can encourage the beginning teacher to take the lead, supporting them to ensure that the objectives/outcomes are addressed.

- Based on your experience, share with the beginning teacher any misconceptions that you think could arise in this lesson and talk through how these might be addressed.
- Talk about the pupils; how will the needs of individuals be met? How will you ensure that all pupils can achieve the learning outcomes?
- Consider assessment; how will you know whether the intended outcomes have been achieved?
- Discuss the practicalities. Who will prepare the resources? Who will teach each part of the lesson?

Collaborative planning with a beginning teacher in the early stages of ITE is a way of helping them identify where their own learning about pupils, learning theory and cognitive science comes together and impacts on their practical classroom work and subject considerations. However, it is something that you may wish to continue over time to further support and challenge your beginning teacher's thinking as they strive to refine their skills and approach. Through this you can model more complex and sophisticated thinking about teaching and learning in RE, allowing beginning teachers to see beyond generic considerations to focus on pedagogical questions in a subject context.

The role of the mentor

Your support and the school context are crucial in supporting beginning teachers to develop their planning skills and move on from 'copying' planning practices to becoming autonomous practitioners who can plan independently. This is one of the most challenging aspects of being a mentor – giving too much freedom too soon will leave the beginning teacher floundering, but being overly controlling can stifle their ability to become autonomous practitioners.

Mentors should be aware of three attitudinal roles which beginning teachers might adopt when planning, outlined in Table 11.1. You should seek to ensure that they are not adopting a 'task manager' role, (i.e. planning activities to keep pupils busy throughout the lesson). This is not a commonplace position given the wealth of resources and pedagogical guidance available to teachers, but some beginning teachers become task-focused when they first start planning lessons. More commonplace is the role of 'curriculum deliverer' whereby the beginning teacher is competent but relies on resources and materials prepared by others. This may lead to a focus on content knowledge with consideration of pedagogical principles being sidelined. The attitude towards planning which we advocate, and which should be the goal of your work to develop your beginning teacher's skills, emphasises the manipulation and use of subject knowledge as a 'skills and concepts builder' where a mentor nudges the beginning teacher towards autonomous planning rather than curriculum delivery. Mentors should encourage beginning teachers to draw on theoretical understanding and develop into effective skills and concept builders (Twiselton and Elton-Chalcraft, 2018) because, if this is stifled, they might feel disengaged and disillusioned when planning. If the beginning teacher has an emerging understanding of theoretical and pedagogical strategies coupled

Table 11.1 Intersection of mentor control and beginning teacher autonomy in lesson planning.

	Limited theoretical/ pedagogical understanding of planning	Emerging theoretical/ pedagogical understanding of planning	Developing theoretical/ pedagogical understanding of planning
Acute mentor control/ *limited beginning teacher autonomy*	**TASK MANAGER** Feels **underprepared, reliant** on mentor's/ external planning models	feels **competent** in developing strategies, but **constrained** by mentor's/ external planning models	Feels **confident but disillusioned** because mentor discourages the implementation of innovative/risky planning ideas
Partial mentor control/ *Emerging teacher autonomy*	Feels **underprepared,** and **defaults** to mentor planning	**CURRICULUM DELIVERER** Feels **technically competent** following mentor planning models	Feels **confident yet limited** by opportunities to deviate from mentor's planning models
School provides freedom/ *Developing teacher autonomy*	Feels **underprepared and overwhelmed,** feels mentor should provide planning models	Feels **competent but directionless,** feels mentor should provide explicit feedback on planning	**SKILLS /CONCEPTS BUILDER Confident, reflective, autonomous planning with** professional interchange between beginning teacher and mentor

Adapted from Elton-Chalcraft et al. (2020) and Twiselton and Elton-Chalcraft (2018)

with a supportive mentor, they will be able to plan creative and engaging lessons. While many beginning teachers may become technically competent curriculum deliverers in their lesson planning, a supportive mentor can push them towards the optimum position on the matrix (Table 11.1) adopting a role of skills and concepts builder to ensure the lessons they plan are more sophisticated than merely regurgitation of subject knowledge (Twiselton and Elton-Chalcraft, 2018, Elton-Chalcraft et al., 2020).

The role of the mentor is crucial; you must gauge your beginning teacher's level of competence and provide the correct level of support to facilitate their development. They need freedom, but they also need encouragement to engage with pedagogical strategies in their lesson planning to grow into a skills and concept builder in their planning.

The lesson planning process

To ensure that beginning teachers have a clear understanding of the planning process it is important they plan some lessons from scratch. There are several key aspects of the planning process around which support can be given by a mentor.

Understanding the context

Before they can start planning lessons, mentors need to help beginning teachers understand the structure and sequencing of the school's curriculum and the rationale that underpins it.

They also need to be aware of the key concepts running through the curriculum and how they are developed over time. These conversations should also extend to explore the rationale for the choices made in the selection of GCSE and A level specifications, the options selected within those specifications and how their content builds on the schemas established by pupils in Key Stage 3.

Over time lessons should build the pupils' substantive knowledge by linking new knowledge to that which they already know because, when learning, pupils are building schemas in which "the mind connects new information with pre-existing knowledge, skills, and concepts thereby developing existing schemas" (Education Endowment Foundation, 2021, p. 31). In RE, this will mean understanding where different religions and worldviews are covered and then revisited within the curriculum. It may also mean understanding how disciplinary knowledge is built over time. Understanding the 'bigger picture' enables beginning teachers to know how the content they are covering extends and builds on the learning that has gone before.

This approach, which is intended to build knowledge schemas over time in a carefully sequenced way, has implications for the planning of individual lessons. Research from cognitive science demonstrates the importance of asking pupils to retrieve key knowledge at regular intervals (Agarwal et al., 2021). This means that opportunities to revisit key ideas need to be built into schemes of work and, subsequently, into classroom activities.

Aims and objectives

When a beginning teacher is told that they are going to plan a lesson about a particular topic, they sometimes immediately focus on what they are going to ask the pupils to do. This activity-focused approach – in which they assume the role of 'task manager' – can lead to pupils being busy but without any sense of what they have learnt and how it fits into their developing schema in RE. Therefore, mentors sometimes need to start by impressing on beginning teachers that when planning lessons, they should start with the end; they should begin by identifying their aims and intended outcomes and then select or develop activities that help meet that goal. Hattie (2012) calls this 'backwards design'; the planning starts with the teacher knowing their desired outcomes and then working backwards to where the student is at the start of the lesson.

Exactly how the aims and outcomes might be included on the lesson plan will vary between different contexts (e.g. sometimes phrases like 'objectives', 'learning intentions' or 'success criteria' are preferred). Some lesson plan proformas require the identification of an overarching aim. It is often helpful for beginning teachers to express this as a question (e.g. Why are the five pillars important to Muslims? Which is the most important Christian Festival? How might their beliefs affect the daily life of a Sikh?). The aim of the lesson then becomes for the pupils to develop their knowledge and understanding so that they can answer the enquiry question (Walshe, 2018). In thinking about aims and outcomes some schools prefer to focus on the former (what am I setting out to achieve in the lesson) whilst others prefer to focus on the latter (what will I see from pupils who have made progress in the lesson), and there are other terms or acronyms that could be used instead. Therefore, it is important that you help your beginning teacher understand the terms used in your context and guide them to write intended outcomes in an appropriate way.

Beginning teachers must understand that it is important they have a clear goal. If you are working with a beginning teacher who is finding it hard to understand the importance of identifying the overall aim for each lesson, work through Task 11.4 with them. It offers a scenario for talking about lesson aims to help a beginning teacher understand how they impact on the writing of outcomes and the design of activities and, therefore, why this must come first.

Task 11.4 Clear aims and appropriate activities

Martin Luther King, Jr. is a figure who is often included in RE schemes of work. However, what might be taught about him, and the activities used to do this, will vary depending on the context of the lesson. Below are the enquiry questions for three different lessons that might involve teaching about Martin Luther King, Jr. Discuss with your beginning teacher the activities which might be used in each of the lessons.

- What can we learn from Martin Luther King, Jr. about Christian responses to racism?
- Is non-violent protest effective?
- How can belief affect action?

In the discussion, highlight that only the first of these lessons may require pupils to learn about Martin Luther King, Jr. in detail, with a focus on his faith. The second example explores an aspect of violence and the third is focused on the impact of belief. In these lessons, he is used as an example and activities might need to draw on other key figures to allow for the development of detailed responses to the questions. These lessons are not *about* Martin Luther King, Jr., and this is something that should be reflected in the activities.

Designing the activities

Structure

Once the beginning teacher has identified appropriate aims and learning outcomes, they need to start planning the classroom activities that will allow pupils to meet these goals. However, it is important that, for each task, they can articulate how it enables pupils to achieve their intended outcomes. Activities need to draw on prior learning and link new content to that which they already know (Deans for Impact, 2015) so that pupils are developing their RE knowledge schema. The beginning teacher also needs to consider the structure of the activities as they think about how to scaffold more complex tasks so that each pupil is presented with an appropriate level of difficulty (Coe et al., 2020).

As a mentor, you need to check that the beginning teacher can explain why each activity is included in the lesson plan and that they can account for the sequencing of the activities. You may also need to support the beginning teacher to review the plan from the perspective of individual pupils within the class to consider whether there is appropriate scaffolding within activities to ensure that all pupils can access the learning.

Explanations

Beginning teachers are likely to have been taught about a range of theoretical strategies and pedagogies including Sweller's (1988) cognitive load theory. The Great Teaching Toolkit (Coe et al., 2020) asserts that good teaching involves "limiting the number and complexity of new elements; breaking complex ideas or procedures into smaller steps; helping students to assimilate concepts into – and extend – existing schemas" (p. 32-33). Therefore, beginning RE teachers need to give thought to how they are going to explain new ideas and concepts, particularly abstract concepts. Examples are a common way of helping pupils understand abstract concepts, but beginning teachers need to select those which will best support the development of conceptual understanding. Mentors can act as a sounding board for beginning teachers as they develop creative strategies for explaining new content and concepts to their pupils.

Questioning

Many frameworks with which beginning teachers are familiar (e.g. Rosenshine, 2012) encourage teachers to incorporate questions into their lesson activities. However, it is important that, at the planning stage, beginning teachers think about the types of questions being asked, the time given to them, how they can ensure deep thinking on the part of the pupils and how the teacher will develop the responses (Coe et al., 2020). In RE, the use of questions, particularly following the Socratic approach, is often used as a way of promoting deeper and more complex thinking. Helping beginning teachers develop the ability to ask questions effectively and generate dialogue that allows pupils to develop their thinking is an example of a way in which the mentor can move the beginning teacher from being a curriculum deliverer to a skills and concepts builder. Beginning teachers often find it difficult to lead discussion as it requires them to think and reflect in the moment. Therefore, where their lesson plan allows time for questioning, check that the beginning teacher is clear about their intention and the ways in which they hope to develop the pupils' understanding. It is a good idea to ask them to add some examples of the kind of questions they intend to ask to their lesson plan. This ensures that they have thought carefully about this part of the lesson and does not leave them trying to come up with questions in the middle of the discussion.

Adaptive teaching

The activities planned in the lesson must be appropriate for all the pupils in the group. However, for RE specialists, who teach hundreds of children each week, the challenge of finding out about the needs of individuals in their classes and understanding how those needs can be met is particularly challenging. Therefore, it is an area where beginning teachers often need additional help from their mentors. In addition to reviewing special education needs and disability (SEND) data before they start planning lessons, beginning teachers on ITE courses may benefit from an opportunity to sit with class teachers to discuss the needs of individual pupils in each group. These conversations can allow the beginning teacher to find out about the pupils, including those not on the SEND lists but who, nevertheless, may benefit from additional support.

How beginning teachers use this knowledge of their classes to inform their planning will depend on the needs of their classes and their own targets. For example, some beginning teachers may start by planning scaffolding into their tasks, whereas others need to focus on strategies for developing literacy skills. The latter is an example of an issue that requires the beginning teacher to consider subject-specific pedagogical issues in their lesson planning. For example, if pupils need to engage with religious texts or read extracts of religious scholarship beginning teachers will need to think about whether these texts are accessible to their pupils and may conclude that, in the sequencing of the lesson, they need to first teach the pupils some relevant subject-specific vocabulary (Ofsted, 2021). Whatever the next step it is likely that they will need support from their mentor to plan this, to both identify appropriate strategies and understand how to make them work in their context.

Reviewing aims

The lesson plan should include opportunities for reviewing the lesson outcomes, both to see if they have been achieved, and to assess the progress made by pupils to inform the planning of the next lesson in the sequence. Whilst some lessons inevitably include an element of summative assessment, it is formative assessment that is key in supporting the development of beginning teachers' lesson planning skills. There is a range of strategies that might be used to gather this information and mentors are best placed to share those that work effectively in their context. However, beginning teachers are likely to want to explore things like the use of questioning, low-stakes quizzes and mini-whiteboards as they learn to gauge how effective their lesson has been. They need to look for indications as to whether the pupils have achieved the intended learning outcomes and whether there are any developing misconceptions (Ofsted, 2021).

A subject-specific approach

The reality is that, when you are discussing lesson plans with a beginning teacher, the discussions do not fall into the neat categories outlined earlier. All the elements of the planning process impact one another and underpinning them all are questions about subject-specific challenges and pedagogy. The challenges that present themselves often require the consideration of more than one aspect of planning at once. Task 11.5 offers a case study to help you reflect on this and consider the multifaceted nature of subject-specific support.

Task 11.5 Sources of wisdom and authority

Hannah has been teaching Christianity to a Year 10 GCSE group and introducing them to the biblical texts listed in the specification. However, she is frustrated that her pupils are not using them more effectively when answering exam-style questions. They are constantly re-using the same two or three passages and are not writing about them in a way that indicates a great deal of understanding. They are simply being used as proof texts (i.e. short passages of the Bible used to support arguments without any reference to their context).

What are the potential issues with Hannah's planning that could be addressed to help her tackle this issue? Consider the following:

- Subject-specific pedagogical questions – How are the texts being introduced in lessons? In her planning is Hannah using pedagogical strategies based in herme-neutics (Bowie, 2020; Pett and Cooling, 2018) that help ensure pupils have a thor-ough understanding of the texts and how they link to their existing knowledge?
- Structure – How is Hannah scaffolding tasks when she introduces new texts? Are all pupils are revising from accurate, detailed information?
- Modelling – Do the pupils know what a good response to an examination question looks like? Does Hannah's planning include opportunities for modelling this?
- Adaptive teaching – Are all the pupils using the texts as proof texts? Is she plan-ning enough support for lower ability pupils and enough challenge for higher abil-ity pupils?
- Reviewing aims – Hannah is assessing her pupils' understanding through the framework of exam-style questions. Are there other ways she could check pupils' understanding of the texts?

Planning using existing resources

To address the workload of both trainee and qualified teachers, it has been clearly stated that they should not be expected to plan all lessons from scratch and one suggested solution is to focus on amending and adapting existing resources (DfE, 2018). Increasingly, planning across departments or even multi-academy trusts (MAT) means that beginning teachers have access to schemes of work which are fully resourced with lesson plans for every lesson. For many, there is an expectation (or even requirement) that they will use these as their starting point. However, this is not a new concept for the RE subject community. In a subject where lessons are often taught by non-specialist teachers, for a long time, RE departments have ensured that there is a full plan (with resources) for every lesson on the curriculum. However, because of this, many RE teachers are also aware that it can be very difficult to teach a lesson based on a someone else's planning. Using lessons planned by others can lead to a focus on ensuring content is addressed rather than on the needs of the pupils in your own class. There can be pressure to get through the material, even when the teacher feels (or knows) that it's not working.

Amend, adapt and improve

For this reason, a clear approach to using existing resources as a starting point is needed for beginning RE teachers to ensure they do not resort to 'curriculum deliverer' mode. One approach is to give the beginning teacher the plans and resources but tell them that you expect them to 'amend, adapt and improve' them as they plan their lessons. This means that all the features of lesson planning outlined above must still be considered in the preparation of lessons, but rather than starting with a blank proforma, they are amending, adapting and improving what is already there to ensure they have a plan they understand and can confidently teach in order to build the pupils' skills and understanding of concepts (Elton-Chalcraft et al., 2020; Twiselton and Elton-Chalcraft, 2018).

'Amending' lesson plans allows beginning teachers to think about the context of the lesson. Do they need to amend the activities to ensure that they achieve the given aims/outcomes? For example, if part of the lesson relies on questioning, can they identify the kinds of questions that they might ask? Have they thought through the examples that they might use to explain key knowledge and are they aware of any potential misconceptions? Initially, a beginning teacher may need the mentor's support to talk through these issues as they develop their confidence and skills.

'Adapting' requires the beginning teacher to think about the needs of the individual pupils in their class. Preplanned lessons are, by definition, broad in their content as there is an assumption that each teacher will tailor them to the needs of their own class. Beginning teachers need to look at the needs of individuals and consider whether any activities need to be adapted for their classroom. For example, they might consider whether activities are sufficiently scaffolded to support their pupils, whether their literacy levels will allow them to access the given resources or whether there are any tasks that would benefit from being modelled for their class. Conversations with their mentor will be invaluable in helping them understand their pupils better so that they can more effectively tailor lessons for particular groups.

Suggesting that the pre-existing plans might be 'improved' offers encouragement to the beginning teacher that they may have something to offer to this lesson plan that will make it more effective (at least for their class). This may mean developing or replacing an activity, developing a resource, or adding something new to the scheme (in line with the aims/outcomes). Beginning teachers are exposed to new ideas and research (through university input or CPD sessions) which they may need encouragement to utilise in their teaching.

As beginning teachers gain experience, they may see things they want to change but need support in deciding how to go about this. Task 11.6 offers a case study so that you can consider how you might handle such a situation. On the whole, beginning teachers are grateful for the opportunity to draw on plans and resources designed by colleagues with more experience. As they develop their skills in amending, adapting and improving them you may wish to think about how you want them to document this. One option might be to ask them to annotate the existing lesson plans to indicate where they have made changes or added more detail. This approach offers an opportunity to keep the workload manageable for the beginning teacher, whilst still allowing you to monitor how their lesson planning skills are developing.

Task 11.6 Teaching shared lesson plans

Mark is an early-career teacher who has settled into his new post, a school which is part of a large MAT. The MAT has recently done a lot of work on the curriculum and developed a well-sequenced curriculum, supported by lesson plans and resources, that is used in all schools in the trust. Mark is currently teaching Islam to his Year 8 classes.

However, in one of his groups, which includes many pupils with low literacy levels and some with educational needs, the pupils in the class are struggling to access the content of the lessons. In next week's lesson, he is supposed to cover the Five Pillars, but he has asked to speak to his mentor about this. He feels that this is too much content for a single lesson with this group.

What could his mentor do to support him with his planning with this situation?

There are, of course, no easy answers, but it is encouraging that Mark has developed the confidence to make judgements about what will and will not work for his pupils and an eagerness to, potentially, replan a lesson for them. This is important as effective mentoring should seek to ensure that beginning teachers are not simply trained to deliver a curriculum but become skills and concepts builders (Elton-Chalcraft et al., 2020).

Developing planning skills

Mentors can support a beginning teacher to develop their ability to plan autonomously by encouraging them to think about creativity, consider their own agency, and reflect on their own development, in order to move them on from being a curriculum deliverer to a skills and concepts builder in their planning (Elton-Chalcraft et al., 2020; Twiselton and Elton-Chalcraft, 2018).

Creativity has been variously defined as an abstract noun with particular characteristics (NACCCE, 1999), an active verb (e.g. creative thinking) or as the application of imagination to produce something new (an idea, a performance or a product). Whichever conceptualisation is adopted the mentor can support a beginning RE teacher to draw on theoretical ideas to plan creative lessons which engage and challenge their pupils. Creative and engaging lessons encourage pupils to be curious and present opportunities for them to explore, investigate and experiment with ideas, as well as challenge them to critically examine their own and others' viewpoints about a particular topic (Claxton, 2007). A teacher's autonomy and agency are important determinants when considering their ability to be creative, and mentors can support beginning RE teachers by considering how the classroom environment and ethos enhance creative and transformative RE. Therefore, beginning teachers should be encouraged by their mentors to consider the pace, content and ethos in their planning. For example, the topic might be introduced in the first part of the lesson where learners are introduced to a concept. This could then be followed by an investigation of the topic (drawing on resources such as newspaper articles, pictures, artefacts, etc.), a quiz would test knowledge and misconceptions, followed by a debate in which the teacher creates an atmosphere where all young people are encouraged to voice their opinions about the topic.

Some challenges?

However, there is a potential issue if RE is creative and 'fun' but lacks challenge or depth (Elton-Chalcraft and Mills, 2015). A teacher might plan a lesson on the festival of Passover with Year 7 for example, with a variety of interactive activities including making Charoset; creating their own Seder plates with their special foods and planning a Seder meal, without really considering why Passover is so important for many Jews; and how this fits into other lessons in a unit of work. Focusing on the externals of religion can detract from the more important internal meaning or beliefs that underpin these. A mentor needs to encourage the beginning teacher to recognise that religions are complex, and practised, experienced and interpreted at individual, local and cultural levels, as well as globally understood; this needs to be reflected in their planning. It is important to show what unites people of the same religion, as well as help pupils understand and experience the diversity within them. In supporting the beginning teacher to recognise this, the mentor can move the beginning teacher on from curriculum deliverer to skills and concepts builder as they develop more sophisticated aims for the lesson. The resources and approaches a teacher selects should portray this unity and diversity to help pupils challenge their own assumptions and stereotypes about religions and build a more well-rounded understanding of their complexity. A beginning teacher will need to be encouraged to develop their own understanding of this first, to enable them to be able to reflect this complexity in their planning, the resources they use (e.g. photos, pictures, music) and expand and develop the way they teach about religions.

RE teachers are sometimes accused of presenting an overly positive view of religions and avoiding the difficult issue of the negative face of religion. This is particularly the case in discussing terrorism in the name of religion, to which pupils are exposed regularly through the media. It is important that lesson plans are flexible enough to allow pupils to raise and discuss these kinds of perceptions and that the reality of religion, is acknowledged (Revell, 2019). Task 11.6 offers some scenarios you can discuss with your beginning teacher to help you explore with them how they can plan for similar questions.

Task 11.7 Planning for the complexity

Discuss the following comments that might be made by pupils in lessons with your beginning teacher.

> *'I thought Buddhists were supposed to be peaceful miss. I saw them fighting on the news in Myanmar'.*

> *'My neighbour is a Christian Miss. They are the most horrible and unkind person I know. Are they a proper Christian?'*

- Does your beginning teacher have any examples of similar questions or comments they have encountered?
- Had they anticipated them in the planning of their lesson?
- Is there anything that can be done at the planning stage to prepare for incidents like these?

Mentors need to help beginning RE teachers be prepared and, at the planning stage, anticipate that challenging questions may arise. If a pupil suddenly says something which could take the lesson off at a tangent, a beginning teacher may be reluctant to deviate from their plan, whereas an experienced teacher would have a feel for the class and make a professional judgement. The mentor can help the beginning teacher interrogate their planning and consider what they would do if, for example during a lesson about Islam with Year 8 a pupil says, "My dad thinks Muslims are terrorists". While tempting to stick to the plan, it is important to address controversial issues (see Chapter 16). However, when working with a GCSE group, beginning teachers are less likely to be willing to deviate from the lesson plan because of a need to cover the content. These dilemmas need to be addressed by the mentor with the beginning teacher; with an appreciation of the experience, competence and confidence of the beginning teacher, the mentor should provide the appropriate level of freedom to ensure they develop as autonomous skills and concepts builders.

Summary and key points

Beginning teachers must learn to think through every aspect of a lesson in their planning. This ensures that they have a clear understanding of the features of an effective lesson and so that, with experience, their planning skills will become more intuitive. In time it is hoped that they will become skills and concepts builders who are confident, reflective and autonomous in their planning and who can deal with the challenges inherent in teaching RE.

- Supporting a beginning teacher to teach part of a lesson can be an effective 'first step' in developing their lesson planning skills.
- Collaborative planning is a way of modelling for a beginning teacher the thought processes that underpin effective planning and, over time, helping develop their skills further.
- To support beginning RE teachers to plan a lesson from scratch, there are key elements of a lesson plan that they need to understand.
- It is crucial that beginning teachers understand the wider context of each lesson that they teach to ensure that they can identify appropriate aims and objectives/outcomes.
- When planning lessons, beginning teachers need to carefully consider lesson structure and plan their explanations and their questions and make appropriate adaptions to ensure their lessons are accessible for all learners.
- Making use of existing resources can help make the workload of a beginning teacher manageable. However, it is not always easy to deliver pre-prepared resources and they may need support develop these resources to meet the needs of their own classes.
- Mentors can support beginning teachers progress in planning by supporting them to move away from a curriculum deliverer role to a skills and concepts builder role in their planning, ensuring lessons are creative and engaging.

Further resources

Education Endowment Foundation - https://educationendowmentfoundation.org.uk/

The Education Endowment Foundation is an independent charity who aim to raise achievement and close the disadvantage gap. One of the ways they do this is by summarising the best available evidence about 'what works' to improve teaching and learning.

Hutton, L., & Cox, D. (2021). *Making every RE lesson count: Six principles to support religious education teaching*. Crown House Publishing.

This text considers some evidence-informed approaches to classroom practice in an RE context. It looks at features of effective lessons that can be applied to beginning teachers' own practice.

Kirschner, P., & Hendrick, C. (2020). *How learning happens: Seminal works in educational psychology and what they mean in practice*. Routledge.

This text takes key pieces of research in psychology and applies them to classroom practice. Each chapter offers an overview of a seminal research paper and then explores implications for classroom practice.

Rivett, R. (2013). *101 great ideas: Strategies for spiritual and moral development in the RE Classroom*. RE Today.

A practical classroom guide that offers classroom strategies and activities that could be used to aid lesson planning.

References

Agarwal, P., Nunes, L., & Blunt, J. (2021). Retrieval practice consistently benefits student learning: A systematic review of applied research in schools and classrooms. *Educational Psychology Review*, 33(4), 1409–1453.

Bowie, R. (Ed.). (2020). *The practice guide: Classroom tools for sacred text scholarship*. Canterbury Christchurch University.

Claxton, G. (2007). Expanding Young People's Capacity to Learn. *British Journal of Educational Studies*, 55(2), 115–134. https://doi.org/10.1111/j.1467-8527.2007.00369.x

Coe, R., Raunch, C., Kime, S., & Singleton, D. (2020). *The Great Teaching Toolkit: Evidence Review*. Evidence Based Education. https://assets.website-files.com/5ee28729f7b4a5fa99bef2b3/5ee9f507021911ae35ac6c4d_EBE_GTT_EVIDENCE%20REVIEW_DIGITAL.pdf?utm_referrer=https%3A%2F%2Fwww.greatteaching.com%2F [Accessed 10/03/22]

Deans for Impact. (2015). *The science of learning*. Deans for Impact.

Department for Education (DfE). (2018). *Addressing teacher workload in Initial Teacher Education (ITE): Advice for ITE providers*. Department for Education.

Education Endowment Foundation (EEF). (2021). *Cognitive science approaches in the classroom: A review of the evidence*. Education Endowment Foundation.

Elton-Chalcraft, S., Copping, A., Mills, K., & Todd, I. (2020). Developing research-informed practice in initial teacher education through school-university partnering. *Professional Development in Education*, 46(1). https://doi.org/10.1080/19415257.2018.1550100

Elton-Chalcraft, S., & Mills, K. (2015). Measuring challenge, fun and sterility on a "phuno-metre" scale: Evaluating creative teaching and learning with children and their student teachers in the primary school. *Education 3-13*, 43(5), 482–497. https://doi.org/10.1080/03004279.2013.822904

Hattie, J. (2012). *Visible learning for teachers: Maximizing impact on learning*. Routledge.

National Advisory Committee on Creative and Cultural Education. (1999). *All our futures: Creativity culture and education*. https://sirkenrobinson.com/pdf/allourfutures.pdf

Ofsted. (2021). *Research review series: Religious education*. https://www.gov.uk/government/publications/research-review-series-religious-education/research-review-series-religious-education

Pett, S., & Cooling, T. (2018). Understanding Christianity: Exploring a hermeneutical pedagogy for teaching Christianity. *British Journal of Religious Education*, 403, 257–267.

Revell, L. (2019). Teacher practice and the pre-crime space: Prevent, safeguarding and teacher engagement with extremism and radicalisation. *Practice*, 1(1), 21–36.

Rosenshine, B. (2012). Principles of instruction: Research-based strategies that all teachers should know. *American Educator*, 36(1), 12–19, 39.

Sweller, J. (1988). Cognitive load during problem solving: Effects on learning. *Cognitive Science*, 12(2), 257–285.

Twiselton, S., & Elton-Chalcraft, S. (2018). Unit 2.4 moving from novice to expert teacher. In Arthur, J. & Cremin, T. (Eds.), *Learning to teach in the primary school* (4th ed., pp. 88–100). Routledge.

Walshe, K. (2018). Lesson planning. In Barnes, P. (Ed.), *Learning to teach religious education in the secondary school* (3rd ed., pp. 33–55). Routledge.

12 Supporting the delivery and evaluation of lessons

Rebecca Davidge and Lisa Vickerage-Goddard

Introduction

The purpose of this chapter is to look at how you can support beginning religious education (RE) teachers with the delivery and evaluation of their lessons. The chapter is designed initially to help you think about the prior experiences of the RE teacher who you will be mentoring and where they may be in terms of their confidence in the classroom. Once a mentor understands what a beginning teacher already knows, they can effectively support them in their practice and enable them to deliver and evaluate their lessons. The chapter starts by looking at case studies of beginning RE teachers and explores the different stages they may be at when you start working with them. The case studies provide you with space to reflect on beginning teachers as individuals and the different ways in which you might wish to support them to develop their practice.

The second section looks at stages of development as an RE teacher and identifies guiding principles which will allow beginning teachers to flourish and succeed in their practice. This part of the chapter is written as a guided journey to embark on with your mentee. It supports you in helping a beginning teacher to visualise the teaching process, set clear learning objectives and measure pupils' prior learning and gives practical ways in which they can measure progress during and at the end of the lesson. Strategies for supporting the beginning teacher to develop the ability to evaluate their own teaching are also explored.

By the end of this chapter, you should be able to:

- Consider the prior experiences your beginning teacher has had delivering lessons and how this will direct your support for them.
- Reflect on central practices that have allowed experienced teachers to thrive and understand how these can be applied to mentoring your beginning teacher.
- Be able to support your beginning teacher in delivering a lesson and evaluating its success.

The prior experiences of beginning RE teachers

When beginning RE teachers arrive at schools, they come from a range of backgrounds with varying amounts of teaching experience and a range of religious understanding. You may be mentoring trainee teachers, early career teachers or those from other subject areas teaching RE as an additional subject. Some are theists, some atheists and some agnostic. Some see the subject as an academic pursuit, and some see it as a vocation. Mentors must

DOI: 10.4324/9781003191087-15

recognise the uniqueness of the beginning teacher in front of them and, in order to support them in delivering and evaluating lessons, know their starting point.

There is no typical beginning teacher, and your role as a mentor is to work with them as individuals. The amount of experience they have had before starting will influence their confidence during their time in school. Task 12.1, 'Reflecting on the background of beginning teachers', highlights the variety of starting points that you may encounter in your work as a mentor. It provides you with an opportunity to reflect on the differing levels of support beginning teachers might need in the delivery and evaluation of their lessons.

Task 12.1 Reflecting on the background of beginning teachers

Case Study 1 – Jatinder

When Jatinder finished her undergraduate degree in theology and education studies, she worked as a teaching Assistant (TA) for two years before applying for her Post-Graduate Certificate in Education (PGCE). Once she had secured a place on the course, she began working for a school as a cover supervisor to gain experience and earn money before the course started. During her PGCE year, she undertook two contrasting school experiences. Her first school experience was at a school in an affluent area, where many parents were professionals, and the school had a reputation for high academic standards. Her second contrasting school was in an area of deprivation with little social mobility. Teachers worked hard at this school to raise aspirations and encourage pupils to be the first in their families to go to University. During her second school experience, she interviewed for and was offered a teaching position in her placement school.

As an early-career teacher, Jatinder may feel more confident in the classroom than colleagues who came to teaching straight from the university or other careers. She is well experienced and has already spent time building relationships with her pupils during her time as a PGCE trainee at the school. Her experience and the length of time she has spent in the classroom mean she will have a good sense of whether learning has occurred and some understanding of pupil progress. In terms of mentor support in delivering and evaluating lessons, it may be helpful for Jatinder to have an early lesson observation to identify the level of support she might need. If she is observed to be confident in the classroom and has good relationships with her class, her mentor can focus on further professional development. For example, having been shown some examples, she could be encouraged to produce differentiated materials for a range of needs in the lesson. She could also be guided to engage with form tutors and support staff in school to learn more about the individual needs of pupils in her classes. The mentor could also support Jatinder by identifying a class and asking her to complete a weekly reflective journal that focuses on her delivery. Time should then be made to talk through the reflections and offer advice and guidance on future practice.

Case Study 2 - Simon

Simon has always wanted to work with children and young people. He is a late applicant to the PGCE course and did an undergraduate degree in Applied Theology and Youth Ministry. He has worked in youth clubs and churches with children and young people, but he has not had any experience of teaching in a classroom. It was too late for him to gain experience in a school setting before his training programme commenced.

Simon's experience working with children and young people comes from a youth work setting, which is very different from the classroom. Relationships between a youth worker and a young person differ from that of the pupil and teacher. Simon will need support in recognising the difference between these roles. In this scenario, Simon's mentor may need to model good relationships and ensure that he knows that there is a difference in professional boundaries between a youth worker and a teacher. A teacher is not 'alongside' a young person in the way a youth worker is. It may be that Simon needs to observe and then team-teach lessons before taking responsibility for a full lesson. His mentor might also consider concentrating on year seven and eight classes allowing him more time to observe year nine and beyond to build confidence. A key issue for Simon might be understanding whether learning has taken place and to what extent. It is good practice for beginning teachers to have a notebook to hand to each class teacher to write brief comments during informal lesson observations. For Simon, it might be helpful for teachers to write what went well (WWW) and even better if (EBI) for each lesson, highlighting areas of good practice and making suggestions for next time.

Case Study 3 - Sara

Sara comes from a religious background and has a degree in theology. She would like to be a head of RE within two years of qualifying. She is aware of others who have achieved this and feels she is able. Throughout her undergraduate studies, she has kept in touch with the Ofsted-recognised outstanding Church Secondary school that she attended. She has undertaken work experience there.

Sara's situation is different again. Although she has had experience in school and feels confident in her knowledge of religious studies, her experiences are limited to one school setting. Sara needs to know that all schools are different and that teaching practices vary not only between schools but between classes. Sara is very confident in her abilities, and it is important that at the start of her teaching practice, she is encouraged to recognise her strengths and areas for improvement without her feeling criticised. A clear understanding of the importance of the evaluation process and how reflecting on practice and developing a range of skill sets in the classroom will enable her to achieve her longer-term goals. Sara needs to know that those things take time and that teaching practice is called practice for a reason.

These three case studies illustrate that all beginning teachers have different starting points in delivering and evaluating lessons. This means mentors need to dedicate some time to ask questions that will elicit the teacher's relevant experience and training needs. Consider the following questions to support your reflection on the case studies provided and the starting point of the beginning teacher with whom you are working.

- Consider each of the case study examples of beginning teachers. Now you are aware of their backgrounds, what specifically do you feel you need to do to support the individual in delivering and evaluating their lessons?
- Think about the possible opportunities and advantages their experience and perceptions could bring to their lesson delivery and evaluation.
- Think about your own mentee and their experience to date. What do you need to be mindful of when meeting with them to discuss the delivery and evaluation of their lessons. What specific things do they need to develop further? Are they realistic in evaluating their own practice? What can you do to encourage and support them further?

The components needed for effective delivery and evaluation of lessons

Becoming a teacher and learning how to deliver and evaluate lessons takes time; however, with structure and guidance, the journey can be one of discovery and fulfilment, with plenty of success along the way. In their review of the underpinning research of 'What makes great teaching?' Coe et al. (2014) offer six components of great teaching that can be used to support beginning teachers in delivering and evaluating their lessons.

Using these six components as a starting point, we have identified seven areas for you to consider in the context of your work with beginning teachers. These areas are utilised to enable you to support your beginning RE teacher throughout this chapter:

- Subject knowledge
- Imparting knowledge
- A safe learning space
- Managing the classroom
- Adapting practice
- Teacher identity
- Being professional

Subject knowledge

Strong subject knowledge is critical in delivering effective lessons. Not all RE teachers have a degree in RE or theology, and even those who do may not have covered the material needed to teach a range of world religions. It is important to ensure beginning teachers have both access to and understand the syllabus your school follows, or the locally agreed syllabus and

General Certificate of Secondary Education (GCSE) exam board specifications. You can do this by ensuring that they have access to short-, mid- and long-term planning materials, providing them with GCSE textbooks and having subject content as an agenda item in meetings so that there is an opportunity to discuss upcoming topics. Building confidence in a beginning teacher's subject knowledge supports them in the delivery of their lessons and should also be part of lesson evaluation.

Imparting knowledge

Good teaching in RE has questioning at the core of lessons. Rich, open, problem-based questions posed by the teacher and the pupils help shape and move the lesson forward. As Astley and Barnes (2018) argue, a good questioning technique in RE helps pupils explore the diversity of opinions in society and religious communities. When supporting beginning teachers to deliver and evaluate their lessons, it is important to assist them in developing the quality of their questioning. You can support beginning teachers in their delivery by providing them with an opportunity to discuss, question and observe you teaching your classes. Observing others can also support beginning teachers in developing their ability to deliver effective instructions and assess learning.

A safe learning space

Delivery of lessons will not always be effective, and mentors need to create a safe space that allows for mistakes to be made. Beginning teachers will learn by making mistakes and, as a mentor, you need to remember that your role is to create a safe space and positive environment for beginning teachers to practice their delivery. You can create this space for your beginning teacher through the effective use of positive praise. Resilience and determination are as important to beginning teachers as they are to pupils.

The RE curriculum covers a range of sensitive topics. The classroom environment and teachers' interactions with pupils must allow the opportunity for valuable, safe discussion to take place. Beginning teachers may feel uncomfortable at first teaching topics such as abortion, euthanasia or contraception. As you well know, pupils can sometimes make comments which may cause distractions or even upset. You must support your beginning teacher in the delivery of sensitive topics. You can do this by allowing the beginning teacher to observe you and your colleagues in delivering sensitive subject matter and/or ensuring you talk through these lessons in detail, considering what could go wrong.

Managing the classroom

It is important for beginning teachers to establish clear expectations, rules, and boundaries with their pupils. With rules and boundaries in place, they can effectively evaluate their practice against expectations. An important step in supporting beginning teachers in delivering their lessons is to remind them of the school's behaviour policies. Encouraging beginning teachers to use the school's behaviour policy to manage low-level disruption should mean that lessons are delivered effectively. Furthermore, reflecting with beginning teachers on their use of the school's behaviour policy can support in highlighting where things may or may not have gone well.

Adapting practice

We are all unique. Teachers, beginning teachers, teaching assistants, and pupils all bring different thoughts, beliefs and needs to the classroom. One of the areas beginning teachers find difficult and need support in is adapting their practice for all of those within their classrooms. They may fail to recognise that, in addition to adapting practice for those with a range of special educational needs and disabilities, they need to remember the protected characteristics of those within their classroom from different faith and cultural backgrounds as part of their adaptive practice. There will be those in a school community who come from non-traditional family backgrounds, and there will be a range of sexual orientations. When delivering RE lessons that may be considered controversial, the beginning teacher must recognise that school communities are made up of a range of unique individuals. Mentors need to recognise and point out to beginning teachers that, when delivering lessons, they must be mindful of the wide range of needs of those within their care and adapt their practice accordingly.

Teacher identity

Mentors need to support and guide beginning teachers as they develop and form their identity as a teacher and, for an RE teacher, this may involve reflecting on the way that personal faith and beliefs might impact their teaching. Although beginning teachers learn theory and pedagogy during training, it is through their classroom practice that they begin to understand their identity as a teacher. We can all identify different kinds of teachers through how they deliver their lessons. Pointing this out to beginning teachers, reflecting on their delivery with them, and discussing what kind of teacher they want to be will help them establish their own identity as a teacher.

Being professional

Reflecting on delivery and evaluating lessons is part of the role of a teacher as a professional. As a mentor to a beginning teacher, you must remind them to remain professional when delivering lessons. The unique nature of the role of an RE teacher means that sometimes there is a risk of over-sharing or perhaps being more lenient than we should. It is important that beginning teachers remain professional in their delivery and that you support them as they explore the importance of this for effective teaching and learning.

Although all these components may be needed for the delivery of effective lessons, there will be times when you find it is necessary to focus on some more than the others. Task 12.2 offers you an opportunity to reflect on these aspects of effective teaching in relation to the support you offer beginning teachers.

Task 12.2 Reflecting on components needed for effective delivery and evaluation of lessons

Think about your time in the classroom supporting beginning teachers and consider the following questions:

- When have you had the opportunity to engage with these components?
  o Subject knowledge
  o Imparting knowledge
  o Classroom environment
  o Managing the classroom
  o Adapting practice
  o Teacher identity
  o Being professional
- What comes naturally?
- What do you need to develop further?

Central practices to support beginning RE teachers

Experienced teachers Knight and Benson (2014) provide a series of questions that can be used to reflect on the delivery of good lessons. They ask:

- What do pupils need to understand?
- What will they do to create that understanding?
- How will the teacher and pupils know they have been successful?
- What feedback will pupils receive at each stage of the lesson?
- How will pupils demonstrate their learning, both during and at the end of the lesson?

(Adapted from Knight and Benson, 2014, p. 34)

Utilising these questions as a foundation, Task 12.3 provides a subject-specific opportunity to reflect on central practices that will specifically support beginning RE teachers evaluate their teaching and support their delivery.

Task 12.3 Developing practices to help beginning teachers deliver effective lessons

Complete the Table 12.1, considering each question in turn. Reflect on how each practice would support the delivery and evaluation of effective lessons and the kind of targets you might set a beginning teacher to help them develop this aspect of their practice.

Now consider the case study given in Task 12.4. Discuss Alex's lesson with your beginning teacher.

Table 12.1 Central practices to support beginning RE teachers

Central practices that will help beginning RE teachers deliver effective lessons	How might this support the delivery and evaluation of lessons?	Targets and actions to embed these in the delivery of a lesson
1. RE develops pupils' thinking through delivery that is based on honesty, receptivity, wisdom and truthfulness.		
2. Good questioning techniques in RE help pupils to explore a diversity of opinions.		
3. RE is enquiry based and enables pupils to reflect on their own worldviews and evaluate their own enquiries.		
4. Drawing on support from the RE community and the resources they publish will ease the delivery of lessons.		
5. Meaningful learning is promoted through interaction between pupils and religious content.		
6. Help pupils learn about religions and allow pupils to make personal reflections on their learning.		

Task 12.4 Case study

Alex wanted to introduce Sikhism to his Year 8 class. He decided to use an infographic, copied one between two, to explore data about Sikhs in the UK and beyond. He used this information to develop a quiz for the students: how many Sikhs do pupils think they are in the world/UK? In which countries do they think most Sikhs live? How many Sikhs wear the 5Ks? How many Sikhs have experienced discrimination?

Alex knew he needed to extend the questions he asked pupils beyond what, who, where, when and how, so he decided to throw it open to the pupils to develop deeper questions about the infographic. He gave them some question stems (a revised version of Bloom's taxonomy by Anderson and Krathwohl, 2001) so that, to help pupils analyse the data, they could ask, "Is the information on ... relevant?"; to evaluate, "How would you feel if ..."; to create, "What generalisations can you make about ..."

Once pupils had made some inquiries about Sikhism, Alex wanted them to think about some important values to Sikhs. He introduced Kirat Karni (honest living), Vand Chakna (sharing with others), and equality as teachings that focus on living without being self-centred. He asked pupils to use research and role-play to think about how these values might affect the day-to-day lives of Sikhs. To allow pupils to reflect personally on these values, Alex asked them to consider which values are important in their own lives. He encouraged pupils also to find out which Sikh values were compatible with the school values.

Alex used resources published by RE Today to support his lesson (Diamond-Conway, J [ed.] 2019; Pett, S. (ed.), 2019)

Discuss this case study with your beginning teacher and ask them the following questions:

- Can they identify any central practices in RE that would help Alex deliver a good RE lesson?
- What do they think might have worked particularly well in this lesson?
- Can they see any pitfalls or issues that may have arisen in this lesson?

Supporting beginning RE teachers to reflect on the delivery and evaluation of lessons

The journey

It may help beginning teachers to use metaphor to help them visualise the delivery and evaluation process. Many teachers will recognise the allegory of teaching being like a journey that involves - to some extent - preparation, action and fulfilment. The preparation is helped by having a destination in mind. The action may end up at that destination by a straight or winding path. The fulfilment may come when you have got your feet up reflecting on the photographs! The journey is only productive if we assess our progress as we go along. It is no use moving towards the destination if half your fellow travellers have gone off in a different direction. Delivering and evaluating a lesson involve regular checks that the intended route is clear, that the destination is still in sight and that your fellow travellers remain with you. Haydn (2016) reminds us that research suggests teachers need to be clear with pupils on the objectives for the lesson. A magical mystery tour may sometimes be exciting, but generally, a journey requires a clear destination! So, encourage the beginning teacher to share the learning objectives with pupils. The teacher can then measure whether pupils have moved towards it at the end of the lesson.

Identifying the objectives

The route and the destination the lesson will take, often referred to as aims and objectives for the lesson, necessitate measuring a pupil's prior learning. Research tells us that prior knowledge plays an important role in pupils' learning and suggests teachers learn how to break complex material into smaller steps. This involves 'discussing and analysing with [the mentor] how to sequence lessons so that pupils secure foundational knowledge before encountering more complex content' (Department for Education [DfE], 2019, p. 11). In the learning 'journey', beginning teachers need to know their pupils' starting point. Some pupils may be closer to the destination (the desired outcome for the lesson) before the teaching starts. Below are some practical examples you could share with beginning teachers to help them deliver a lesson to reach the destination in RE lessons:

➤ Ask pupils, "How much do you know about karma?" Provide closed answers and ask pupils to show you with their hands:
  1. I have never heard of this word.
  2. I have heard of this word but do not know a definition.
  3. I can give a definition for this word.
  4. I can explain how this word is linked to reincarnation.
➤ Design a quiz, use a digital format or old-fashioned pen and paper! Ask pupils:
  1. "How do you think you spell karma?"
  2. "What do you think it means?"
  3. "Which religion(s) do you think it is associated with?"
  4. "How do you think karma affects a believer's life?"
➤ Give pupils a statement to respond to using red, amber, green (RAG) cards or thumbs-up/-down – the important thing is that they show you and you can quickly assess their prior knowledge:
  1. "I know what karma means and how it is linked to the concept of reincarnation".
  2. "I understand how the concept of karma may affect the life of a believer".
  3. "I can give my personal views on the concept of Karma".

Measuring pupil progress during the lesson delivery

Once the lesson is underway, progress checks are needed to ensure pupils are moving towards fulfilling the objective. Remind your beginning teacher that the teaching and learning may take a straight or winding path, but they are looking for some movement towards the destination! Research (Sweller et al., 2011) indicates that working memory can be overloaded and beginning teachers need to understand the implications of this for their practice. To avoid this, teachers need to avoid overloading working memory by "discussing and analysing [with mentors] how to reduce distractions that take attention away from what is being taught (e.g. keeping the complexity of the task to a minimum, so that attention is focused on the content)" (DfE, 2019, p. 11). Strategies to avoid memory overload may include chunking information, not presenting too much information at once and giving pupils regular opportunities to practise skills. Task 12.5 allows you to reflect on how you might approach these conversations with a beginning teacher.

Task 12.5 Measuring pupil progress

Read and reflect on the following case study of how this teacher measures pupil progress when delivering their lesson

Case Study

Nicky was teaching a Year 7 group about the Five Pillars of Islam. She had used some 'hands-up' and targeted teacher questioning and ascertained that pupils had mixed prior knowledge of these. Nicky presents the 'big question' for the lesson – What are the Five Pillars of Islam? Some knew the names, and others knew definitions. Some knew nothing. She used a card sort activity to ask pupils in pairs to match up the names and definitions of the Five Pillars. Following this, Nicky paused the class and asked for feedback, checking all pupils had them matched correctly. She decided to give pupils a choice of activities: draw and label a diagram on which pupils had to add the names and definitions of the Five Pillars or explain why Shahadah is the first Pillar of Islam or evaluate which might be the most demanding Pillar to follow and why. She uses mini-whiteboards to ask pupils to respond to the 'big question', and after one minute, pupils show their progress.

- Reflect on this teaching episode with your beginning teacher and think about how pupil progress was measured. Can they identify good practice?
- Can your beginning teacher suggest other ways Nicky could have checked that all pupils had made progress?
- What does this quote about diagnostic assessment from the Education Endowment Foundation (2019) tell us about the purpose of monitoring pupil progress?

"A helpful distinction can be made between using assessment to monitor a pupil's progress and using it to diagnose a pupil's specific capabilities and difficulties. Monitoring can be used to identify pupils who are struggling or whose progress can be accelerated, and diagnostic assessments can suggest the type of support they need from the teacher to continue to progress. When an assessment suggests that a child is struggling, effective diagnosis of the exact nature of their difficulty should be the first step and should inform early and targeted intervention".

Measuring progress at the end of a lesson

It is important to involve pupils in measuring their progress. Haydn suggests asking pupils the extent to which they have fulfilled the learning outcome, marking each other's work, or drawing up a mark scheme and success criteria. He asserts that "You cannot do the learning for the pupils; they have to do it themselves, and your job is to show them how to do this" (Haydn, 2016, p. 462). This is reflected in a recent policy report which states that beginning teachers should be 'Discussing and analysing with expert colleagues how to ensure feedback is specific and helpful when using peer- or self-assessment' (DfE, 2019, p. 24).

Supporting beginning RE teachers to evaluate their lessons

Avoiding negative talk (or misplaced positives) in post-lesson analysis

It is good practice to discuss the lesson with the beginning teacher as soon as possible after they have taught it; we all know the feeling of waiting with nervous anticipation for feedback. Also a discussion soon after the observation can ensure that the events of the lesson are easily recalled and targets can be set before the next lesson is planned. However, giving *time* for reflection will also bring fresh insight to the beginning teacher and the mentor. This wait can also help to clarify strengths and areas for development and identify the effective features of the lesson.

Three main aspects of focus in post-lesson reflection are, first, to consider if the lesson has been effective; second, to identify implications for future practice; and, finally, to record the learners' educational progress. Holmes (2003) suggests using a checklist after a lesson to help beginning teachers consider the effectiveness of the lesson. There are many examples of similar checklists in literature (see e.g. Kyriacou, 2009). However, Table 12.2 is specific to RE teachers.

A checklist like this could help a beginning teacher analyse how their lesson went in an objective way. Some beginning teachers will be predisposed to recognise the aspects of the lesson that did not go according to plan or that learning was missed. Others may be more inclined to declare that a lesson went well as it fulfilled the lesson plan, even if effective

Table 12.2 Post-lesson RE Checklist (Adapted from Holmes, 2003)

	✓	✗
Subject knowledge		
Did I use keywords? Did I refer to specific beliefs, teachings and practices? Did I use key sources of wisdom and authority? Did I refer to forms of expression and ways of life?		
Imparting knowledge		
Did I share the lesson objectives? Did I check prior learning? Did I include regular assessment points? Did I use a range of questioning techniques? Did I model and scaffold new learning? Did I review the learning objectives at the end of the lesson?		
Classroom interactions		
Did I maintain high expectations? Did I regularly interact with all pupils? Did I provide an appropriate level of challenge? Did I recognise the effort pupils make?		
Managing the classroom		
Did I follow the school behaviour policy? Did I manage the pupil's behaviour appropriately? Did I make effective use of the classroom space and prepared resources? Did I ensure pupils were on task and actively engaging in learning?		
Adapting Practice		
Did I adapt practice where necessary? Did I recognise individual pupils' needs?		
Teacher identity		
Did I recognise any bias I might bring to this subject matter?		
Being professional		
Did I act as a positive role model to pupils? Did I treat pupils with respect? Did I communicate effectively with pupils and other adults in the room? Did I set myself targets for further improvement?		

learning did not occur. So, to avoid unnecessary negative or overly positive talk, a checklist will help ensure a lesson's successful implementation serves the intended learning outcomes (Kyriacou, 2009).

The post-lesson discussion

At the start of the journey, many beginning teachers are concerned about their own role within the lesson instead of the pupils' learning. It is important for mentors to guide beginning teachers, both trainee and early-career teachers, from a place of concern over their role in the classroom to a pupil-focused position. A beginning teacher needs to be able to evaluate their own lessons in order to make progress from self-focused to student-focused, and reflection is an important part of this process. Your role as a mentor will be to support the beginning teacher in evaluating their progress and becoming a reflective practitioner, so Task 12.6 suggests questions you can use to prompt post-lesson discussion.

Task 12.6 Post-lesson discussion

Discuss these questions regularly with your beginning teacher and establish them as good self-reflection habits:

- How do you know a pupil has learned? What can you use as evidence?
- What do pupils know at the end of the lesson that they did not know at the beginning, and how was this evidenced?
- What were the common misconceptions, and how could you plan for these?
- What methods of assessment did you use to assess progress, and were they effective?
- If you had to teach the same lesson to the same group again, would you do it differently?

What other questions do you think could help your beginning teacher to reflect on their lesson?

Further ideas to support the evaluation of lessons

Different strategies can be useful at different times and in different situations. You may want to consider some of the following strategies to help beginning teachers evaluate their lessons and demonstrate their progress over time. For example, setting targets might be used throughout the mentoring process, whereas RAG rating might be particularly useful in the early stages of supporting your beginning teacher.

What Went Well (WWW) and Even Better If (EBI) journal

Give beginning teachers WWW and EBI on all lessons and learning episodes. Ask them to do the same.
Use these to support beginning teachers in reflecting on their lessons and progress.

RAG rating lessons

Red Amber Green (RAG) rating lessons in a teacher's planner can help beginning teachers self-reflect on the success of their lessons, identifying where the need additional planning or support.

Setting targets

Encourage beginning teachers to set sharp, not blunt, targets for their future practice.

Think about the following examples. These are blunt targets because they are written in very general terms:

Set high expectations for my class
Plan homework activities for my classes
Stretch and challenge my pupils

To make these sharp targets, they need to be specific, achievable and measurable, for example:

Plan a homework activity for 7X next lesson which is focused on helping pupils understand why Muhammad (pbuh) fled to Madinah.

Stress importance of plenary sessions and end-of-unit assessments

Be clear with beginning teachers about the importance of plenary sessions at the end of every lesson or learning stage as an opportunity for reflection and evaluation.

Use of assessment and data to support evaluation of lessons

Although a welcome addition to the subject for some, assessment has been a controversial issue in RE (Blaylock, 2000). However, as identified in many government policy documents, assessment is critical to effective teaching (DfE, 2019). Monitoring and assessment produces data that can be used to support planning, teaching and evaluation. School systems can provide teachers with data giving information about, for example, reading age, special education needs and disability provision, or Pupil Premium status, and it is important to introduce beginning teachers to these data as soon as possible. This provides them with information that can help them decide upon their seating plans, focus their lesson planning and help them measure progress. Task 12.7 offers a structure for the way that you might approach this with your beginning teacher.

Task 12.7 Collating and using data to support teaching

- Discuss with your beginning teacher the data that are available to teachers within your school and make sure they know how to access this.
- Talk them through each data set, explaining how it might be used to support effective planning and evaluation of lessons.
- Co-plan a lesson where you use the data to inform the choices made (in the selection of resources, the structuring of tasks and the adaptions made for individual pupils)
- After the beginning teacher has taught the lesson ask them to produce a written evaluation where they link lesson outcomes to the data that were originally used.
- Encourage them to think about the following questions when evaluating their lesson:
    - o   How did the data impact on the planning of the lesson?
    - o   Is there anything that you did because of the data that went particularly well?
    - o   Is there anything you would like to know that the data couldn't tell you?
    - o   Have you generated any data in the lesson that helps you understand whether or not individual pupils have made progress?

Summary and key points

This chapter has explored how you can support a beginning RE teacher in the delivery and evaluation of their lessons as they learn to manage teaching and learning, and reflect on their experiences. In particular, the following points have been highlighted:

- The importance of the prior experiences your beginning teacher has had delivering lessons and how this will direct your support for them
- The identification of central practices that have allowed experienced teachers to thrive and an understanding of how these can be applied to mentoring your beginning teacher
- The opportunity to engage with case studies and practical strategies, which will aid you and your mentee measure the pupils' progress when delivering a lesson and evaluating its success.
- Understanding the importance of using data and assessment to help your mentee plan, teach and evaluate their lessons.

Further resources

Bowman, T. (2017). *88 Ideas to Teach More Effectively*. Routledge.

This is a little book with lots of helpful, practical and accessible ideas.

Quigley, A. (2016). *The Confident Teacher: Developing Successful Habits of Mind, Body and Pedagogy*. Routledge.

This book is useful in providing both practical and research-focused guidance in developing pedagogy and the effective characteristics needed in the classroom.

References

Anderson, L. and Krathwohl, D. (2001). *A Taxonomy for Learning, Teaching and Assessing: A Revision of Bloom's Taxonomy of Educational Objectives.* https://www.uky.edu/~rsand1/china2018/texts/Anderson-Krathwohl%20-%20A%20taxonomy%20for%20learning%20teaching%20and%20assessing.pdf

Astley, J. and Barnes, L. P. (2018). The role of language in religious education. In Barnes, L. P. (Ed.), *Learning to Teach Religious Education in the Secondary School* (pp. 73–88). Routledge.

Blaylock, L. (2000). Issues in Achievement and Assessment in Religious Education in England: Which Way Should We Turn? *British Journal of Religious Education, 23*(1), 45–58. https://doi.org/10.1080/0141620000230106

Coe, R., Aloisi, C., Higgins, S., & Elliot Major, L. (2014). *What makes great teaching? Review of the underpinning research.* Durham University.

Department for Education [DfE]. (2019). *ITT Core Content Framework.* https://assets.publishing.service.gov.uk/government/uploads/system/uploads/attachment_data/file/974307/ITT_core_content_framework_.pdf

Diamond-Conway, J. (Ed.) (2019). *Inspiring RE: No5 Sikhs.* RE Today Services.

Education Endowment Foundation. (2019). *Assessing and Monitoring Pupil Progress.* https://educationendowmentfoundation.org.uk/tools/assessing-and-monitoring-pupil-progress/ampp-introduction/#diagnostic-assessment

Freathy, R., Doney, J., Freathy, G., Walshe, K., and Teece, G. (2017). Pedagogical Bricoleurs and Bricolage Researchers: The case of Religious Education. *British Journal of Educational Studies, 65*(4), 425–443. https://doi.org/10.1080/00071005.2017.1343454

Grimmitt, M. (2000). *Pedagogies of Religious Education: Case Studies in the Research and Development of Good Pedagogic Practice in RE.* McCrimmon.

Haydn, T. (2016). Assessing pupil progress: what do we know about good practice? In Capel, S., Leask, M., and Younie, S. (Eds.), *Learning to Teach in the Secondary School* (7th ed., pp. 447–470). Routledge.

Holmes, E. (2003). *The Newly Qualified Teachers Handbook.* Routledge Falmer.

Knight, O. and Benson, D. (2014). *Creating Outstanding Classrooms: A Whole School Approach.* Routledge.

Kyriacou, C. (2009). *Effective Teaching in Schools Theory and Practice.* Nelson Thornes.

Pett, S. (Ed.) (2019). *Examining Religion and Belief: Sikhs.* RE Today Services.

Sweller, J., Ayres, P., and Kalyuga, S. (2011). *Cognitive Load Theory.* Springer.

Wright, A. (2004). *Religion, Education and Post-Modernity.* Routledge Falmer.

13 Observing beginning religious education teachers' lessons

Jane Savill and Alexis Stones

Introduction

Observing beginning teachers is one of the most important processes for both the mentor and beginning teacher to support the development of professional understanding and classroom practice. It provides a framework for you both to interact as professionals as the beginning teacher moves from student teacher into the early years of their career and beyond. Being observed can be daunting for a beginning teacher and is a time-consuming activity for you as the mentor. In this chapter, we hope to give you ideas about how to make the most of your observations for you and your beginning teacher.

Getting used to being observed is an important skill for beginning teachers as they will need to be observed throughout their careers for job interviews, quality assurance, progression and peer support. As the process sits in between discussions around the beginning teacher's lesson planning and feedback, it is important that observations are focused so that both parties know how, why and what is being observed.

Sometimes the beginning teacher can feel disheartened if a lesson has not gone as well as it should because pupil behaviour was challenging, timing went awry or a plenary could not be completed and so on. As the observer you can support the beginning teacher in learning from lessons which have not gone so well, as well as those which have been very successful. Reflection on the latter allows beginning teachers to continue to learn when things go well, identifying the features of a successful lesson so they may be continued in the future. With your experience, you can model approaches to reflective practice that lead to your beginning teacher's professional development.

Religious Education (RE) is a unique subject in its ability to foster sensitive, controversial and challenging conversations. It requires in-depth knowledge beyond a single undergraduate degree and faces pressures of a lack of consistency in its nature and purpose across schools and year groups. Understanding how to navigate these challenges is of huge value to the beginning teacher. When observations shed light on these issues, the more you can be transparent and communicative about the reasons for your subjective perspective, the more they will be able to reflect on their practice for themselves.

At the end of the chapter, you should be able to:

- understand the purpose of lesson observations and how you can support a beginning RE teacher in developing their classroom skills.

DOI: 10.4324/9781003191087-16

- confidently employ a cyclical approach to observations for pre- and post-lesson activities.
- plan effectively for future observations to give a beginning RE teacher the best chance of success.

Approaching observations

It is important to think about how lesson observations are organised. Expectations need to be established that both the observer and the beginning teacher can meet. To allow you to reflect on your current practice, Task 13.1 invites you to think about how and why you observe lessons.

Task 13.1 Approaching observations

Consider these questions to reflect on how and why you are currently observing lessons:

- What are your reasons for observing a beginning teacher's lessons?
- How do you and your beginning teacher prepare for the observation process?
- How is observing a beginning teacher different/similar to observing a colleague?
- How and where do you record your observations?
- How do you follow up with the beginning teacher on your observations?
- In what ways can observation be a valuable part of the mentoring process?
- How do observations impact the mentor/mentee relationship?
- How are observations of RE lessons different/similar to other lessons?

In your role as an observer of RE lessons, you have the opportunity to 'stand back' and observe your subject being taught. The knowledge and skills of an RE lesson are very distinct. For example, an RE lesson on animal rights will include content and awareness of religious and non-religious perspectives as well as ethical and philosophical dimensions. This requires a beginning RE teacher to draw on a range of substantive and disciplinary knowledge that is very specific. It is important to remember that they are just at the beginning of this process to develop their RE knowledge and skills, and your observations are key to their professional development.

My role as an observer

Why observe?

Your observations form a crucial aspect of your support of the beginning teacher in their journey. They are considered an expectation during training and the early years of a teaching career as they allow you to see the beginning teacher's teaching 'in action', acknowledge progress, give instant and individual feedback, identify strengths and targets and direct the next steps for teacher development. From the beginning teacher's point of view, your support is necessary, both in terms of their work in the classroom and the discussions you have around this. Indeed, meaningful observations make significant links between the past, present and future of the beginning teacher's journey which supports them in developing reflective practice as teachers of RE.

How do I observe: Judge or co-constructor?

An observer who is a 'judge' can be perceived as someone who is looking to find fault when completing the observation. An observer who is a 'co-constructor' is someone who takes on a more collaborative and supportive approach to an observation.

This categorisation relates to the question of whether learning to teach is conceived as an apprenticeship or a process of co-construction. There is considerable evidence that judgemental observing is not helpful to the beginning teacher (Manning and Hobson, 2017b). Although it can be tempting to find 'quick fixes' as you observe, research indicates that beginning teachers find that judgemental observations hinder both the development of a positive relationship with their mentor and their ownership of their individual learning process (Manning and Hobson, 2017b). A way to avoid judgemental observing, which prioritises the mentor's experience and perceptions over the beginning teacher's, is to decide on the focus for the observation *with* the beginning teacher. This highlights the purpose of the observation for both parties and gives you and the beginning teacher a united intention in which they enact the focus and you observe. By deciding on a focus (or more than one focus) the beginning teacher feels less on show and more encouraged to meet the challenges of the focus (or foci).

Task 13.2 invites you to reflect on your own experience of both being observed and observing others to consider the potential impact of different approaches to observation.

Task 13.2 Different approaches to observation

Consider the following questions as ways to reflect on different approaches to observation:

- What kind of observing did you experience as a beginning teacher?
- Which approaches did you find useful?
- List examples of judgemental and co-constructive approaches to observation.
- Is it ever right or useful to judge when you observe?
- How will the beginning teacher benefit from co-construction?

Observation cycle

In order for observations to be the most beneficial for the beginning teacher's development, a helpful approach can be to follow the observation cycle (Figure 13.1), to break down the individual aspects of the whole process. Being observed can make beginning teachers feel exposed and very vulnerable. At each stage of the observation cycle, there should be transparency so that you and the beginning teacher can discuss any worries or hopes before, during and after the observation.

Figure 13.1 The stages of the observation cycle

(Adapted from Laurence, Low and Phan, 2019, p. 185)

Hobson (2016) highlights the fact that how someone observes depends on their attitude to how they learn as teachers. He argues that supportive, non-judgemental, individualised and growth-oriented mentoring through observation creates a positive learning environment for beginning teachers to develop their own professional journey in a way that will last the whole of their career. Your supportive approach to observing allows professional and personal needs to be part of the process too as beginning teachers will only develop if they feel safe and supported. At the end of the day, you want the beginning teacher to both value the observation process and be able to make the most of each observation and following the observation cycle can help you achieve this.

In the next section of this chapter, we consider each stage of the observation cycle in more detail.

Pre-observation activities

To ensure that your beginning teacher finds the observation process supportive, it is important that discussion and planning take place prior to the lesson. Task 13.3 offers a framework for this preparation and invites you to plan an observation using this approach.

Task 13.3 Preparing for an observation

Work through the following process with the beginning teacher prior to your observation:

- Based on feedback from previous lesson observations and discussions, in a pre-lesson meeting agree on next steps to inform the beginning teacher's new lesson plan.
- Ask the beginning teacher what they want to get out of the lesson observation.
- Discuss intentions and concerns about the lesson, class and individuals.
- Agree on your focus/foci for observation.

- Invite the beginning teacher to ask you questions about aspects of the lesson where they are less certain. These questions are examples that relate to components of various professional development frameworks:
  - o Do the activities relate to the learning objective?
  - o Are the success criteria accessible?
  - o Do you think the activities will engage all pupils?
  - o How do you create a positive learning environment?
- Agree a time for the beginning teacher to give you the necessary paperwork for the observation, for example the final lesson plan, a copy of the resources, and the seating plan.
- Agree on a time to reflect and discuss feedback after the lesson.

The activities outlined in Task 13.3 relate both to the beginning teacher's individual journey and your agreed intentions for this lesson. By engaging in these conversations *before* the lesson you will be in a position to intervene if you see anything that would benefit from being amended. There is nothing worse than observing a lesson that could have been improved through your intervention at the lesson planning stage! Intervening at the draft lesson planning stage is also an opportunity for the focus/foci of the observation to be discussed.

You will feel more able to support the beginning teacher if you encourage them to share any concerns and hopes they might have regarding the particular lesson that is to be observed and perhaps any more general issues. Honest communication generates empathy which, in turn, helps you to feel less judgemental and for the beginning teacher to feel less judged. The beginning teacher may want 'the right answer' when they discover a problem in the pre-observation stage. You can call on your experience to demonstrate that professional development is an ongoing process of reflective practice rather than problem-solving technical tools or protocols (Winch, Oancea and Orchard, 2015). To help them understand this, invite the beginning teacher to observe the process when you are being observed by a peer and to listen in to the discussion that follows the lesson when possible developments are considered. There are approaches, attitudes and values that you can demonstrate in your planning, teaching and reflecting that the beginning teacher should want to emulate. Discussions *before* the lesson allow you to demonstrate your investment in the process as you both want to see how the plans play out in practical terms.

The lesson observation

Being observed can be challenging for the most experienced teacher and certainly a beginning teacher will want to 'get it right' in front of an observer. Reminding them about the nature and purpose of the observation is important to reassure them of the relevance of the process to their professional journey.

The formality or informality of the observation may depend on the stage of the beginning teacher's development and the mentor/mentee relationship. An informal observation – when you might just write a few notes and offer general feedback without having agreed any main focus with the beginning teacher – will allow your beginning teacher to get used to the process. You might consider completing some informal observations of parts of lessons before a more focused observation is planned. On the other hand, a formal observation with a clear focus/foci may feel like a more secure start for the beginning teacher and there may be an expectation that you complete a particular number of formal observations during the time you are working with your beginning teacher. There are benefits and shortcomings for both approaches, and it is worth bearing these in mind in case you wish to draw from both forms. As the mentor, you need to decide which type of observation you are conducting in order to support your beginning teacher and make it clear to them which approach you are taking. You may choose to combine elements of both so, using Table 13.1, consider the advantages and disadvantages of each as you plan your approach. Then consider Task 13.4.

Table 13.1 Points to Consider when Conducting Informal and Formal Observations

	Advantages	Disadvantages
Informal	• Suitable for a single activity rather than a whole lesson; • less intimidating; • chance to get used to the process; • open-ended and exploratory; • feedback is verbal or informal; • lower stakes; • pre-observation activities can be more open-ended.	• The beginning teacher can feel exposed; • Mentor has not agreed on what to look out for or comment on; • preparation can be less relevant; • too subjective and prone to bias; • post-observation discussion can be overwhelming, • irrelevant or difficult to apply; • feedback is too informal.
Formal	• Clear focus/foci; • both mentor and beginning teacher know what is being observed; • uncontrollable factors are less important; • preparation, observation and follow-up activities are specific and connected; • feedback/comment proformas; • opportunity to record events in chronological order; • potentially more objective.	• The beginning teacher can feel judged; • if things don't go to plan, the beginning teacher can feel defeated; • (as with informal observations) – too subjective and prone to bias; • a clear focus/foci might overshadow unplanned areas of development; • if feedback proformas list events in chronological order it can be difficult for the beginning teacher to understand how this can support progress.

Task 13.4 An observation checklist

Whether you are conducting an informal, formal or joint observation (see the following), we suggest you consider the following as a brief checklist. Use this in the next observation that you arrange to ensure that you have a clear sense of purpose and appropriate arrangements.

•   Am I clear on my focus/foci for the observation?
•   Has the beginning teacher agreed to the chosen focus/foci?

- Is this an informal or formal observation?
- Is the beginning teacher prepared for me to observe and give feedback?
- Have I agreed on a time and venue for my follow-up conversation and feedback with the beginning teacher?

Conducting the observation

Whether it is an informal or formal observation it is important that the beginning teacher is given every opportunity to do their best and show what they are capable of in the classroom. Before the observation decide with the beginning teacher where you will sit and what your interaction with the pupils will be: Will you support a pupil who may value the help, will you move around the classroom to observe pupils working at an appropriate time or will to observe without interacting with the pupils? If you know that there will not be time to talk with the beginning teacher immediately following the observation, tell them a time when it will be possible to have a conversation about the lesson you have observed.

Recording your observations

How you record your observation will depend on whether an observation is formal or informal. An informal lesson observation doesn't have a particular structure, while a formal observation is likely to be on a proforma provided by the initial teacher training (ITT) provider or your school. How you use the form is another decision to make. Some mentors will use the 'Notes' section to list events as they occur and will then identify strengths and targets. Recording events as they occur can be a double-edged sword. On one hand, they provide evidence for discussion and allow the observer to be more objective as they look through what happened after the lesson as a way of reflecting on strengths and targets. On the other hand, they can be perceived as a catalogue of failures if the lesson didn't go as the beginning teacher planned! You might decide to list the events during the observation and keep them for yourself to use in the post-observation activities. However, it is also important to note down successes. Beginning teachers will learn from what went well as well as things that did not work as they had hoped. It is important to note progress and encourage reflection on how and where this might be replicated and developed further.

Triangulation and observing with another professional

Daly and Milton (2017) recommend that mentors mentor each other and highlight a number of principles which enable mentors to develop their mentoring skills and so support beginning teachers in their professional development. The first of these is to "harness diversity of experience among mentors – a mentor learning community thrives on difference" (Daly and Milton 2017: 13). A peer mentoring culture means that mentors are observed by colleagues and thus are reminded what 'being observed' feels like. It also recommends that joint observations (where you and a colleague observe the beginning teacher together) are conducted.

Joint observations are useful, not only for the beginning teacher but also for you as mentor. They will give you the chance to discuss and articulate your reflections before and alongside another professional. They can also give you the chance to be aware of your own subjectivity which, in turn, helps you to develop professionally. Prior to a joint lesson observation, it is useful to have a face-to-face conversation or an email exchange so that the focus/foci of the lesson can be discussed. Task 13.5 offers a framework for you to structure your approach to and planning of a joint observation.

Task 13.5 A joint observation

Consider the following questions when planning a joint observation with a colleague.

- Are both observers and the beginning teacher clear about the purpose of the observation?
- Are both observers making notes or is it more appropriate for one observer to 'observe' and leave note-taking to the other?
- Is the beginning teacher clear about how the observation will be discussed and recorded following the lesson?
- What can you – as the mentor – do to prepare the beginning teacher for a joint observation and ensure that they are comfortable with the process?
- Who will conduct the feedback following the lesson?
- Will you make time with the colleague to reflect on the joint observation process and consider the impact of the process – both for the beginning teacher and for you as the mentor.

Post-observation discussion

Post-observation discussion is an important part of the observation. It might be easy for the beginning teacher to want to feel the hard work is done after the actual lesson is over, and you may need to reiterate the importance of reflection and feedback as part of the observation cycle (Figure 13.1). You have both heard and seen what pupils have said and done. Some lessons will involve written work, as well as oral contributions, and this should also inform your reflections.

Depending on your relationship with the beginning teacher and their level of confidence, you may want to reassure them immediately afterwards. Then, we suggest you ask the beginning teacher to take five minutes, or thereabouts, to reflect on what happened. You could ask them to write some notes in answer to the following questions which can then go on to support the post-lesson discussion:

- Did pupils meet the learning objectives?
- Were there any surprises in the oral feedback to questions asked or in any written work seen?

- Were the success criteria appropriate and met by the pupils?
- Is it evident that pupils have gained the necessary knowledge and understanding to move on?
- How can pupils' written work inform your next steps?

In addition to the notes you have made, you will be able to draw on your own classroom experience when discussing the lesson you have observed. The beginning teacher may begin their reflection of the lesson they have taught with a focus on how attentive pupils were or how much they engaged in the activities they were asked to do, for example. As the mentor, you can guide them to reflect on the learning which took place, whether the learning objectives of the lesson were met and whether they used the available time wisely – even if not all tasks were completed. As a subject-specialist mentor, you also need to ensure that you encourage them to reflect on the RE content of the lesson and the pedagogical decisions they made when approaching their planning. As beginning teachers grow in confidence, they will become more reflective and analytical about their lessons and able to focus more clearly on learning from them.

There are many loose frameworks you can use for structuring post-lesson discussion, and whatever you decide to use, it is a good idea to follow the same framework so you can compare your perspectives. Some possible frameworks for reflection of an informal observation could be:

- What went well (WWW) and Even Better If ... (EBI)
- Strengths and targets
- Three stars and a wish (three positive aspects of the lesson and one thing to improve)
- Questions relating to the pre-existing professional development frameworks, for example: "How did the lesson meet the requirements of..."
- How does pupils' written work inform your reflections and questions?

Reflections relating to the focus that was agreed in advance of the observation will relate directly to the pre-observation activities and elements of the lesson that you and the beginning teacher have agreed to discuss. If you have agreed to combine aspects of a formal and an informal observation, we suggest you commit to reflecting on the agreed-on focus as well as any unexpected issues which have arisen. Any unexpected issues will allow you, the mentor, to support the beginning teacher with whatever is needed, and this may be your observation of areas of strength or an area that needs further support. The point is the more ways you have to reflect with the beginning teacher on their classroom practice, the more balanced and supportive feedback you will be able to offer to together identify next steps. It is important that you do not have too many points for development for the beginning teacher to take on board as they could become overwhelmed. Task 13.7 presents some questions to aid your own reflections about how you could support your beginning teacher following an observation.

Task 13.6 Post-observation reflection

When you reflect on your observations, you could use the following questions to help you focus on how you can best support the beginning teacher:

- Are my reflections non-hierarchical and is the beginning teacher sharing with me what they need professionally and personally?
- Have I remained non-judgemental and so established trust?
- Am I considering the well-being of the beginning teacher and supporting self-reflection and not self-deprecation?
- Am I treating the beginning teacher as an *individual* and remembering that they are on their own journey to developing the knowledge and skills of an RE teacher?
- Have I remained positive and reflected on how the beginning teacher can develop and make progress rather than what they might have done wrong?
- Have I created an environment where the beginning teacher can reflect on their own reflections and ability to identify ways to improve?
- Have I inducted the beginning teacher into the benefits of professional and peer observation as a form of professional development?

Adapted from Hobson (2016)

Practical 'observational' tools

Being a mentor of a beginning teacher is a privilege and the skills and knowledge gained will be of benefit to both you and your beginning teacher as you go forward. The following observational tools are some suggestions to ensure a positive school experience for both you as the mentor and the beginning teacher. Task 13.7 then invites you to consider how these suggestions could be incorporated into your practice.

- Share with the beginning teacher a draft timetable outlining when formal observations will take place – recognising that this can be adapted as the term unfolds. Make it clear that when formal observations take place a detailed lesson plan and a copy of resources should be available for the observer.
- Give the beginning teachers opportunities to observe the learning and teaching in your classroom and that of other RE specialists – thus giving them the opportunity to see different styles of teaching. This is especially useful if you are teaching the same topic as a colleague, but you teach it in different ways and apply different pedagogies.
- Give the beginning teacher opportunities to observe learning and teaching in other departments, giving them the opportunity to see how classrooms in other subjects are organised.
- Explore lenses and frameworks for the beginning teacher to use as they observe. For example, they can observe what makes questioning effective, how particular pupils are supported in their engagement with their learning or how the learning objective is met through particular activities and how this might be improved.

- Give the beginning teacher opportunities to observe the learning and teaching in other departments – perhaps with a focus on time management or behaviour strategies – thus giving them the opportunity to see how alternative classrooms are organised.
- Together with the beginning teacher look at samples of pupils' work following a lesson observation. Ask the beginning teacher to reflect on the learning which has taken place and reflect on where pupils have achieved their objectives (or not).
- Suggest the beginning teacher keeps a notebook in which you as mentor can record informal observation notes and they can use to record evaluations of their lessons or their observations of other teachers.

Task 13.7 Supporting a positive school experience for both mentor and beginning teacher

1. Draw up a timetable for the beginning teacher to observe different teachers in the RE department and in other areas of the school and so give them an opportunity of seeing a variety of teaching styles.
2. Look at the previous list with the beginning teacher and write an action plan for developing how you can utilise the process of observation.
3. Ask the beginning teacher to identify two or three points from the previous list that they could action in the next half term. Have a target date and deadline when you can review the points together.

Finally, as we noted near the start of this chapter. RE is a unique subject, and as a mentor, you can both inspire and challenge a beginning teacher to want to become an excellent and reflective practitioner. Task 13.8 allows you to consider the impact you might have on a beginning teacher and think about the part lesson observation plays in this.

Task 13.8 Developing teaching strategies in observed lessons

Ruth Marx (2021) says of her ITT mentor, "He showed me his tricks for behaviour, planner management, lesson planning and resource management, but most importantly he trusted and encouraged me. Any lesson ideas I had, he told me to run with them and see how they went. With a very real and genuine interest in my life, he found ways for me to bring my passions into the classroom".

Set up a lesson observation but encourage your beginning teacher to "run" with their ideas when designing the learning activities. You should still follow the observation cycle, including pre- and post-observation discussion. However, you should let the beginning teacher explore their own teaching approach and be ready to help them reflect on how it went through the supportive process of the observation cycle.

Summary and key points

It is important to reflect on your role as mentor when observing RE beginning teachers in the classroom. This includes how you work with the beginning teacher before the observation takes place and how you support the beginning teacher after the lesson observation.

- You need to be clear about the approach you are taking in observations with the beginning teacher of RE. Seeing your role as that of co-constructor may allow a beginning teacher to have ownership of their lesson and, at the same time, learn from you and your experience.
- Viewing the observation process as a cycle allows it to be a supportive activity in enabling to grow in the role of the RE teacher.
- It is important to be clear about whether the approach taken to an observation is formal or informal and share this with the beginning teacher.
- As mentor, it is acknowledged that you have a particular role through observations in supporting the beginning teacher of RE to
  - plan lessons which enable pupils to achieve and make progress in their learning.
  - identify areas for development that may be a particular focus/foci for the observation.
  - learn from observations by other professionals who will offer different perspectives.
  - reflect on the learning which has taken place in order that appropriate lessons can be planned for pupil progress in the future.
  - reflect on the effectiveness of the teaching and pedagogical strategies which were used to support pupil progress.
  - keep a record of their observations to help them learn from both the strengths and targets which may have been identified.

Further resources

Manning, C. and Hobson, A. (2017a). Judgemental and developmental mentoring in further education initial teacher education in England: Mentor and mentee perspectives. *Research in Post-Compulsory Education*, 22(4), 574–595. https://doi.org/10.1080/13596748.2017.1381377

This article presents findings from a study which sought to identify the extent to which trainee teachers and their mentors considered their mentoring experiences and approaches to be judgemental or developmental. It will help you think about supporting a beginning teacher and being a co-constructor.

Marx, R. (2021). Inspired by . . . Paul Tyler my Student Teacher Mentor. *RE:ONLINE*. 19 January 2021. [Blog] Available at https://www.reonline.org.uk/2021/01/19/inspired-by-paul-tyler-my-student-teacher-mentor-ruth-marx/ (Accessed 22 March 2022)

This is a reminder that, as a practised and experienced RE teacher, a mentor can have a lasting effect on a beginning teacher. Hopefully, as Ruth discovered, your beginning teacher will be inspired by what and how you teach the unique and empowering subject of RE.

References

Daly, C. and Milton, E. (2017). External mentoring for new teachers: Mentor learning for a change agenda. *International Journal of Mentoring and Coaching in Education*, 6(3), 178–195. https://doi.org/10.1108/IJMCE-03-2017-0021

Hobson, A. J. (2016). Judgementoring and how to avert it: Introducing ONSIDE mentoring for beginning teachers. *International Journal of Mentoring and Coaching in Education*, 5(2), 87–110. https://doi.org/10.1108/IJMCE-03-2016-0024

Laurence, J., Low, K., and Phan, J. (2019). Observing physical education teachers teaching. In Capel, S. and Lawrence, J. (Eds.) *Mentoring physical education teachers in the secondary school* (pp. 184–194). Routledge.

Manning, C. and Hobson, A. (2017b). Judgemental and developmental mentoring in further education initial teacher education in England: Mentor and mentee perspectives. *Research in Post-Compulsory Education*, 22(4), 574–595. https://doi.org/10.1080/13596748.2017.1381377

Marx, R. (2021). Inspired by... Paul Tyler my Student Teacher Mentor. *RE:ONLINE*. 19 January 2021. [Blog] Available at https://www.reonline.org.uk/2021/01/19/inspired-by-paul-tyler-my-student-teacher-mentor-ruth-marx/ (Accessed 22 March 2022)

Winch, C., Oancea, A., and Orchard, J. (2015). The contribution of educational research to teachers' professional learning: Philosophical understandings. *Oxford Review of Education*, 412, 202–216. https://doi.org/10.1080/03054985.2015.1017406

14 Post-observation discussions and target setting

Helen Sheehan

Introduction

Although much public discourse is based on the belief that learning to teach is best done 'on the job', if teaching experiences are going to turn into meaningful opportunities for a beginning religious education (RE) teacher to learn and develop their skills, they need opportunities to reflect on and discuss their classroom experience. Earlier chapters have considered the importance of the conversations that might take place before a formal observation, both in supporting beginning teachers with their lesson planning (Chapter 11) and in agreeing on a focus for observed lessons in advance (Chapter 13). Following the observation cycle, this chapter assumes that these activities have taken place and that observations have been organised so that the beginning teacher is clear about the approach taken, the focus of the observation and the targets they are addressing.

This chapter focuses on post-observation discussion and target setting, the next step in the observation cycle. These conversations help beginning teachers make sense of their experiences and identify targets to develop their practice going forward. Although initially beginning RE teachers may need help to analyse their experiences and identify steps for development, it is important that they develop the ability to reflect on their own practice as this forms the basis of their contributions to post-observation discussions. This also may help avoid "judgementoring" (Hobson and Malderez, 2013) where feedback conversations focus on the beginning teacher being told what they need to do to improve. This chapter considers different models of mentoring to explore how mentors could approach these professional conversations so that post-observation discussions are a collaboration between the mentor and the beginning teacher.

The chapter then explores the practicalities of post-observation discussion and the features of an effective, developmental conversation. It is acknowledged that, sometimes, these conversations can be difficult and strategies for dealing with this are considered. Finally, the importance of setting focused, developmental and RE-specific targets is explored.

By the end of this chapter, you should be able to:

- Understand the importance of reflective practice to ensure beginning teachers can contribute in a meaningful way to post-observation discussions.
- Have considered your approach to post-observation discussions to avoid 'judgementoring' and utilise more collaborative and supportive approaches.
- Have considered practical arrangements for post-observation discussions.

DOI: 10.4324/9781003191087-17

- Have reflected on the nature of post-observation conversations and considered how they might go beyond simple, chronological discussion surrounding the events of the lesson.
- Be conscious that, sometimes, post-observations discussions can be challenging and consider how you might approach this.
- Have considered the role that the weekly mentor meeting might play in drawing together the outcomes of post-observation discussions as the basis of a broader discussion about progress and targets.
- Have reflected on the importance of target-setting as the outcome of post-observation discussions and as a process that should go beyond offering top tips and 'quick-fix' strategies.

Reflective practice

A key purpose of post-observation discussions is to support the development of beginning teachers as reflective practitioners. Reflective practice is considered necessary for beginning teachers to ensure they can learn from their own experiences and develop their practice going forward (Lane *et al.*, 2014). Commonly used frameworks to support reflective thinking include those offered by Gibbs (1988), Kolb (2015) and Schön (1983), and one of these may be used in your context as a basis for asking beginning teachers to reflect on their practice. However, if you are not currently using a particular model, a simple way of getting beginning teachers to engage with the process is to use the one proposed by Rolfe *et al.* (2001) which is based on three questions: What? So what? and Now what? Consider each question and how it might be turned into a reflection on a teaching experience for a beginning teacher.

- **What?** – This encourages the beginning teacher to describe a particular situation or event – positive or negative – that stands out from within the lesson, reflect on why it stands out and consider any emotional responses to the incident or section of the lesson they identified.
- **So what?** – This asks the beginning teacher to think about what they have learnt from the incident. Why did this happen? Why is this a notable incident? What questions does it raise for classroom practice? Is it a positive incident they could replicate and develop?
- **Now what?** – This moves the thinking to what has been learnt and next steps. The beginning teacher is encouraged to think about what they might do differently in the future to develop their skills and practice.

Encouraging beginning teachers to ask these or similar questions of their experiences will help them develop the ability to identify strengths and areas for development in their teaching and consider possible solutions for further development. Initially they may need guidance from you to recognise progress or to identify appropriate next steps. The following tasks offer an opportunity to be explicit in your exploration of this with your beginning teacher. Task 14.1 invites you to engage with this process with your beginning teacher using the model offered by Rolfe et al., and Task 14.2 offers a way to develop this aspect of your work and thinking further.

Task 14.1 Encouraging reflection

Following an observed lesson ask your beginning teacher to reflect on their teaching using the 'What? So what? Now what?' approach, in the light of the agreed focus of the observation.

Invite them to open your discussion by sharing their responses to the three questions, and then structure your conversation around their reflections. The intention is to focus on positive aspects of the lesson or areas of concern identified by them rather than structuring the discussion around your thoughts about the lesson.

Try to develop the conversation by asking questions to push their thinking further, particularly where you think they overlooked positive elements of the lesson, not identified the key issues or where there are next steps they have not considered.

Task 14.2 Developing reflection

Working with your beginning teacher, explore an alternative model of reflection (this may be one that they are already being encouraged to use or one you select together). The online resource *Getting Started with Reflective Practice* (see Further Resources) may provide a useful starting point.

In another planned formal observation, follow this reflective model and discuss with your beginning teacher whether they found it practical and helpful. Consider if there are useful prompts encouraged by this model that were missing from the 'What? So What? Now What?' model.

Avoiding judgementoring

A reflective approach, particularly one in which the mentor is prepared to listen to the beginning teacher's own evaluation of the lesson, avoids the problems that can be caused by a judgementoring approach. As explored in chapter 13, this is when the mentor reveals "too readily and/or too often her/his own judgements on or evaluations of the mentee's planning and teaching (e.g. through "comments", "feedback", advice, praise, or criticism)" (Hobson and Malderez, 2013, p. 90). In post-observation feedback, this is characterised by discussion in which the mentor does not explore the beginning teacher's perceptions of the lesson but instead lists all the things they have identified that need to be addressed and improved. Hobson (2016) highlights this can, potentially, leave beginning teachers feeling judged, stressed and in a position where their observer is "directive" and provides too much "practical advice" (p. 102). Better approaches may be offered by other conceptions of mentoring, such as *educative mentoring* and *ONSIDE mentoring*, both of which focus on the establishment of effective working relationships between the mentor and beginning teacher.

Educative mentoring

The concept of educative mentoring was first outlined by Feiman-Nemser (1998), who describes it as "mentoring that helps novices learn to teach and develop the skills and dispositions to continue learning in and from their practice" (p. 66). Rather than viewing the mentor as the 'expert' offering solutions, in educative mentoring conversations are seen as a dialogue, and mentors and beginning teachers become co-inquirers as they seek to develop good teaching practice (Windsor *et al.*, 2020).

Following their study that explored mentors' experiences of engaging in educative practices, Stanulis *et al.* (2019) argue a post-observation discussion becomes educative when the mentor both considers what the pupils have learnt and helps the beginning teacher learn from their experience of the lesson to identify next steps. This discussion should be based on evidence gathered during the observation (e.g., the mentor's notes, the pupils' responses) to explore the identified focus but all the time encouraging the beginning teacher to share their own reflections. The mentors involved in their study found that a focus on educative practices changed their approach to post-observation discussion. In particular:

- Mentors recognised that, previously, in post-observation discussion they tended to share *everything* they had noticed about the lesson. The educative approach led them to focus on one or two elements of the lesson.
- Mentors had previously focused on offering judgements and giving advice in post-observation discussions. Instead, the use of key questions, based on the things they had noted during the observation, was found to be more effective in helping the beginning teacher recognise what they needed to address and how they might approach this.

These observations exemplify some of the key principles that can guide an educative mentoring stance. The approach sees mentoring as a 'bi-focal' practice which focuses on the immediate needs of the beginning teacher whilst, at the same time, keeping the longer-term goal – meaningful and effective learning for all pupils – in sight (Norman and Feiman-Nemser, 2005; Schwille, 2008). This helps avoid the practice of sharing everything in a post-observation discussion, as the focus on the long-term goals helps identify the elements of the lesson that should drive the conversation at this point in the beginning teacher's professional development. An educative approach also requires the mentor and the beginning teacher to work collaboratively. Post-observation discussions are an opportunity for meaningful and productive dialogue in which the beginning teacher leads the conversation and the mentor asks questions to help them reflect on the lesson rather than simply sharing their perspective.

ONSIDE mentoring

Another holistic mentoring framework is offered by Hobson who introduces the concept of ONSIDE mentoring. This is a research-based framework that seeks to allow the beginning teacher to develop as a reflective practitioner and "does not assume that the mentor always knows best" (Hobson, 2016, p. 100), instead promoting a non-hierarchical working relationship. As the name of the model implies, it is based on the view that mentors are "allies, champions and advocates" (p. 100) for beginning teachers. Other features of the model are described in Table 14.1.

Table 14.1 ONSIDE mentoring

Off-line	Mentoring should ideally be separated from line management or supervision, so the mentor is not in a position where they need to formally assess their mentee's work. Obviously, this cannot usually be avoided when mentoring beginning teachers. If you are required to contribute to assessments of their performance, it is worth reflecting on the extent to which this impacts your approach to mentoring and your relationship with the beginning teacher.
Non-evaluative and non-judgemental	A mentor should seek to establish a trusting mentor/mentee relationship, avoiding an evaluative or judgemental approach.
Supportive of mentees' psychosocial needs and well-being	Mentors should consider beginning teachers' emotional well-being rather than focusing solely on their 'performance'.
Individualised – tailored to the specific and changing needs of the mentee	Mentoring should acknowledge that all beginning teachers are different and will respond in different ways to similar situations.
Developmental and growth-oriented	Mentoring should encourage beginning teachers to manage their own learning and allow them to be appropriately challenged rather than focus on correcting problems.
Empowering	Mentoring should support beginning teachers to find their own solutions so that, over time, they become more autonomous.

(Adapted from Hobson, 2016, p. 101)

Both educative and ONSIDE mentoring focus on the working relationship between the mentor and the beginning teacher. Whilst their emphasis might be different, they both encourage an approach where the mentor is working alongside the beginning teacher to develop their practice, rather than telling them what to do next. Task 14.3 asks you to reflect on your experiences as a mentor to consider how you would characterise your approach to post-observation discussions.

Task 14.3 Clarifying your approach

Following a lesson observation, reflect on the post-observation discussion using the following questions:

- Who 'led' the discussion, you or the beginning teacher?
- What percentage of the time were you talking? How much input did the beginning teacher have?
- Did your part in the discussion have any of the characteristics of educative mentoring?
  o Did you focus on one or two aspects of the lesson, or did you share everything you noticed?
  o Was the discussion focused on pupils and their progress?
  o Did you consider long-term, as well as short-term, goals?

- Did your part in the discussion have any of the characteristics of ONSIDE mentoring?
  - o Did you try and support the beginning teacher's development at their own pace?
  - o Did you consider the emotional impact of the lesson (particularly if it was a formal observation) as well as their 'performance'?
- Having considered these models, and after reflecting on your own practice, is there anything you might modify in your approach going forward?

Practical arrangements

Having considered your approach to post-observation discussion it is important to consider practical arrangements. Where and when these conversations take place can send important messages to beginning teachers about the status and value of the process.

Time and place

An informal observation (see Chapter 13) might be followed by an informal conversation about the lesson. This is often particularly true in small RE departments where the mentor and beginning teacher are together much of the time and there are lots of opportunities to talk about teaching experiences and reflect on progress (Chapters 12 and 13 explore possible approaches to structuring informal feedback). Although these conversations are not necessarily structured and are not part of a reflective cycle or the process of target setting, it is the case that they can be important and valuable in developing beginning teachers' thinking (Jones *et al.*, 2018).

However, it is important that verbal feedback following a formal observation is arranged as a scheduled meeting. It is not something that should be done as you and the beginning teacher are walking out of the room or in the middle of a busy corridor or staffroom; these conversations need a quiet space so that you can both focus and reflect on the events of the lesson. For this reason, it may also be best if the conversation does not take place as soon as the lesson ends. If an educative or ONSIDE approach is to be adopted it is important that the beginning teacher can contribute to the discussion; to do this in a meaningful way, they will need time to reflect on their experience, consider the key events and think about next steps.

Therefore, if the conversation is not going to take place immediately, agree in advance on a time and a place to talk so that your beginning teacher is not left anxiously wondering what you thought of the lesson. Sometimes there is a temptation to leave the discussion until your next weekly meeting, but this is not usually appropriate. First, it is best to discuss the lesson soon after it has taken place (preferably within 24 hours) to ensure you can both still clearly remember the events of the lesson. Second, in a context where you are required to meet with a beginning teacher weekly, this is usually so that space can be given for a broad discussion focusing on progress in more general terms, not on individual lessons. If all post-observation discussion takes place in the weekly meeting, there will never be time to discuss anything else.

Written feedback

Whilst this chapter focuses on post-observation discussion, mentors are often required to produce written feedback, particularly for formal observations. Some of the practicalities of this have been considered in Chapter 13. However, in the context of this chapter, the relationship between the two types of feedback should be considered. It may be that written feedback is compiled during the observation itself before the post-observation discussion. However, if there is to be a focus on working with the beginning teacher to develop their reflective skills and their classroom practice, it might be better for the formal observation notes to be written after the post-observation discussion. This presents an opportunity for the notes to reflect jointly agreed conclusions and targets.

Of course, for many mentors, written feedback must be produced during the observation as this is an efficient use of time; there is not the luxury of time after a post-observation discussion to reflect and produce written notes. However, a compromise would be to leave space to add to your notes during the post-observation discussion. This way additional issues raised or points made by the beginning teacher could be added and targets could be jointly agreed.

Shaping the discussion

The chapter now turns to focus on the content of the conversation. Inevitably, the substance of this will be based on the reflections of the beginning teacher, your own observation notes, and it should address your agreed focus. It is hoped that, as suggested earlier, using the beginning teacher's own reflections as a starting point will ensure the conversation is a collaborative discussion, led by them. The intended outcome is that next steps are jointly agreed rather than the beginning teacher being offered solutions and a list of things to demonstrate in the next observation. However, there are other things you may wish to bring to the discussion to support the beginning teacher in developing their skills as a specialist teacher of RE.

RE-specific discussions

Subject mentors bring a unique perspective to a post-observation discussion as they help beginning teachers reflect on and develop their substantive subject knowledge, ensuring it is accurate and used effectively in their lessons. However, in addition to this, you can also help them develop their pedagogical content knowledge (PCK; Shulman, 1986, 1987). This is knowledge developed by teachers about how to teach subject-specific content in appropriate ways to enhance pupils' understanding. It is knowledge about how learning in RE is structured and how it should be presented to pupils. This will involve a beginning teacher understanding curriculum decisions about, for example, whether units of work present religions systematically or thematically and the way in which disciplinary knowledge is developed over time. It includes the informed decisions teachers make about what to include and what to leave out of a lesson and how to present RE content. How are key concepts such as salvation, moksha or tawhid explained, and which examples can be used when illustrating complex ideas? What are the misconceptions the beginning teacher is likely to encounter and how can these be addressed? Improving understanding of PCK is key to a beginning teacher's development as an RE specialist and post-observation discussions offer an opportunity to explore this in detail, based on specific experiences.

However, Puttick and Wynn (2021) note that observers' comments (in written feedback) tend to focus on teaching as a craft or technical activity and that feedback rarely addresses the subject explicitly. Even for a subject specialist mentor, it can be difficult to see beyond issues such as behaviour and classroom logistics, and targets are often generic, focusing on issues such as teaching and learning, classroom presence and relationships with pupils. This misses an opportunity for supportive discussions that explore subject-specific considerations of planning in relation to the content covered in the lesson (Puttick and Wynn, 2021). Task 14.4 asks you to reflect on the feedback you have given following observations and consider the extent to which you have focused on RE.

Task 14.4 Written observation feedback

Look back over the written feedback you have produced following formal lesson observations. Consider the following questions:

- Would it be clear to someone reviewing this feedback that you were observing an RE lesson?
- Are there missed opportunities to help a beginning teacher think about and develop teaching and learning in RE?

Observations present an opportunity to draw on your subject-specialist knowledge, and the post-observation discussion is a space where you can make visible your curricular and pedagogical thinking (Healy, Walshe and Dunphy, 2020), going beyond the immediate challenges of classroom management and lesson structure. Following Shulman's concept of PCK, this could include conversations about the selection of content, decisions about the parameters of the lesson (i.e. what was included and why), how effectively RE concepts were explained, the rationale for the examples used and how misconceptions were identified and dealt with. RE-specific observations also allow for consideration of challenges that might arise in an RE classroom, such as how a beginning teacher deals with unexpected, emotive or challenging situations. Task 14.5 offers a potential structure to support both an observation which is focused on subject issues and the post-observation discussion that follows it.

Task 14.5 RE-focused post-observation discussion

Identify a lesson observation which you and your beginning teacher agree will focus solely on subject knowledge and pedagogy. Use the following questions (or some selected from the list) as the focus of the observation.

- Was the substantive RE knowledge clearly outlined in the lesson objectives?
- How did the beginning teacher ensure understanding of religious vocabulary or concepts addressed in the lesson?

- Was there awareness of disciplinary knowledge in the planning and teaching of the lesson?
- Were there any issues to do with the beginning teacher's own positionality that impacted the lesson?
- Did the pupils have opportunities to develop their understanding of either their own worldview or the worldviews of others?
- Did any misconceptions arise in the lesson? How were these addressed?
- Did the lesson take into account the wider curriculum and prior learning?
- Was it clear to the pupils how this lesson fits into their broader study of religion and worldviews?

Following the observation ask the beginning teacher to reflect on the lesson in relation to the selected questions. In the post-observation discussion, through questioning around these issues, guide them to think deeply about the subject-specific aspects of their lesson.

Links to research

The professional frameworks used to support the development of knowledge and skills for beginning teachers are based on educational research. Therefore, beginning teachers' classroom experiences can (or should) be an opportunity to reflect on the link between 'research and practice'. Winch *et al.* (2015) argue that, particularly in initial teacher education (ITE), there should be a positive relationship between educational research and practice.

You can also support a beginning teacher to develop as an RE specialist by encouraging engagement with current research and thinking about the subject. For example, when discussing how they have used sacred texts in a General Certificate of Secondary Education (GCSE) lesson you may direct them to the work that has recently been done around hermeneutical approaches (Bowie, 2020; Pett and Cooling, 2018) or when they have been dealing with controversial or emotive subject content you might encourage them to engage with pedagogical approaches that support this (see Chapter 16). To help you consider how you can, through post-observation discussion, support your beginning teacher in making links between their classroom practice and educational research, undertake Task 14.6 following a lesson observation.

Task 14.6 Connecting Discussion and Research

In one of your post-observation discussions reflect on your contributions to the conversation with your beginning teacher. Consider the following:

- What knowledge is informing your analysis of the lesson?
- What is the source of the ideas that underpin your suggestions for 'next steps'?
- Can this be linked to RE-specific research?

Having identified the knowledge that informs your own judgements about the lesson, identify research that supports the position you are taking. Share this with the beginning teacher and ask them to consider the link between this and their practice. This could also support the setting of developmental targets going forward.

Don't forget the praise

Although this chapter advocates a collaborative approach to post-observation discussion sometimes beginning teachers need reassurance. As Hobson (2016) reminds us in the ONSIDE framework, it is important that mentors pay attention to beginning teachers' well-being. In research that explored what beginning teachers (in this case ITE students) found helpful in lesson feedback one participant commented they wanted "positive comments and constructive criticism", and another added "some praise so I don't feel too awful" (Stevens and Lowing, 2008, p. 188). Although it is important to ask beginning teachers to identify and reflect on both the positive and negative aspects of their lessons, some beginning teachers tend to focus on what went wrong, not necessarily taking a balanced view of their experience. Therefore, post-observation discussions are an opportunity for a mentor, through a collaborative approach, to guide a beginning teacher to recognise what went well and areas of progress, as well as help them decide how they are going to address the identified areas for development.

Many mentors instinctively offer a 'praise sandwich' in post-observation discussions, where they start and end the feedback with a focus on the positive comments and in between to discuss ways in which the lesson could have been improved. However, many beginning teachers expect (and want) constructive criticism and, as long as positives are acknowledged, do not necessarily need areas for development to be 'sandwiched' by positive comments in this way. Stevens and Lowing found that many of their participants "hoped that their tutor would use specific examples from lessons to evaluate progress, giving encouragement and praise" (Stevens and Lowing, 2008, p. 188). Approaching the discussion in this way may be effective where a more collaborative, educative approach is being used; the focus should be on identifying the strengths of the lesson with reference to specific examples, encouraging beginning teachers to build on this going forward.

Considering the broader context

Stevens and Lowing's research also highlighted that some beginning teachers hope the feedback from individual lessons will be set in the context of their broader professional development. It is important to beginning teachers that they see each lesson as a step on the road to achieving a larger goal. This helps them understand that one bad lesson is not the end of the world; today it went badly, but, overall, progress is being made. Although it may be important for the beginning teacher to discuss what they will do to address the issues raised in the next lesson in the sequence, it is also a good idea to step back from this particular lesson and consider it in the context of progress in broader terms. Are the issues arising from this observation the same as those encountered in other lessons? Is the progress seen in this lesson just with this class, or is a pattern of progress across all classes being observed? This kind of discussion can help prioritise the focus of targets when there is more than one thing to work on.

This approach also helps a beginning teacher take a realistic view of their progress. In the same way that one bad lesson is not the end of the world, one good lesson does not mean they have solved all their issues and there is nothing to work on. It is important they can recognise their success but, in doing so, also identify how this contributes to their broader development. They should still be able to engage in meaningful conversation about their next steps.

A beginning teacher's development as an RE specialist should also be considered in broader terms. For example, if they are working to develop their substantive knowledge of a particular religion or worldview, they may be teaching this content (albeit with different levels of detail or complexity) to pupils in different year groups. Therefore, it might be helpful to consider their progress in relation to a particular aspect of subject knowledge across a number of different lessons. Post-observation discussions also present an opportunity to consider different aspects of subject-specific pedagogy in a more holistic way; it is much easier to discuss disciplinary approaches, questions of positionality or the development of pupils' personal knowledge when a lesson is considered in the context of other teaching experiences.

Weekly meetings

It may be the case that these broader issues are picked up and developed in weekly mentor meetings. Many mentors are expected to meet with their beginning teacher weekly to focus on progress and development in more general terms; the importance of this was highlighted in Chapter 3. The conversations will, of course, be informed by teaching experiences and observations, but they should set this into the broader context and support the setting of developmental targets.

A crucial element of these weekly meetings should be a check on the beginning teacher's well-being, a key component of ONSIDE mentoring. Hobson (2016) highlights the intense pressure teachers experience during the early years of their career, arguing that the provision of scaffolded support to ensure beginning teachers develop their confidence (and do not feel they are failing) is central to their well-being. Weekly mentor meetings are an important opportunity to check on the beginning teacher's well-being and, based on this, consider the nature of the support they need going forward.

The professional development frameworks being followed by some beginning teachers may mean they have been given an agenda for their weekly mentor meeting. This means the focus of these meetings cannot solely be on the discussion of lesson observations; given agendas are a way of ensuring you engage in professional conversations that span different aspects of teaching. The nature of these conversations will also change as the beginning teacher gains more classroom experience. Whilst some of these scheduled agenda items are likely to be generic in nature (e.g. behaviour management, use of data to support pupils who have special education needs and disabilities, effective use of teaching assistants) there are others that anticipate you exploring aspects of teaching with your beginning teacher in a subject-specific context (e.g. curriculum and lesson planning, adaptive teaching). Task 14.7 encourages you to consider how you might use this book to develop your RE-specific support in weekly mentor meetings.

Task 14.7 Weekly mentor meeting activities

Through the chapters of this book, there are tasks that are either designed specifically as a focus for a mentor meeting or that could be used in this way. Review the tasks in other chapters and identify some which you might use in one of your meetings.

Challenging situations

A post-observation discussion or weekly mentor meeting are both opportunities for a beginning teacher to share their concerns. Although most beginning teachers are eager to engage in collaborative discussion about their progress, there are occasionally those who find their work in the classroom challenging and, even with support, seem unable to either identify or action their next steps. Sometimes beginning teachers become disheartened when they feel that they are repeating their mistakes and become aware that they are not making progress in the development of their teaching skills. Post-observation discussions feel like an evaluation; a confirmation that things are not going well with limited hope of moving forward once the initial suggested strategies have not worked. Expertise does not come through simply amassing experience (Ericsson *et al.*, 1993); sometimes a different approach is needed. Task 14.8 offers a case study for you to consider and reflect on how you would respond as the mentor in this situation.

Task 14.8 A difficult conversation

Stevie is a trainee teacher who is finding her current placement challenging. Her mentor feels that all advice and feedback is being ignored and is frustrated that all of Stevie's host teachers are making the same points in the discussions that follow observations again and again. The situation has now come to a head after Stevie complained to another member of the department that she is not being given useful feedback and that no one is helping her to improve her practice. If you were Stevie's mentor, how would you tackle this situation?

Consider:

- Does feedback need to be presented differently? If so, how? Does anything else need to change?
- How should the conversation with Stevie be approached?
- What are the issues here? There is a complaint about feedback, but are there other issues (e.g. her perception of what "help" looks like) that need to be considered?

Even though several colleagues are observing and engaging in post-observation discussions with her, Stevie is not understanding the issues or finding ways to develop her practice in the light of this. Also, the fact that she feels "no one is helping her" needs to be explored further. Lots of people are trying to help, but she is not recognising this, or it does not feel as if this is the case. Some discussion around what she perceives as helpful is needed.

Drawing on Stevie's own reflections, the discussion should explore ways in which support can be made more effective. Hobson (2016) highlights that, in the context of ONSIDE mentoring, scaffolded support is important as it can stop a beginning teacher feel as if they are failing. He notes that scaffolding can be reduced as the beginning teacher gains more experience but that it can be reintroduced if necessary to support their emotional well-being. For example, with a class that they are finding difficult, it might be appropriate to return to a period of observation to focus on how a more experienced colleague handles the group. Alternatively, collaborative approaches to planning could be utilised (Chapter 11) or arrangements could be made for the beginning teacher to co-teach some lessons with the host teacher.

Stevie's mentor could also consider the approach being taken to target setting. They could review the feedback from the host teachers and look at the nature of the targets that have been identified. Are they specific? Is it easy for Stevie to measure her success in relation to them? Are they similar to those set by other members of the team? If they are similar, following an educative mentoring approach, the mentor should bring them together in one clear target that is communicated to all host teachers and is a target across all lessons. All the teachers working with Stevie need to understand that she cannot effectively work on lots of different targets simultaneously.

Target setting

The end goal of a post-observation discussion (and a weekly mentor meeting) is likely to be the development of appropriate targets that acknowledge progress and clarify next steps. The ideas explored in this chapter have outlined some principles that might underpin effective target setting. For example, the idea that targets should be co-constructed, encouraging beginning teachers to draw on their own reflections to help identify their next steps (rather than simply being given solutions or strategies to try out) has been emphasised. Also, the importance of developing overarching targets and then identifying the steps necessary to scaffold progress has been noted. Finally, Hobson (2016) reminds us that all beginning teachers are different and will progress at different rates; targets therefore need to be focused on what each individual needs at that time, rather than being driven by an external agenda.

When working with beginning teachers it is usual to focus on professional development frameworks when seeking to construct targets. This is an appropriate approach as these frameworks generally try to draw on research evidence to identify the key features of effective teaching. Other research-based practices that support whole-school approaches to teaching and learning may also inform the target setting (e.g. Rosenshine's Principles, retrieval practice, etc.). However, it is important that these frameworks do not lead to targets that focus on 'correcting problems' (Hobson, 2016) and offer quick-fix solutions; post-observation discussion can ensure that this is not the case. For example, consider the following targets:

1. Try out think–pair–share to start discussion.
2. Make sure there is some retrieval practice at the start of every lesson.
3. Scaffold written activities to support lower ability pupils.

These targets may be in danger of presenting a beginning teacher with 'top tips'; things they must demonstrate that they are including in a lesson. However, if they have been agreed upon as the result of a post-observation discussion which has considered in detail the difficulty of engaging pupils in discussion (target 1), the importance of sequencing and connecting learning (target 2) or the development of adaptive teaching (target 3), they become mutually agreed developmental targets. The professional conversation is important in shaping the target and ensuring that the beginning teacher has been involved in identifying and framing the target and understands both how it will address current concerns and how it will move their practice forward.

A helpful approach may be to distinguish between targets (long-term goals) and actions (linked to short-term concerns). If we take one of the earlier examples – scaffold written activities to support lower ability pupils – a distinction could be made between the broader target (to adapt teaching to ensure that all pupils can access the lesson content) and the short-term concern (some lower ability pupils in one class are not able to access the set tasks). The conversation around this should go beyond 'what shall we do with this class next week' (i.e. an action). It might consider the nature of adaptive practice, what the subject-specific issues are and then the practical strategies that could be used with this and other classes.

Professional frameworks usually make explicit reference to subject knowledge, pedagogy and curriculum. As a subject-specialist mentor, it is your responsibility to ensure that there are targets that focus on these areas and not solely on generic issues and craft skills. Task 14.9 offers some guidance to help you think about what might be addressed through subject-specific targets.

Task 14.9 RE-specific targets

Take some time to think about a beginning teacher that you are currently working with and reflect on the targets for development that you have recently identified. Did any of them focus on subject knowledge, pedagogy or curriculum in RE?

If not, having thought about their strengths and areas for development, consider what would be an appropriate subject-specific target. You could consider the following areas to help you formulate the target(s):

- Developing substantive subject knowledge
- Disciplinary knowledge (or ways of knowing) – could they approach a topic through a different lens?

- Helping pupils identify and understand other worldview perspectives
- Selecting appropriate substantive content
- Sequencing of content in lessons
- Links to prior learning
- Selecting appropriate examples
- How misconceptions are addressed and dealt with
- Pedagogical approaches taken

Summary and key points

This chapter has highlighted the importance of approaching post-observation discussions as a collaborative activity which acknowledges successes as well as areas for development and maximises opportunities for meaningful engagement with the subject-specific aspects of classroom practice. Next steps should be articulated in clear targets that move beyond a focus on the immediate to acknowledge long-term goals and consider RE-specific content and pedagogical knowledge.

- Beginning teachers can use a given model to structure their own reflections on the lesson and input into the post-observation discussion.
- Educative or ONSIDE approaches to mentoring can be helpful models to support the development of a collaborative approach that puts the beginning teacher at the heart of the process.
- Adequate time and space need to be given to post-observation discussions.
- Post-observation discussions develop from straightforward discussions of the events of the lesson to consider broader questions, such as what has been learnt from a subject-specific perspective and links to wider research. These conversations can be developed further in weekly mentor meetings.
- Targets set as the cumulation of post-observation discussions should avoid offering 'top tips' and instead focus on developmental targets arising from a discussion that not only uses professional frameworks but also considers long-term goals and the nature of teaching and learning in RE.

Further resources

Cambridge-community.org.uk. (2022). *Getting started with reflective practice*. https://www.cambridge-community.org.uk/professional-development/gswrp/index.html

This is a useful webpage that offers a clear overview of reflective practice for teachers.

O'Leary, M. (2020). *Classroom observation: A guide to the effective observation of teaching and learning* (2nd ed.). Routledge.

This general text focuses on all aspects of observation. Chapter 7, which focuses on the importance of critical reflection, might be of particular interest.

References

Bowie, R. (Ed.) (2020). *The Practice Guide: Classroom tools for sacred text scholarship.* Canterbury Christchurch University.

Ericsson, A., Krampe, R., & Tesch-Römer, C. (1993). The role of deliberate practice in the acquisition of expert performance. *Psychological Review*, 100(3), 363–406. https://doi.org/10.1037/0033-295X.100.3.363

Feiman-Nemser, S. (1998). Teachers as teacher educators. *European Journal of Teacher Education*, 21(1), 63–74. https://doi.org/10.1080/0261976980210107

Gibbs, G. (1988). *Learning by doing: A guide to teaching and learning methods.* Further Education Unit. Oxford Polytechnic: Oxford.

Healy, G., Walshe, N., & Dunphy, A. (2020). How is geography rendered visible as an object of concern in written lesson observation feedback? *Curriculum Journal*, 31(1), 7–26. https://doi.org/10.1002/curj.1

Hobson, A. (2016). Judgementoring and how to avert it: Introducing ONSIDE Mentoring for beginning teachers. *International Journal of Mentoring and Coaching in Education*, 5(2), 87–110. https://doi.org/10.1108/IJMCE-03-2016-0024

Hobson, A. & Malderez, A. (2013). Judgementoring and other threats to realizing the potential of school-based mentoring in teacher education. *International Journal of Mentoring and Coaching in Education*, 2(2), 89–108. https://doi.org/10.1108/IJMCE-03-2013-0019

Jones, L., Tones, S., & Foulkes, G. (2018). Mentoring associate teachers in initial teacher education: The value of dialogic feedback. *International Journal of Mentoring and Coaching in Education*, 7(2), 127–138. https://doi.org/10.1108/IJMCE-07-2017-0051

Kolb, D. A. (2015). *Experiential learning: Experience as the source of learning and development* (2nd ed.). Pearson Education, Inc.

Lane, R., McMaster, H., Adnum, J., & Cavanagh, M. (2014). Quality reflective practice in teacher education: A journey towards shared understanding. *Reflective Practice*, 15(4), 481–494. https://doi.org/10.1080/14623943.2014.900022

Norman, P. & Feiman-Nemser, S. (2005). Mind activity in teaching and mentoring. *Teaching and Teacher Education*, 21(6), 679–697. https://doi.org/10.1016/j.tate.2005.05.006

Pett, S. & Cooling, T. (2018). Understanding Christianity: Exploring a hermeneutical pedagogy for teaching Christianity. *British Journal of Religious Education*, 40(3), 257–267. https://doi.org/10.1080/01416200.2018.1493268

Puttick, S. & Wynn, J. (2021). Constructing "good teaching" through written lesson observation feedback. *Oxford Review of Education*, 47(2), 152–169. https://doi.org/10.1080/03054985.2020.1846289

Rolfe, G., Freshwater, D., & Jasper, M. (2001). *Critical reflection for nursing and the helping professions: A user's guide.* Palgrave.

Schön, D. (1983). *The reflective practitioner how professionals think in action.* Basic Books.

Schwille, S. (2008). The professional practice of mentoring. *American Journal of Education*, 115(1), 139–167. https://doi.org/10.1086/590678

Shulman, L. S. (1986). Those who understand: Knowledge growth in teaching. *Educational Researcher*, 15(2), 4–14. https://doi.org/10.1177/0022057419300302

Shulman, L. S. (1987). Knowledge and teaching: Foundations of the new reform. *Harvard Educational Review*, 57(1), 1–22. https://doi.org/10.17763/haer.57.1.j463w79r56455411

Stanulis, R., Wexler, L. J., Pylman, S., Guenther, A., Farver, S., Ward, A., Croel-Perrien, A., & White, K. (2019). Mentoring as more than "cheerleading": Looking at educative mentoring practices through mentors' eyes. *Journal of Teacher Education*, 70(5), 567–580. https://doi.org/10.1177/0022487118773996

Stevens, D. & Lowing, K. (2008). Observer, observed and observations: Initial teacher education English tutors' feedback on lessons taught by student teachers of English. *English in Education*, 42(2), 182–198. https://doi.org/10.1111/j.1754-8845.2008.00015.x

Winch, C., Oancea, A., & Orchard, J. (2015). The contribution of education research to teachers' professional learning: Philosophical understandings. *Oxford Review of Education*, 41(2), 202-216. https://doi.org/10.1080/03054985.2015.1017406

Windsor, S., Kriewaldt, J., Nash, M., Lilja, A., & Thornton, J. (2020). Developing teachers: Adopting observation tools that suspend judgement to stimulate evidence-informed dialogue during the teaching practicum to enrich teacher professional development. *Professional Development in Education*, 1-15. https://doi.org/10.1080/19415257.2020.1712452

15 Supporting beginning teachers to teach GCSE and A level religious studies

Rachael Jackson-Royal

Introduction

The study of religious studies at the General Certificate of Secondary Education (GCSE) level and Advanced level (A level) is incredibly rewarding both for pupils and teachers. Many considerations regarding how this will be approached are the same as those that impact teaching in other key stages, but there are some elements that are particular to teaching at this level. This includes a greater emphasis on having excellent subject knowledge, in terms of both substantive knowledge and those elements of knowledge which are more proximal (i.e. additional knowledge that will help pupils make sense of the specification content and highlights links to other areas of the curriculum), as well as understanding how to teach pupils the skills they need to answer examination-style questions. This chapter begins with a discussion of what should be considered when teaching examination classes, regardless of the key stage, followed by specific recommendations that apply to A level. This chapter refers to the subject as religious studies (RS) because this is the title that appears on all the examinations taken in this area, whether this is at GCSE or A level.

At the end of this chapter, you should be able to:

- Articulate the importance of beginning teachers developing a clear understanding of examination specifications when teaching RS at the examination level.
- Support a beginning teacher in understanding the requirements and content of the examination course(s) they will be teaching.
- Identify ways in which you can support beginning teachers to develop the required subject knowledge.
- Help beginning teachers understand the way that the content of the specification is organised into schemes of work and how this is developed.
- Help beginning teachers plan effective lessons for GCSE and A level classes.
- Demonstrate an awareness of the additional requirements of teaching A level RS compared to teaching at GCSE level.

Initial conversations: Teaching examination specifications

Before reading any further, undertake Task 15.1.

DOI: 10.4324/9781003191087-18

Task 15.1 Mentor reflection: getting started

- Which examination boards offer GCSE and A level qualifications in RS? Where do you find up-to-date, reliable information about specifications?
- What examination board does your department follow and which specification (if applicable)?
- Why did you/your department select this board and specification?

Share your answers to these questions with your beginning teacher. This will help them understand the wider picture of the range of content and how RS is examined, as well as enable them to appreciate your vision and rationale for the choices that you have made for the pupils at your school.

Regardless of whether a beginning teacher is teaching GCSE or A level, a good place to begin to develop an understanding of teaching at the examination level is to explore the various examination boards which offer a qualification in this subject. This will give beginning teachers a better grasp of the format of the examination system, which is useful for both their current setting and any future school they may work in. Such an exploration should highlight how there is not only more than one examination board for the subject but also that each board might offer a number of options. This can include the choice of more than one specification and sometimes a choice of units within that specification. You should visit the webpages of the various boards with your beginning teacher to ensure that they know where this information is to be found and explain the rationale for the choices your department has made; such conversations help the beginning teacher 'buy in' to the decisions of the department. Possible reasons that underpin these decisions could include

- the topics are more relevant to the expertise of staff and the background of the pupils;
- the department already has a lot of resources that link to this specification (an important consideration when budgets are tight);
- the belief that the question structure in the examination is more accessible to the learners in the particular school;
- the department is already familiar with this particular examination board; or
- the level of support that is available from this examination board is viewed as being better when compared to others.

Conversations about this will also enable the beginning teacher to realise that, ultimately, the decision was made because it was believed that this will enable the staff to support pupils to obtain the best grades possible; something it is important for them to remember when ultimately teachers are there to help pupils realise their potential.

Exploring the content of an examination course

After the various examination boards have been explored and your beginning teacher has been introduced to the one(s) your department is using, the focus should move onto investigating in more depth the course they will be teaching. Discussions in these areas should focus on the range of content: how many papers there are and what the differences are between them, what kinds of content must be covered in each paper, what synoptic links are expected to be made in the various sections of the course, what kinds of skills or assessment objectives the learners need to demonstrate and how these skills link to the examination format. At this stage, it may be helpful to explore together the resources on the examination board website, explaining the purpose of each section and when it may be useful to consult these in further detail as the course is taught. Good resources to look at will include the specification, any exemplar schemes of work (if the board has them), past papers and model answers and examiners' reports. This does take time, but it is invaluable as it means a beginning teacher is more self-sufficient in being able to find the necessary materials for themselves when the need arises. It is also beneficial to draw attention to the subject officer for the examination board and to explain how teachers can contact this person, perhaps outlining some examples of the types of questions that might be posed to them if the need arises. This is often an overlooked source of support yet it can be an invaluable one, especially when the beginning teacher is undertaking preparation outside of school hours when they are not able to speak to their mentor.

It is important that beginning teachers are familiar with the content of the specification and are aware that *everything* listed there will need to be covered (even if this has been overlooked in a textbook) including the technical language mentioned, as examination questions will be generated from this material. A useful distinction at this stage is to introduce the beginning teacher to the difference between substantive and proximal knowledge. The substantive knowledge is that information which has been listed on the specification, that is what the pupil has to know. In this chapter, the term proximal knowledge is used to describe the surrounding knowledge that will help pupils make sense of this key knowledge and show them how it links to other areas of the curriculum. Proximal knowledge is not listed on the specification, but it is still important that this is covered (for a fuller description of substantive and proximal knowledge see Ofsted, 2021, where the latter is discussed in the context of the development of schemas). Thus, both need to be explored and taught for the pupils to succeed in the subject area, but the teacher has to make informed decisions about which proximal knowledge is necessary and which is not. Task 15.2 encourages you to reflect on how you have developed your own knowledge for teaching GCSE and A level.

Task 15.2 Mentor reflection: developing adequate subject knowledge

- Reflect on your own experience of teaching at the examination level; what additional activities and research did you undertake to ensure you subject knowledge was secure?
- What is your understanding of the difference between the substantive knowledge and the proximal knowledge you need? Why are both important?
- Make a list of the common resources you would recommend a beginning teacher to enable them to teach the specifications you use effectively.

Share your responses with the beginning teacher as this modelling will enable them to see more clearly what kinds of reflections and actions will help them to be successful in the classroom.

To help the beginning teacher develop their knowledge, you can provide a selection of books and other resources (if you have a knowledge organiser for the unit this should be shared as well as any other useful material). Textbooks are useful for beginning teachers to read to gain an overview of the main areas they will be covering and sometimes there are handbooks specifically designed to help teachers improve their subject knowledge of a particular examination (e.g. see Jackson-Royal et al., 2017). In addition to books, explore with the beginning teacher any online sites aimed at supporting pupils' understanding (see further resources) and any notes or lesson resources that the department has already created. It is very important that a beginning teacher fully understands how significant it is that they have a good understanding of the content they will be teaching, particularly at A level where greater depth of knowledge and understanding how the various elements link together are needed. To help your beginning teacher think about the strengths and areas for development in their knowledge work with them to complete Task 15.3.

Task 15.3 RAG rating subject knowledge

Ask your beginning teacher to evaluate their existing knowledge of the content by taking an examination specification and colour coding each section red, amber or green (RAG) based on whether they feel their knowledge is not secure, is developing or is very competent. The areas identified as being red will then be their immediate area of focus, followed by those which were coloured amber.

Progress in making this knowledge more secure could be a focus of weekly mentor meetings where you, as the mentor, can help the beginning teacher to deepen their knowledge further through sharing your experience in the area (especially in making decisions about what kinds of proximal knowledge are important and which are not). To prevent cognitive overload for the beginning teacher if many areas have been highlighted red, it may be a good idea to focus on one unit at a time (to understand cognitive overload both for beginning teachers and pupils, see Lovell, 2020).

Organising the content

Before you read any further Task 15.4 invites you to reflect on how you organise the content outlined in the specification being followed in your context.

Task 15.4 Mentor reflection: organising the material for teaching

- Look at the schemes of work that have been created in your department. Consider why the content was organised in this manner; what decisions were made when organising the material in this way? Have time constraints in the timetabling influenced these choices?
- What is your understanding of the curriculum acting as a progress model? How does your scheme of work ensure this occurs?
- How does the scheme of work ensure that all the substantive and proximal knowledge is covered? Where are the opportunities for pupils to develop the key skills or assessment objectives?

Share your responses with the beginning teacher as this modelling will enable them to see more clearly what kinds of reflections and actions will help them to be successful in the classroom.

Once the beginning teacher has a secure knowledge of the content they will be covering in the first unit or section of material from the specification, they will need to understand how this has been or can be organised into a unit of work that will be taught to the pupils. An important place to begin is to explain how many lessons will be dedicated to the teaching of this unit and, if you have one, share the curriculum map which indicates which parts of the specification for that unit will be focused on in each lesson so that the whole course (i.e. the substantive knowledge) is covered. Explain why the content has been organised in this way, especially if this is not the order that it appears on the specification. This may be because this is the most logical manner for enabling the content to flow, because this is the best way to activate what has been taught previously or because this positioning of the material enables a more holistic comprehension of what must be covered. Reflecting on curriculum design so that pupil progress can be secured is an important consideration for a beginning teacher and one that it is worth spending time discussing (for a fuller discussion of this area see Ashbee, 2021; Howard and Hill, 2020; and Sealy and Bennett, 2020). In addition, as the curriculum is discussed, it may be that some topics for a unit will have to be set for independent study if time is too short to cover them all in the lessons. If this is the case, explain why these topic areas were selected (normally because they are more straightforward) and the scaffolds or supports that have been put in place to ensure pupils can undertake this work without the immediate support of the teacher.

The scheme of work or curriculum map should ideally highlight both the substantive and proximal knowledge that should be focused upon in each lesson. It should also indicate when and where time will be given to develop the skills or assessment objectives pupils need for the examination. It may be the case that these skills will not be addressed in every lesson, particularly at the start of the course. It may also be that the ways in which they will be explored will not resemble the final skill but will focus on aspects of this so that pupils can gradually become more competent in their use. This is especially the case for assessment objectives which require more extended writing and where time will need to be spent mastering individual elements rather than writing a whole essay in one go (this is briefly considered later, but for further information on how to effectively teach extended writing in stages, see Hochman et al., 2017, and for effective assessment in general, see Christodoulou, 2017).

If the department does not already have a scheme of work or curriculum map in place and the beginning teacher is being asked to create this, re-direct them to the examination board website as there are often examples on there for teachers to use. Another place where these might be found is on different social media platforms where some teachers have freely shared their materials (however it is worth indicating to the beginning teacher that not all of these will be of the same high standard and ideally it is better to adapt those they find to what will work in their situation and to carefully check them for mistakes). It may also be helpful to share examples of schemes of work from other departments and to provide a blank proforma which the beginning teacher could complete, initially with your help and, later, on their own once they feel more competent. Progress in this area should be discussed at weekly mentor meetings where you can offer advice on how they can be improved. Furthermore, even if they are not going to create such a scheme of work, it is useful to explain to the beginning teacher how this is organised for their own professional development and so that they can understand this when they are teaching the scheme themselves. Such conversations will enable the beginning teacher to have greater 'buy in' to what you have already put into place and will mean that their teaching of units will be smoother.

Planning lessons for the GCSE and the A level

Before the beginning teacher begins to teach a unit of work for an examination class, it is important that there is consideration of the best ways that the content can be explored in each individual lesson. These discussions should occur regardless of whether the lesson activities have already been created by the department or whether the beginning teacher is expected to create these with your help as they will learn so much about the teaching process from this undertaking. The conversations should include an exploration of why different lesson activities are more suitable for the content than others. For example, would a community of enquiry approach be a suitable format for a given lesson or would a didactic approach be more effective? Explaining and modelling the methods chosen is helpful, but it is important that within these conversations time is spent exploring why one method was selected over another. Indeed, observing how other, more experienced teachers in religious studies teach examination classes is an invaluable method of helping beginning teachers to develop, especially if one or two areas are selected as a focus for these observations. Watching colleagues in other subjects and even those teaching the subject in other schools (perhaps in your own multi-academy trust chain if this is applicable) can also be useful. Once these observations have been undertaken, these should be discussed in weekly mentor meetings where there is a particular focus on how this could improve the beginning teacher's own teaching of examination classes.

An important aspect of conversations surrounding teaching strategies is the inclusion of practices which cognitive psychology has shown to be effective. Weinstein et al. (2019) indicate this includes

- spaced practice (where you come back to things over time rather than covering them once),
- interleaving (where you mix up the topics you cover rather than focusing solely on one),
- elaborative interrogation (asking and explaining how and why things work),
- concrete examples (when abstract concepts are explained through concrete examples),
- dual coding (combining words with visuals) and
- retrieval practice (bringing learned information to mind from the long-term memory which is much more effective than rereading notes).

Some of these methods are more significant in daily teaching than others and this is particularly the case for retrieval practice. Discuss with the beginning teacher the benefits of retrieval as well as the different methods that can be employed (including the best ways to do this). Jones (2019) gives examples of effective retrieval methods which include brain dumps (where pupils write all they can remember about a topic), quiz/quiz/trade (where there are question cards with answers on the back; pupils ask each other questions and trade the cards when they have them correct) and cops and robbers (where they do a brain dump then read someone else's and then 'rob' what they have forgotten and add it to their own). It is also important for pupils to reflect at the end of the lesson on the key takeaways and be encouraged to consider how their new knowledge and skills can be aligned to what they have learnt previously and/or if there are still any areas in which they do not feel confident; Rosenshine (2012) identifies this review of previous learning as one of the 10 principles of effective instruction.

Another of Rosenshine's 10 principles highlights the importance of using examples, particularly concrete ones, to help understanding; this is particularly important when teaching the A level as there tend to be more abstract concepts, especially in the units focusing on the philosophy of religion and ethics. Once again it is important to spend time in mentor meetings helping beginning teachers to find concrete examples, as well as the other elements highlighted above, as they may find this difficult to do on their own (indeed, Daniel Willingham, 2010, calls this the difference between novices and experts in a particular domain).

The use of effective questioning is another of Rosenshine's 10 principles of instruction because it is a way in which a teacher can check for deep rather than shallow knowledge (helping move information from working to long-term memory; see Willingham, 2010). It is important that a beginning teacher understands the purpose of different types of questioning, as this will influence when and where they are used. For example, are questions being used to ascertain whether pupils can remember basic facts? If so, perhaps some quick closed questions might be appropriate. Are they being asked in order to develop ideas or to tease out meta-cognitive thinking? If so, more open-ended questions might be more useful (for a fuller discussion on meta-cognitive strategies see Webb, 2021). When exploring effective questioning, also discuss how the asking of questions can be truly inclusive of all pupils. For example, one useful strategy for a beginning teacher could be to display a few questions they are going to ask on the board before pausing to allow pupils to consider their response to these either individually or in small groups (which a beginning teacher chooses will depend on what level of scaffolds are needed). Perhaps the beginning teacher will also state in advance that pupils will be selected randomly both to answer these and to comment on the points made (i.e. cold calling). Explore with the beginning teaching the strengths and limitations of using more inclusive methods of facilitating pupils in the answering of questions as well as an evaluation of other methods.

Undertake Task 15.5 to reflect on how you approach lesson planning for GCSE and A level classes.

Task 15.5 Mentor reflection: exploring how to teach individual lessons

- Reflect on the kinds of activities that the department already utilises when teaching units of work to examination classes. Why have these been chosen?
- What is your knowledge of how pupils learn (i.e. how content and skills can move from working memory to long-term memory)?
- How does your knowledge of how pupils' learn impact on your teaching?
- Are there any teaching and learning strategies used in your school because cognitive psychology has shown them to be effective? If so, how are they used in RS?

Share your responses with the beginning teacher as this modelling will enable them to see more clearly what kinds of reflections and actions will help them to be successful in the classroom.

As already indicated, lessons should also include opportunities for pupils to develop the skills needed to answer different styles of examination questions (i.e. they need to learn to be competent in the assessment objectives). It is therefore important that you spend time with beginning teachers exploring what kinds of activities will enable these skills to be developed. Such activities may focus on one aspect of a skill that is required especially if the skills are composite (i.e. made up of parts which can be taught separately). In addition, discuss how, as pupils become more familiar with the content and the skills, they may answer questions under timed conditions. These should be accounted for within each scheme of work (however, do not limit these to the current unit that is being studied, as previous content can be included as another way of embedding retrieval and overcoming the forgetting curve (Jones, 2019)). In addition to discussing when these skills will be covered, time should be spent explaining how this work will be marked so that, as far as possible, it is in line with how external examiners will grade pupils' work. However, it is important for the beginning teacher to note that not all work set has to be practising the examination skills. Indeed, Jones (2022) indicates homework that has greatest impact includes practising, retrieval and preparation, all of which can be set as classroom or homework tasks. It is recommended that you model how this is undertaken with the beginning teacher as they will learn much from understanding the reasoning behind why you have marked work in the way that you have. This could be followed by team marking before the beginning teacher moves on to completing this independently, with support in place to double-check a sample in the first instance. If funds permit, offering the beginning teacher the opportunity to attend courses run by the examination board or others where they mark together is always a very useful exercise (or indeed being a marker themselves).

As the beginning teacher starts to employ the strategies outlined earlier in their teaching, time should be dedicated in the weekly mentor meetings to reflect on how they are progressing. Lesson observations could focus on one or two areas that arise from these conversations. Discussion in mentor meetings should also explore how the work and test results of pupils can be analysed and how this can provide useful indications of what should be focused on in future lessons. In these conversations you can explain different ways of analysing test results: how they can be compared to how the pupil has performed in other subjects, whether pupils have gained their target grade, how the department has fared compared to other similar schools and previous years and whether there is an area that needs to be addressed (e.g. the marks are lower for a question which demonstrates a particular skill or a topic on the specification appears to gain fewer marks compared to others). Discuss with the beginning teacher what kinds of strategies might be adopted in light of this analysis and why they have been chosen. As with other topics of discussion in weekly mentor meetings, it is important to ask beginning teachers for their thoughts and reflections before you share your own views. These conversations can also occur after end-of-unit tests or during internal school examinations (if these are applicable).

Teaching RS at A level

Before reading any further, reflect on the questions in Task 15.6.

Task 15.6 Mentor reflection: teaching at A level

- Reflect on your own experience of teaching A level. Consider how this is different from teaching at GCSE.
- What would you consider to be the three most important aspects of teaching A level?
- Reflect on how, over time, you have changed the way you teach A level.
- Similarly, reflect on what you think is effective when you teach A level.

Share your responses with the beginning teacher as this modelling will enable them to see more clearly what kinds of reflections and actions will help them be successful in the classroom.

The main area of difference when teaching A level compared to GCSE is that the subject knowledge of the beginner teacher needs to be more substantial. It is really important that this is stressed in any conversations and that time is spent discussing the kinds of resources would be helpful in aiding the beginning teacher in this area (the RAG activity recommended in Task 15.3 would be an excellent exercise to undertake with the beginning teacher as there will probably be elements of the A level specification with which they will be familiar; this exercise can also help you ascertain which topics, if any, they will teach the pupils). Sometimes it may be necessary for the beginning teacher to enrol on a course to develop their subject knowledge (good examples are those run by Future Learn, Open Learn or RE:ONLINE, as well as the A level subject seminar series organised by the Theology and Religious Studies department at Chester University), or it could be that further reading is all that is required (some examination boards provide recommendations). It is also necessary for the beginning teacher to become familiar with the higher level skills the examiner is expecting learners to demonstrate in the examination. This is normally a long essay where the skills are more complex than those required at GCSE. Time will need to be spent enabling pupils to master individual aspects of these skills gradually rather than expecting pupils to demonstrate them all in one go such as writing a full essay from the start; it is recommended that your beginning teacher could follow the approach of Hochman et al. (2017) to support this. Beginning teachers might find it helpful to look at exemplar essays produced on the exam board website and any scripts that have been recalled from pupils who have sat the examination previously. Once again discussion in weekly mentor meetings should centre on what the beginning teacher has learnt from these exercises and how they think this will inform their teaching of the subject. It may be useful within these conversations to outline why an essay gained the mark that it did as modelling can be a very powerful scaffold through which beginning teachers can learn.

Participation in additional activities can help pupils gain higher grades at A level and spending time with the beginning teacher exploring possible ways this can be achieved can be useful. Discussions with the beginning teacher could focus on what is already happening within your own department, why these have been chosen, and the benefits they can bring to the pupils. For example, perhaps the department promotes A level essay competitions, arranges attendance at free or low-cost courses delivered by the local university, or promotes online learning opportunities. You might also recommend further reading or podcasts for pupils to listen to (good podcasts include *Beyond Belief*, *Moral Maze*, and *In Our Time* produced by Radio 4; see further resources for details). Finally, before the beginning teacher starts teaching any A level class, it is worthwhile encouraging them to observe as many A level lessons as possible, not only in RS but in other subjects as well. Once again discussions should follow these experiences giving them an opportunity to reflect on and explore what they have learnt through this process.

Summary and key points

Teaching effectively across any key stage is a complex activity. It requires an understanding of how pupils learn as well as effective teaching strategies which link to the learning process. There are also additional considerations that are needed when teaching an examination specification as it is essential that beginning teachers have a thorough understanding of the assessment requirements as well as a firm grounding in the subject knowledge.

• It is important that beginning teachers have a good understanding of the content of examination courses.

- Beginning teachers should develop knowledge of how the content of each specification is organised in schemes of work.
- Lesson planning needs to take into account, not only the substantive and proximal knowledge that must be included but also findings from cognitive science research about the most effective ways to structure learning activities.
- Subject knowledge is key to effective GCSE and A level teaching. As well as developing their own knowledge, beginning teachers need to understand how they can offer A level pupils additional opportunities to enhance their understanding.

Further resources

The following websites and podcasts are useful sources of information for GCSE and A level RS teachers (and their pupils).

Support for teaching GCSE

BBC Bitesize - www.bbc.co.uk/bitesize/secondary
BBC Bitesize have produced some excellent support materials for GCSE.

True Tube - www.truetube.co.uk/
True Tube produces some excellent clips and support material that is suitable for GCSE.

Support for teaching A level

FutureLearn - www.futurelearn.com/
A website that hosts online courses from a number of universities around the world which might be used by beginning teachers to support the development of their own subject knowledge.

Making links with universities - https://tinyurl.com/4d6rexka
The National Association of Teachers of Religious Education (NATRE) have put together a webpage that enables teachers to make more links with universities.

OpenLearn - www.open.edu/openlearn/
This platform offers free courses from the Open University. Some may be of interest to beginning teachers who are seeking ways to develop their subject knowledge.

Radio 4 podcasts
BBC Radio 4 has excellent podcasts which link to A level. For example:
Beyond Belief (www.bbc.co.uk/sounds/brand/b006s6p6)
In Our Time (www.bbc.co.uk/sounds/brand/b006qykl)
Moral Maze (www.bbc.co.uk/sounds/brand/b006qk11)

RE:ONLINE - www.reonline.org.uk/
This is an excellent website that has several useful areas for A level teachers, including detailed essays to support subject knowledge development, a half-termly digest to support the teaching of A level and ways to link to research.

RE:ONLINE eLearning platform - https://courses.cstg.org.uk/
This is a free online platform for teachers' CPD. It is an interactive way to access free, self-study courses designed to introduce teachers to current thinking in religion and worldviews education.

Theology and Religious Studies in Higher Education (TRS-UK) - https://trs.ac.uk/teachers-of-re/overview/
This website has videos and resources to help with the teaching of A level.

TRS Chester A level webinars - https://tinyurl.com/3h3xdnub
The University of Chester has an excellent selection of webinars for both teachers and pupils at A level RS.

Wi-Phi - https://tinyurl.com/fycmcdw7
Wireless Philosophy has produced some excellent clips that support the A level.

References

Ashbee, R. (2021). *Curriculum: Theory, culture and the subject specialisms*. Routledge.
Christodoulou, D. (2017). *Making good progress the future of assessment for learning*. Oxford University Press.
Hochman, J., Wexler, N., & Lemov, D. (2017). *The writing revolution*. Jossey-Bass.
Howard, K. & Hill, C. (2020). *Symbiosis the curriculum and the classroom*. John Catt.
Jackson-Royal, R., Mogra, I., Ahmedi, W., Ahluwalia, L. & Hewer, C. (2017). *The Oxford teacher handbook for GCSE Islam Oxford*. Oxford University Press.
Jones, A. (2022). *Homework with impact*. Routledge.
Jones, K. (2019). *Retrieval practice: Research and resources for every classroom*. John Catt.
Lovell, O. (2020). *Sweller's cognitive load theory in action*. John Catt.
Ofsted. (2021). *Research review series: Religious education*. https://www.gov.uk/government/publications/research-review-series-religious-education/research-review-series-religious-education
Rosenshine, B. (2012). Principles of instruction: Research-based strategies that all teachers should know. *American Educator*, 36(1), 12-39.
Sealy, C. & Bennett, T. (2020). *The ResearchED guide to the curriculum: An evidence informed guide for teachers*. John Catt.
Webb, J. (2021). *The Metacognition handbook: A practical guide for school leaders and educators*. John Catt.
Weinstein, Y., Sumeracki, M., & Caviglioli, O. (2019). *Understanding how we learn*. Routledge.
Willingham, D. (2010). *Why don't students like school? A cognitive scientist answers questions about how the mind works and what it means for the classroom*. Jossey-Bass.

16 Supporting beginning religious education teachers in approaching controversial issues in the classroom

Abigail Maguire

Introduction

The centrality of controversial issues in contemporary education is particularly evident and pronounced in the context of religious education (RE). The nature of the subject means that pupils are confronted head-on with matters pertaining to life, meaning, reality, belief, justice and ethics. With so many differences of opinion surrounding these matters, it is easy to see how controversy could occur. However, whilst an essential part of RE, the teaching of controversial issues receives mixed reactions from beginning teachers. Some find them to be one of the most enjoyable parts of their school experience as they facilitate pupils' learning through lively debate and discussion. In contrast, others find the teaching of controversial issues more challenging due, in part, to the capacity for them to create division and discord amongst pupils, teachers and society at large. As mentors, it is your role to help beginning teachers to navigate this terrain.

In order to help you in this role, the chapter starts by exploring what makes something controversial, and which criteria might be used. It then 'zooms out' to take a wide-angle look at the purpose of teaching controversial issues within religious education (RE), reflecting on their place within the subject, why they are studied and what teaching such issues hopes to achieve. Finally, it considers ways in which you are able to support beginning teachers by helping them to reflect upon the practical, personal and pedagogical aspects of tackling controversial issues.

At the end of this chapter, you should:

- Have a greater understanding of what makes a topic controversial, and the criteria that can be used to define this.
- Have considered why we teach controversial issues in RE.
- Have reflected on the ways in which you can support beginning teachers by addressing practical, personal, and pedagogical concerns.

DOI: 10.4324/9781003191087-19

What makes something controversial?

Controversial issues, by very nature, are dynamic which makes establishing an exact definition problematic. They are highly contextualised; dependant on geographical and cultural considerations. What is controversial for a group of pupils in one part of the world may differ from another. For example, teachers in South Africa consider issues such as HIV/AIDS and corporal punishment to be controversial, whereas the hijab and inter-ethnic conflict are more prominent in Turkey (Chikoko et al., 2011; Ersoy, 2010). In the UK, controversial issues include the relationship between religion and terror (Jerome and Elwick, 2020), the Holocaust (Ofsted, 2021), gender and sexual orientation (Woolley, 2020), and abortion and euthanasia (Pace, 2021). However, even within a specific culture and geography, teachers may hold different views on what should be considered controversial (Hess, 2002). To add to this, controversial issues are often amenable to change over time. Wellington, in his 1986 book *Controversial Issues in the Curriculum*, included nuclear armament as a 'hot topic' of his time. However, this rarely appears on an RE curriculum or syllabus today.

Given such complexity, focus has turned away from providing one all-encompassing or holistic definition of controversy. Instead, it has turned towards establishing 'criteria' that can be used to ascertain whether or not an issue should be taught as controversial. As a mentor, having an understanding of these criteria is useful as you work with your beginning teacher to identify which issues might be controversial and assist them to consider appropriate strategies in order to tackle such issues effectively.

Below is listed a summary of several key criteria which are also summarised in Figure 16.1. It is worth noting that there is considerable debate surrounding the use and practicalities of each of these criteria, and it is not quite as simple as using them as a checklist. Not all the criteria need to be fulfilled in order for an issue to be deemed controversial and it is likely that some issues will identify more strongly with certain criteria than others. Nevertheless, they do provide some helpful parameters that can be used in mentoring discussions.

The behavioural criterion

Something is controversial if it causes societal division. This criterion recognises that controversy is something that extends beyond individual disagreement. It involves numbers or groups of people who offer conflicting explanations, behaviours and solutions in relation to an issue (Bailey, 1975; QCA, 1998).

The epistemic criterion

The epistemic criterion states that "a matter is controversial if contrary views can be held on it without those views being contrary to reason" (Dearden, 1984, p. 86). In other words, controversial issues are those which the majority of people have not, as yet, reached an agreed consensus in light of available evidence and logical reasoning. They are largely unanswered, and rational disagreement exists about which position is most likely to be right.

The diversity criterion

Recognising that in the context of religion it is not always easy to assess rationality or the availability of evidence, Trevor Cooling puts forward the diversity criterion. This criterion proposes that issues should be taught as controversial when "significant disagreement exists between different belief communities in society where those communities honour the importance of reason giving and exemplify a commitment to peaceful co-existence in society" (Cooling, 2012, p. 177).

The 'politically authentic' criterion

This suggests that controversial issues can be identified when they appear and are deliberated within the public and political sphere. They appear on ballots; in courts; in government debates; as part of substantive political movements; and in legislative chambers (Hess and McAvoy, 2015).

The social criterion

For an issue to be considered controversial, it must be regarded as relevant to pupils' lives (Anders and Shudak, 2016). They are issues that are likely to be important either inside or outside of the classroom; at the present time or in the future. For RE within England and Wales, the role of a Locally Agreed Syllabus is often helpful in this regard where the curriculum is designed to reflect the needs and interests of pupils' local communities.

The psychological criterion

Something is controversial not solely because has the potential to evoke strong feelings and reactions in the lives of the pupils. It also needs to create a sense of intellectual tension that cultivates reasoning skills and learning (Yacek, 2018).

Some of the preceding criteria may seem familiar and natural to you and something that you use almost instinctively in your own practice. However, beginning teachers often struggle to identify which issues are controversial. Accordingly, outlining the key criteria has been included to provide a useful framework to support you in articulating some of these issues to your beginning teacher. Task 16.1 asks you and your beginning teacher to reflect upon some of the key criteria which establish whether an issue is controversial. The questions in the middle of the wheel act as helpful prompts and discussion starters for ongoing conversation with your beginning teacher.

Task 16.1 Reflection: what is a controversial issue?

With your beginning teacher, consider an issue taught in RE that you believe to be controversial. Use the diagram (Figure 16.1), along with the earlier text, to explore the issue. Think specifically about which criteria identify the issue as controversial, and why?

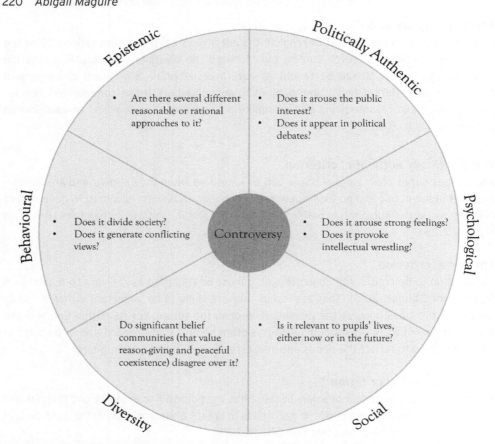

Figure 16.1 Summary 'wheel' of several key criteria used to establish controversiality

Why do we teach controversial issues?

One of the numerous jobs you have as a mentor is to enable your beginning teacher to think reflectively about all areas of their teaching experience. This includes encouraging them to take a step back from teaching lesson-to-lesson to consider the bigger picture. Discovering and discussing the rationale for teaching certain topics, and their place in a scheme of work, is an important part of this reflective process. You will need to support your beginning teacher to ensure they do not overlook controversial issues and their potential to bring about learning and development. As a mentor, you are likely to know first-hand the value of teaching controversial topics. However, the beginning teacher will often need your help to identify the purpose of teaching such topics and the benefits for the pupils in their class. As a result, it is worth taking some time to revisit this for yourself so that you are better able to assist the beginning teacher to think critically about the positive opportunities that teaching controversial issues will present.

There is a sense in which we teach controversial issues simply because they are on the curriculum. They also form a key part of broader educational aims because they assist in preparing young people for the complexities of adult life. The (now-defunct) Qualifications and Curriculum Authority (QCA), for example, stated that "education should not attempt to shelter our nation's children from even the harsher controversies of adult life, but should prepare them to deal with such controversies knowledgeably, sensibly, tolerantly, and morally" (1998, p. 56). Controversy is an established part of the pluralistic culture of which we are a part, and forms a basis for societal and intellectual change. Much of the material that is currently learnt by pupils across all syllabuses, subjects, and ages came to be as a direct result of controversy. As such, controversy, with its capacity to change the direction of human knowledge, cannot really be extinguished from the curriculum.

Nevertheless, RE, by very nature, encounters controversy in greater frequency and intensity than other subjects with wider longstanding debates around the nature and purpose of RE only acting to heighten this reality. Religion is inherently controversial, causing disagreement both within, between, and outside of various religious traditions. Additionally, each of the component 'parts' that frequently make up religion and belief systems: their ideas, teachings, figureheads, practices, ethics and histories are also considered controversial. They have the potential to create friction with other contested understandings within our culture, such as identity, politics, gender, sex, multiculturalism or capitalism. For these reasons, it makes sense that the Commission on Religious Education would advocate as part of the National Entitlement to the study of religion and worldviews, that pupils have are entitled to be taught by teachers who "are capable of addressing misconceptions and misunderstandings and handling controversial issues" (2018, p. 13).

Although not without challenge, it is engagement with precisely such complex issues that is at the heart of good RE. The RE classroom is one of the best places to be able to deal with controversial issues positively. The subject, more than any other, is concerned with that which is fundamental to human nature in all its beauty and messiness. Taught well, RE can help to foster an environment in which pupils are able to openly critically reflect on and discuss their own opinions and experiences, and respond constructively and respectfully to others. It provides the space where stereotypes can be challenged, media bias can be assessed and the tensions between conflicting truth claims can be explored.

Further, the teaching of controversial issues in the RE classroom allows pupils to develop the appropriate skills or competencies that are necessary both within the subject and outside of it. It can promote language, communication and scholarship skills through engagement with verbal and written discussion; higher level thinking skills such as information-processing, deductive reasoning, evaluation, creative problem-solving and critical enquiry; and personal and interpersonal skills such as resilience, responsibility, empathy, and confidence.

Finally, controversial issues are regularly those which pupils find to be most engaging and enjoyable. Young people have an appetite to want to learn about the controversial issues that affect them and their world and are highly motivated to be able to tackle them in an age or stage appropriate way (Oxfam, 2018). Although they must be taught carefully, controversial issues play a key role in addressing pupils' concerns. Accordingly, pupils are capable of dealing with them in the classroom and are ready to discuss and reflect on them in a way that is meaningful and brings about life-shaping learning (Association for Citizenship Teaching, 2015).

Many of the things mentioned above may seem intuitive to you as a more experienced classroom teacher. However, it is likely that beginning teachers may be discovering some of the benefits of tackling controversial issues for the very first time. Task 16.2 asks you use the given table (table 16.1) to help your beginning teacher to understand how controversy can facilitate learning.

Task 16.2 Equipping your beginning teacher to think about the purpose of controversial issues

Ask your beginning teacher to spend some time filling in Table 16.1. Although this task can be used for any controversial issue, it will be most helpful if your beginning teacher chooses an issue which they are currently teaching. Once they have filled in the table, ask them to bring it to your next meeting where you can discuss it together. Particularly, identify anything they might have missed, and help them set targets to apply their reflections to their ongoing teaching experience.

Table 16.1 Table for reflecting on the purpose of teaching controversial issues

Which controversial issue are you teaching?

Where does it appear in the scheme of work or syllabus? Why is it taught here?

In what ways will studying this particular issue bring about the intended learning?

What skills, competencies and/or proficiencies do you want pupils to develop through tackling this issue?

What is the benefit or value of studying this particular issue (either in the short or long term)?

Supporting beginning teachers

There is no denying that preparing to teach a lesson on a controversial issue for the very first time can be daunting; often fraught with practical, personal and pedagogical concerns. One of the biggest apprehensions that beginning teachers have in this area is the (admirable) desire to 'get it right' and the (understandable) fear of 'getting it wrong'. In this, there may be several factors at play, for example

- wanting to succeed in their progression, training and learning including passing any mandatory requirements for qualification;

- wishing to teach in such a way that impresses you as a mentor, especially during lessons that you might be observing or be present in;
- ensuring that they do justice to the controversial subject material they are teaching and are secure in their knowledge of the topic and preparedness to deal with any questions that may arise from pupils; and
- desiring not to cause unnecessary upset to colleagues, pupils or their parents by misrepresenting or misunderstanding the controversial issue or the fear of getting into trouble for doing so.

Addressing practical questions

In order to support your beginning teacher to tackle controversial issues with confidence, it is beneficial to work with them to think through some of the practical aspects of the teaching during the planning stage. Chapter 11 helpfully explores further how to help beginning teachers in planning creative, engaging and religiously literate lessons. In addition, because of the potentially sensitive nature of teaching controversial issues, there are several other aspects that your beginning teacher will also need to consider.

The first of these is to think carefully about the way in which they will take responsibility for managing behaviour to provide a positive environment in which challenging conversations can take place and pupils are able to learn effectively. It goes without saying that legitimate disagreement over controversial issues is acceptable, but there are appropriate ways of dealing with such disagreement. Your school is likely to have clear behaviour policies or strategies for using rewards and sanctions, alongside a code of conduct, which will form a part of your discussions. You may also have specific departmental guidance for dealing with controversial issues. (If not, perhaps consider with your team and beginning teacher how the nature of conversations in RE differs from other subjects and whether it would be helpful to have more formal guidance in place.) Nevertheless, you will also need to support beginning teachers to reflect on the important values they wish to convey in the classroom and how they might utilise a range of strategies, including the setting of ground rules, to promote good behaviour. This is particularly important in dealing with controversial issues where respect, appropriate language, avoiding blame or speculation, inclusivity, empathy, allowing everyone to contribute, openness and being prepared to justify views (amongst others) are fundamental to facilitating proper pupil discussion and reflection. Try to allow your beginning teacher the opportunity to watch you teach a lesson where you are able to model and demonstrate some of your own preferred methods in dealing with difficult discussions. This will be invaluable in helping them bridge the gaps between theory, policy and practice.

The sensitive disposition of some controversial issues also means that your beginning teacher may need to give thought to any pastoral implications that may arise. For example, when teaching a topic such as euthanasia, it is worth supporting your beginning teacher to think through the implications of lesson content in order to minimise distress. There may well be pupils in their class with older adult relatives or who have experienced the death of a loved one or pet. Does your beginning teacher have a strategy of what to do if a pupil becomes upset in a lesson? How will this be communicated to the class? Has your beginning teacher thought about whether they are using any imagery or media that might cause unnecessary discomfort? What will they do, practically, if conversation moves in an unwanted direction? It may be helpful here to role-play a scenario with your beginning teacher to equip them better to deal with these sorts of situations so that they do not face them 'cold' in a lesson.

It is also important to factor in the emotional needs of the beginning teacher whilst coaching them through teaching controversial issues. Inevitably, some issues will be closer to home than others, and it may be that your beginning teacher has been directly affected by one of the issues that they are required to teach. Accordingly, approaching a particular controversial issue may be incredibly challenging for them. Be prepared to make space for them to talk through any personal concerns with you or, if necessary, signpost them to someone who can provide more specific support. Remember, it can be incredibly reassuring for your beginning teacher to hear that it's okay to find certain aspects of teaching tricky. Perhaps consider sharing an example from your own practice – what is it that you find most challenging? How do you deal with this?

Although it is not always easy to pre-empt every pastoral concern as it occurs during a lesson, much can be done in the planning phases to prepare for such an eventuality. Here, encouraging or working with your beginning teacher to develop effective professional relationships and utilise the expertise of other colleagues is vital. Head of years, pastoral leads or form tutors can all provide context or insight to individual pupils' needs that are helpful when determining whether extra care is required. Their advice and specialist support could also be drawn on in the eventuality that a pastoral situation does arise during a teaching session. Accordingly, beginning teachers will need to know when and how to access their support.

In some cases, it will also be appropriate for your beginning teacher to inform pupils' parents of their intentions to teach a particular controversial issue, and the rationale for doing so. Communication to and with parents and carers is an important skill to learn during the school experience. It is especially important in RE where parents are sometimes worried about curriculum content and how it might impact on their family's particular beliefs or worldview. Good communication is a key part of avoiding some of the complications that might arise as a result, such as exercising the right to withdrawal. As a mentor, you play a crucial role in assisting your beginning teacher to identify how best to form and maintain relationships with parents and carers.

Task 16.3 draws together some of these practical issues and provides a framework to help you consider how you may be able to support your beginning teacher in dealing with them.

Task 16.3 Supporting the practicalities of teaching controversial issues

Consider:

- How familiar is your beginning teacher with the pastoral structures of your school? To what extent are they able to effectively draw up on the expertise of other colleagues, and how might you develop this further?

- Is your beginning teacher able to use behavioural management strategies and the setting of ground rules to tackle controversial issues? How could you support them to do so?
- To what extent do you involve your beginning teacher in communication with parents in regard to both curriculum decisions and individual pastoral conversations?
- What values do you think are important to convey in the classroom when teaching controversial issues? How might you incorporate or reference some of these ideas as part of your mentoring discussions?

Dealing with personal questions

In many ways, teaching an issue that is controversial is different from approaching other topics that are settled or agreed upon. Controversial issues directly confront the values that underpin the lives of both pupil and teacher, the ethos of the school, and the values of society more broadly. Therefore, they cannot be approached with the same academic distance, objectivity or sense of detachment that may be appropriate elsewhere (Council of Europe, 2015). For beginning teachers, specifically, it may also be the case that they too are encountering a controversial issue for the first time whilst also attempting to plan and deliver a lesson on it. For example, it may be the first time that they have studied religious approaches to abortion in detail. In so doing, they may well have started to consider (or reconsider) their own personal beliefs and opinions on the topic all whilst trying to help teenagers navigate the same! Nevertheless, for all teachers (regardless of their experience), there are some controversial issues which they will have very clear opinions on, and others where they remain unsure. So, whilst it is important to have an understanding of how beliefs, attitudes and experiences might affect our position on such issues, it is helpful to remind your beginning teacher that it is not a requirement to have a controversial issue 'sorted' before we teach it. To this end, it is beneficial to support your beginning teacher to think deeply about their beliefs (whether firm or not), any potential biases and how they might impact on their teaching approaches.

One common attitude toward confronting controversial issues is for teachers to maintain a neutral stance in the classroom (Oulton, Dillon, and Grace, 2004; Philpott, Clabough, McConkey and Turner, 2011). On the surface, this seems reasonable and is underpinned by contemporary social values of autonomy and freedom of thought in which pupils are free to formulate their own opinions, choices and decisions. It recognises the power dynamics at play between teacher and pupil and attempts to prevent those in authority from imposing their views upon those who are not. The need to avoid indoctrination is of momentous importance in RE, not least in the adherence to legal standards and guidance that stipulate that syllabuses "must not be designed to convert pupils, or to urge a particular religion or religious beliefs on pupils" *(Education Act 1944, s.26(2))*.

However, it is important to prompt your beginning teacher to recognise that neutrality as a solution to indoctrination is problematic. As Hughes and Barnes state, "Non confessional

RE should not be mistaken for a 'neutral' kind of RE" (2008, p. 33). RE is not neutral to the law of the land, the worldviews or opinions of the students or the place and role of religion and the need for RE itself. Like all education, it is not value-free but value-laden in that it presupposes a commitment to a certain set of beliefs and principles. For this reason, it would be appropriate, for instance, to explain to your beginning teacher that teachers should not be neutral towards derogatory or offensive comments. The notion of neutrality is also challenging when considering the teachers' own beliefs. There is no standing outside of a controversial issue and it is impossible to completely divorce a teacher's personal beliefs and values from their pedagogy and practice.

Following on from this, you may wish to build on the input that your beginning teacher receives from their higher education provider to help them answer the question as to whether it is ever fitting for a teacher to share their own opinions on a controversial issue with pupils. Start by reflecting on what you do in your own practice and why. Whilst good RE does not necessitate the sharing of personal beliefs, appropriate self-disclosure can be a "professional asset" (Religious Education Council of England and Wales [REC], 2009, p. 3). The perspective of a teacher can act as a resource to cultivate an atmosphere of trust, communicate the 'lived experience' of a particular worldview, and exemplify the nuances between different schools of thought. However, the classroom environment is one where beliefs and their impact are explored and evaluated. As a result, teachers should act with integrity and openness about their own beliefs, and should not pass judgement on the validity of pupils' beliefs (unless offensive; REC, 2013). Your role as a mentor is crucial in helping beginning teachers to develop their own professional judgement about when it might, or might not, be appropriate to use the sharing of personal beliefs as a resource. By aiding them to consider the implications of self-disclosure on trust, openness, and classroom dynamics, beginning teachers are able to think deeply on issues of positionality. Thus, answering the question, 'What type of teacher do I want to be or values do I want to demonstrate?' Task 16.4 is written to help you to support your beginning teaching to reflect on their positionality in the classroom and explore the different roles or personas they might take on to facilitate learning.

Task 16.4 Teacher roles

Start by reflecting on your own practice. Use Table 16.2 to think about the positions that a teacher might choose to adopt when tackling controversial issues. Consider:

- Which position do you most closely align with in your own teaching?
- In what situations might it be appropriate to adopt the below positions?
- Are there any other positions that you would add to the list?

Revisit the table with your beginning teacher. Talk about the similarities and differences in your approaches and explore these further.

Table 16.2 Potential Teacher Positions on Controversial Issues

Position	Explanation
Neutral Chairperson	The teacher adopts the role of impartial chairperson of a discussion group. Discussion is focused on the students' viewpoints and requires the teacher not to express personal views or allegiances.
Balanced Advocate	The teacher presents students with a wide range of alternative views on an issue. They present each view as persuasively as possible, without revealing their own view.
Committed Impartiality	The teacher explicitly makes their view known. They lead discussion of student's views whilst being willing to advocate for their position.
Challenging Consensus	The teacher consciously and openly takes up the opposite position to that expressed by students or resource material, irrespective of their own viewpoint.
Critical Affirmation	The teacher and students advocate their own stance. This is done in a way that affirms pupils and their views whilst subjecting all views, including the teacher's own, to a close scrutiny, especially regarding implications for the views of others.

Adapted from Fiehn (2005)

Considering pedagogical questions

In this final section of the chapter, we consider several different ways in which the beginning teacher might deliver the content of a controversial issue to a class and your role in offering them support in this. Whilst teaching controversial issues, there is, of course, no 'one-size-fits-all' approach. Teachers are free to adopt their own styles based on individual preference, their specific contexts, and the knowledge of their classes. Many of the general pedagogical approaches to RE are also able to be applied to the teaching of controversial issues. However, more specific methods that involve participatory, problem-based, or enquiry-based learning are also useful. Stradling, Noctor and Baines, in their seminal work of 1984, propose four 'procedures' or strategies that provide a suitable framework in which to situate the teaching of such issues (pp. 113–114). Whilst you are reading through the list below, think about examples and instances from your own practice where you have utilised some or all the 'procedures' effectively. Under which circumstances are you most likely to put them in place?

- *Distancing procedures* can be used if a controversial issue is likely to cause polarisation or division between pupils. It involves the teacher depersonalising the class from the issue to find parallels or analogies elsewhere; from other arenas or areas of curriculum content. Alternatively, the history or contextual backdrop to the issue can be explored. The aim here is not to evade the issue but to critically examine its underlying philosophical, social, political or cultural principles less emotively, before applying them to the controversy. Activities such as case studies, agony aunts, conscience alleys, magazine articles or media clips or utilising P4C, can all prove useful for distancing.
- *Compensatory procedures* are advantageous if there is unquestioning consensus, if views seem based on ignorance, or if it is difficult for the minority voice to be heard. The teacher deliberately offers alternative perspectives to try to rebalance the discussions and enable pupils to think beyond their own current understandings. Compensatory

tools include 'for and against' activities, introducing new material, role reversals or bringing in guest speakers.

- *Empathetic procedures* are most commonly used in classes where the balanced or even-handed view is likely to be unpopular, there is either active or passive discrimination or if an issue is considerably removed from pupils' lives. They are designed to foster a sense of sympathy with, and sensitivity towards, those who hold different viewpoints, thus, giving pupils a more comprehensive understanding of a controversial issue. In addition to those mentioned above, activities designed to increase empathy include role-play, drama, literature and fiction, simulation, 'walking in their shoes' activities and exploring emotions and responses.

- *Exploratory procedures* are adopted for more complex issues that are not clearly defined and may require more extended investigation or study. The teacher is able to incorporate tools such as project work, case studies, fieldwork and guided homework in order to help pupils explore the multifaceted nature of controversial issues.

As a mentor, you will have a wealth of experience as to the types of activities and techniques that may have worked well when you yourself have taught controversial issues. Why don't you give the preceding list to your beginning teacher and ask them to plan an activity that incorporates each of the procedures for one particular controversial issue? Creating and planning engaging activities that enable learning outcomes to be met, alongside tackling broader pedagogical concerns, can sometimes be challenging for beginning teachers. As a result, beginning teachers should be able to draw on your expertise when required in addition to being encouraged to try new and novel activities (even if they don't work as well as hoped!). Nevertheless, it is important to promote an environment where they are able to reflect systematically on the effectiveness of each activity that they choose. Consider any ways in which you can support your beginning teacher to do this. For example, you could 'team teach' a lesson on a controversial topic together and, in the spirit of collegiality, spend some time afterwards critically evaluating each other's practice. You may find that you learn just as much from your beginning teacher as they do from you! Alternatively, you may wish to use some of the literature in the 'further resources' section below to read together, before using it as a tool to help you both appraise one of your lessons, or the lesson of a third party.

Summary and key points

In this chapter, we have examined the role of controversial issues in RE and thought reflexively about some of the complexities that may be encountered when tackling such issues in the classroom. This exploration will have clarified our own understanding of controversial issues and given you some tools or frameworks to be able to better support those who you mentor. Specifically, we have considered the importance of the following:

- Recognising what makes an issue controversial, and which criterion might be used to establish controversiality
- Understanding why controversial issues are taught, the benefits of doing so, and their place within an RE curriculum

- Supporting beginning teachers to address some of the practical and pastoral aspects of tackling controversial issues, including the need to manage behaviour well and communicate with parents and other colleagues
- Reflecting upon our positionality as a teacher and the impact of our beliefs and biases on teaching approaches.
- Helping beginning teachers to develop appropriate strategies for planning and conducting lesson activities

Further resources

Association for Citizenship Teaching. (2015). *The Prevent Duty and teaching controversial issues: Creating a curriculum response through citizenship.* https://www.teachingcitizenship.org.uk/resource/prevent-duty-and-controversial-issues-creating-curriculum-response-through-citizenship

A useful resource that focuses specifically on the role of citizenship education in the prevention of terrorism and extremism. However, it provides helpful material on how to set up a classroom for discussion and debate, as well as strategies for planning, teaching, and assessment.

Council of Europe. (2015). *Living with controversy: Teaching controversial issues through education for democratic citizenship and human rights (EDC/HRE). Training pack for teachers.* https://rm.coe.int/16806948b6

One of the most comprehensive, yet practical, guides that includes an examination of relevant literature within the European context. It aims to equip teachers with the essential skills needed to facilitate good learning in the classroom. Additionally, it contains an extensive pack of resources that can be used in lessons to tackle controversial issues.

Oxfam. (2018). *Teaching controversial issues: A guide for teachers.* OxfamGB. https://oxfamilibrary.openrepository.com/handle/10546/620473

A succinct yet rich guide for teachers of all ages that takes a global citizenship approach to tackling controversial issues. The guide is visually appealing and examines underlying social and political influences. It also supplies several activities that can be used to support teachers to develop their role in the classroom.

References

Anders, P. and Shudak, N. (2016). Criteria for controversy: A theoretic approach. *Thresholds in Education*, 39(1), 20-30.

Association for Citizenship Teaching. (2015). *The Prevent Duty and teaching controversial issues: Creating a curriculum response through citizenship.* https://www.teachingcitizenship.org.uk/resource/prevent-duty-and-controversial-issues-creating-curriculum-response-through-citizenship

Bailey, C. (1975). Neutrality and rationality in teaching. In Bridges, D. & Scrimshaw, P. (eds.), *Values and authority in school* (pp. 122-144). Hodder & Stoughton.

Chikoko, V., Gilmour, J. D., Harber, C., and Serf, J. (2011). Teaching controversial issues and teacher education in England and South Africa. *Journal of Education for Teaching*, 37(1), 5-19. https://doi.org/10.1080/02607476.2011.562013

Commission on Religious Education. (2018). *Religion and worldviews: The way forward. A national plan for RE.* Religious Education Council of England and Wales.

Cooling, T. (2012). What is a controversial issue? Implications for the treatment of religious beliefs in education. *Journal of Beliefs and Values*, 33(2), 169-181. https://doi.org/10.1080/13617672.2012.694060

Council of Europe. (2015). *Living with controversy: Teaching controversial issues through education for democratic citizenship and human rights (EDC/HRE). Training pack for teachers.* https://rm.coe.int/16806948b6

Dearden, R. F. (1984). *Theory and practice in education.* Routledge.

Ersoy, A. F. (2010). Social studies teacher candidates' views on the controversial issues incorporated into their courses in Turkey. *Teaching and Teacher Education*, 26(2), 323-334. https://doi.org/10.1016/j.tate.2009.09.015

Fiehn, J. (2005). *Agree to disagree: Citizenship and controversial issues.* Learning and Skills Development Agency.

Hess, D. E. (2002). Discussing controversial public issues in secondary social studies classrooms: Learning from skilled teachers. *Theory & Research in Social Education*, 30(1), 10-41. https://doi.org/10.1080/00933104.2002.10473177

Hess, D. E. and McAvoy, P. (2015). *The political classroom: Evidence and ethics in democratic education.* Routledge.

Hughes, F. and Barnes, L. P. (2008). Religious education in state and faith schools. In Barnes, L. P., Wright, A., and Brandom, A. (eds.), *Learning to teach Religious Education in the secondary school: A companion to school experience.* (2nd ed., pp. 25–39). Routledge.

Jerome, L. and Elwick, A. (2020). Teaching about terrorism, extremism and radicalisation: Some implications for controversial issues pedagogy. *Oxford Review of Education*, 46(2), 222-237. https://doi.org/10.1080/03054985.2019.1667318

Ofsted. (2021). *Research review series: Religious education.* https://www.gov.uk/government/publications/research-review-series-religious-education/research-review-series-religious-education#fnref:94

Oulton, C., Dillon, J. and Grace, M. (2004). Reconceptualizing the teaching of controversial issues. *International Journal of Science Education*, 26(4), 411-423. https://doi.org/10.1080/0950069032000072746

Oxfam. (2018). *Teaching controversial issues: A guide for teachers.* OxfamGB. https://oxfamilibrary.openrepository.com/handle/10546/620473

Pace, J. L. (2021). *Hard questions: Learning to teach controversial issues.* Rowman & Littlefield Publishers.

Philpott, S., Clabough, J., McConkey, L. and Turner, T. (2011). Controversial issues: To teach or not to teach? That is the question!. *The Georgia Social Studies Journal*, 1(1), 32-44.

Qualifications and Curriculum Authority. (1998). *Education for citizenship and the teaching of democracy in schools: Final report of the Advisory Group on Citizenship.* Qualifications and Curriculum Authority.

Religious Education Council of England and Wales. (2009). *Every one matters in the classroom: A practice code for teachers of RE.* https://www.religiouseducationcouncil.org.uk/wp-content/uploads/2017/09/Practice_Code_for_Teachers_of_RE.pdf

Religious Education Council of England and Wales. (2013). *DFE Teacher standards 2013: An RE exemplification.* https://www.religiouseducationcouncil.org.uk/wp-content/uploads/2017/10/DFE_Teacher_standards_2013.pdf

Stradling, R., Noctor, M. and Baines, B. (eds.). (1984). *Teaching controversial issues.* Edward Armold.

Wellington, J. (1986). *Controversial issues in the curriculum.* Basil Blackwell.

Woolley, R. (2020). Tackling controversial issues in primary education: Perceptions and experiences of student teachers. *Religions*, 11(4), 184. https://doi.org/10.3390/rel11040184

Yacek, D. (2018). Thinking controversially: The psychological condition for teaching controversial issues. *Journal of Philosophy of Education*, 52(1), 71-86. https://doi.org/10.1111/1467-9752.12282

17 Helping beginning religious education teachers develop their professional practice

Paul Smalley

Introduction: Mentoring for professional understanding

In this chapter, we consider the role of the mentor in helping the beginning religious educa-tion (RE) teacher to understand wider aspects of teaching, particularly the link with research and the ever-changing demands placed on those who teach RE. Shulman (2008) suggests that the skilled mentor is required to move beyond simply coaching teaching technique to inculcate a vision for education on the way to the beginning RE teacher developing a new, professional identity. They do this by changing roles from instructor to critical friend or knowledgeable other. Akahito Takahashi (2014) has written about the role of the knowledge-able other in developing teachers. Although his work was based on Lesson Study, a method of professional development for teachers involving collaborative research in the classroom (See Allan *et al.*, 2019), his findings have much relevance to the mentor who acts as a knowl-edgeable other when working with beginning teachers. Takahashi suggests that

> the knowledgeable other is responsible for:
>
> (1)   bringing new knowledge from research and the curriculum;
> (2)   showing the connection between the theory and the practice; and
> (3)   helping others learn how to reflect on teaching and learning."
>
> (2014, p. 13)

This model is used in the first part of the chapter to investigate how you might induct begin-ning RE teachers into the teaching profession and RE community before considering some areas of knowledge that you might encourage beginning RE teachers to explore in order for them to become a reflective, creative RE practitioner.

By the end of this chapter you should be able to:

*   Reflect on the different kinds of knowledge in which beginning RE teachers may need to develop expertise and confidence.
*   Guide the beginning RE teacher to understand the importance of your curriculum intent and how lessons, and sequences of lessons enable pupils to make progress (knowing more and remembering more) towards that.
*   Model critical engagement with RE policy (such as the local settlement of RE) to ena-ble the beginning RE teacher to engage in policy debates throughout their career as a reflective practitioner.
*   Reflect on your role as a mentor.

DOI: 10.4324/9781003191087-20

Bringing new knowledge from research and the curriculum

In order for you to consider your role as the knowledgeable other, each stage of Takahashi's model is examined in turn. The first element of the model is to suggest that a mentor, as the 'knowledgeable other' should help bring in new knowledge from research and the curriculum. There has been, in recent years, an increased pressure on schools to engage with research in order to improve their practice (Stern, 2018). Winch, Oancea and Orchard (2015) have suggested that it should be one of the aims of initial teacher education to ensure that beginning teachers become scholars of educational research. The skilled mentor must be aware of the different forms of knowledge that are required in order to become expert in the classroom. Commonly these are divided into three types of knowledge: subject knowledge, pedagogical content knowledge and curricular knowledge (Shulman, 1986).

In terms of subject knowledge, it is important to encourage the beginning RE teacher to go beyond the knowledge required for the lesson and to use more advanced knowledge sources than they will present to the pupils. Since RE is such a multidisciplinary subject, it is likely that the beginning RE teacher may not start their teaching career as expert in all fields, so you should be ready to recommend further reading to a beginning teacher that develops a wide subject knowledge. This goes beyond substantive knowledge of the content and concepts of the six major world faiths and includes conceptual understanding or disciplinary knowledge (Kueh, 2018). A beginning teacher should understand that 'ways of knowing' in RE (Ofsted, 2021) can be divided along disciplinary lines and may be presented as different types of academic conversations: thinking like a theologian or a philosopher or asking the sort of questions that people who study the lived reality of the human/social sciences would ask. A beginning RE teacher's knowledge of the ways of knowing might also involve them being aware of a variety of tools, methods and processes that can be used to study religion and non-religion and being able to carefully select the correct tools for the job, such as textual (hermeneutical) tools, ethnography, methods in historical reconstruction, participant observation, in-depth interviews or analysis of relevant data.

Developing a beginning RE teacher's pedagogical content knowledge involves inculcating them into a variety of ways of understanding how the material can be taught. Teachers best learn important knowledge with concrete examples, so it is important that the beginning RE teacher is able to see a variety of pedagogical approaches to teaching RE (Grimmitt, 2000). It involves them understanding which parts of the subject are difficult to grasp and which are more straightforward so that appropriate teaching strategies might be chosen. In simple terms, the beginning RE teacher needs to develop an arsenal of different ways of explaining things, so that the pupils will understand the content being delivered. Simply lecturing about such specialised knowledge is not enough.

The beginning RE teacher needs to become adept at understanding the curriculum that they are teaching. This is what Ofsted (2019) means by curriculum intent. They should be ready to show that they have thought about what endpoints the curriculum (either long term or over a sequence of lessons that they are teaching) is building towards, what pupils will be able to know and do at those endpoints and how the curriculum is planned accordingly.

As a mentor, you should be ready to provide new knowledge that relates to the teaching and learning of the topic of the lesson(s) in these three knowledge content areas. This may mean that you signpost the beginning RE teacher to read up on a certain topic before a lesson (or sequence) is planned. You, as the knowledgeable other, will be aware of the ambitious end goals for your RE curriculum and will need to ensure that the beginning RE teacher, like any new colleague, is fully aware of this. Task 17.1 suggests a way in which you may explore this with your beginning teacher.

Task 17.1 Explaining ambitious end goals of the curriculum

Think about the RE curriculum that you are asking the beginning RE teacher to deliver. Can you easily explain your intent, your ambitious end goals? Can you justify the choices you have made in selecting substantive knowledge to be studied and the ways of knowing that pupils will use to learn that substantive knowledge? Can you easily explain this to a beginning teacher?

Showing the connection between theory and practice

The second stage of Takahashi's model involves you as the knowledgeable other helping beginning teachers see the link between theory and practice. New research is constantly being carried out that is relevant to the beginning (and experienced!) RE teacher. Two excellent RE-specific resources are the research pages of the RE:ONLINE website and the Farmington Institute (see Further Resources), both of which aim to enable teachers to use research to improve their practice.

The RE:ONLINE research library aims to make it easy for teachers to access and engage with research in RE. Its main use for teachers is the large number of research reports that it contains. These easy-to-read summaries of published research include suggestions of how the research report may be useful for teachers. There are links to the full version of the published article. There are also opportunities for teachers to get involved in research projects through the website.

The Farmington Institute offers scholarships to RE teachers which pay for them to be released from teaching for the equivalent of a term in order to carry out agreed research projects. These are then written up and are freely available to other teachers. Its website offers a searchable list of all the reports published, and the full report can be requested by email.

These websites offer opportunities for mentors, in the role of the knowledgeable other, to encourage beginning RE teachers to try new ideas based on research and reading. In the best examples, these projects can be done collaboratively. The mentor and the beginning RE teacher might work together to look to improve, for example dialogic skills or pupils' understanding of sacred texts within a religion, having first read one of the research reports online. Task 17.2 offers a suggested approach to engaging in this kind of collaborative work. This may involve going beyond the comfort zone - often of the mentor as well as the beginning RE teacher!

Task 17.2 Using research to inform planning

Select a scheme of work that needs updating and ask your beginning RE teacher to use the RE:ONLINE research library to find a relevant article and summarise it, highlighting how it might be used to inform or develop the scheme. Discuss how the research will inform the lessons.

There are of course many other areas of more general educational research which might be of interest to the beginning RE teacher. Much has been gained from educators' recent engagement with cognitive psychology to help understand how pupils might benefit from, for example adaptive teaching or dual coding or avoiding cognitive overload. What is important is that the beginning RE teacher is encouraged to think deeply and critically about the idea being tested in the research. They should also be encouraged to think deeply and critically about how (and indeed if) the research is relevant to RE. For example, the Ofsted Research Review (2021) suggests that low-stakes multiple choice quizzing is often valuable but not a good way for pupils in RE to recall stories. Task 17.3 addresses the challenges of making links between whole school approaches or generic strategies and the RE classroom.

Task 17.3 Investigating an intervention

Ask the beginning teacher to choose a potential intervention (relating to literacy, special education needs and disability, or one that your school is considering). Encourage the beginning RE teacher to investigate the theory behind that intervention and read reports of the effectiveness of that intervention in other schools. The Educational Endowment Foundation (EEF) toolkit is one location where these reports can easily be found. Discuss with the beginning teacher how to best utilise that intervention in RE.

Keeping abreast of the latest research findings, through engagement with social media, general education newspapers, subject-specific magazines (such as *RE Today*) and journals (such the *British Journal of Religious Education* or the *Journal of Beliefs and Values*) will enable you to be highly effective at directing the beginning RE teacher to find solutions to problems highlighted in lesson observations or their own personal evaluations. The best mentors will want to be engaged in this learning for their own, and their pupils', benefit in any case.

Helping others learn how to reflect on teaching and learning

The final stage of Takahashi's model involves helping the beginning teacher learn how to reflect on teaching and learning. As beginning RE teachers grow in confidence, the art of reflecting on practice should be encouraged. Whilst earlier feedback might have initially been filled with advice, "I want you to try this next lesson", in time they become professional discussions. The emphasis of the mentor's role becomes more of a critical friend, probing the beginning RE teacher to justify pedagogical and curricular choices they have made. So, for example, in a discussion about a particular activity and whether it suitably stretched and challenged the highest ability pupils, you might direct the beginning RE teacher to read some of Mary Myatt's work (e.g. Myatt, 2016, 2018) about challenge in the curriculum to enable to beginning RE teacher to reflect and develop their own understanding of what 'stretch and challenge' might mean.

RE pedagogy, an all-encompassing theory of delivering the subject's aims through a particular methodology, is very much a live matter, and in the very recent past, we have seen authors suggesting an approach to RE rooted in six Big Ideas (Wintersgill, 2017; Wintersgill, Cush & Francis, 2019), a Dialogue with Difference (O'Grady, 2018), or based in critical realism (Easton et al., 2019). The Ofsted Research Review into RE (2021) lists seven approaches and suggests that "although aspects of each of these pedagogical models could be useful, any one model alone would be insufficient". Although you may not be an expert in all these approaches, it is important to be aware of them, their particular strengths and their potential shortcomings. The beginning RE teacher may want to experiment by trying out one of these approaches, or you may wish to challenge them to try one they are not familiar with, again, moving outside of their comfort zone. Task 17.4 offers a potential starting point for this discussion.

Task 17.4 Understanding pedagogical approaches

Work with the beginning RE teacher to look at a sequence of lessons or scheme of work. Can they identify the pedagogical approach used in the sequence? Make sure that they understand how this sequence builds towards your curriculum end goal.

Recently Ofsted (and others) have started to emphasise that it is important for pupils to make progress over time, and the phrase first used by Michael Fordham (2020) , "the curriculum is the progression model", explains what is meant by progress. Pupils should know more and remember more of the planned curriculum over time. The intent, or ambitious curriculum end goal, is what the curriculum should build towards.

So far, we have suggested how some forms of knowledge might be key to helping the mentor develop the beginning RE teacher into a 'whole' teacher. By this we mean a critical, reflective, research-informed teacher. The examples we have used so far have been firmly rooted in the major aspect of a beginner teacher's concern, that of the actual RE lesson. In the latter half of the chapter, we explore how a mentor might seek to induct the beginning RE teacher into the wider RE community.

Connecting with the world of teaching

Due to its historic local nature, RE, often more than any other subject, has opportunities to collaborate and share with teachers from other schools. It is worth encouraging the beginning RE teacher to make contact with the Standing Advisory Council on RE (SACRE) in your area. SACRE meetings are open to the public, and SACREs are keen for more RE teachers to become involved. Many SACREs run teacher networks, and again, this is one way that you can encourage your beginning RE teacher to widen their support network. There are also similar networks and continuing professional development (CPD) opportunities provided by both Catholic and Anglican Dioceses and the Jewish Board of Deputies.

National Association of Teachers of RE (NATRE) has always supported and encouraged RE teacher networks. Its aim is that every teacher of RE should have a local group within 10 miles (or 30 minutes) of where they live or teach. These offer further opportunities for the beginning RE teacher to engage with a variety of practitioners and hear about good practice that is going on locally. The teacher meetings often have a specific focus: teaching a particular religion, writing extended GCSE answers, including literacy in RE, or even a visit to a place of worship (without the pupils!).

RE is well served by conference opportunities: NATRE and Culham St Gabriel's both run annual RE conferences with NATRE also running a wide variety of day courses. University theology and religious studies departments can be a useful source of information for the beginning RE teacher to develop their subject knowledge. The examination boards, of course, often provide training specific to their specifications.

Social media itself can be a very valuable source of support for the beginning RE Teacher. For a number of years, NATRE has held a monthly Twitter event: #REChatUK. The subject of the chat is always topical and relevant to the beginning RE Teacher. Podcasts, such as the *Panpsycast Philosophy Podcast*, BBC Radio 4's *In Our Time* or the *RE Podcast* (see Further Resources) are an easy way to develop a very wide subject knowledge. There are Facebook groups (such as Respect RE) which often provide lots of support opportunities, although sometimes can become a bit argumentative. You might need to warn the beginning RE teacher that posters may have strong opinions about what is right and wrong in RE (and teaching generally) and can be quite blunt in expressing those opinions. They might also need warning that people sometimes enjoy debating (and criticising) truth claims on social media and, on occasions, have been known to take the debate rather too far. However, do encourage the beginning RE teacher to use social media professionally. There are huge benefits to such sites, and the support can be invaluable. You might advise them to 'lurk' (reading but not posting or commenting) for a while to get a feel for the particular virtual environment.

These sorts of networks do not have to be confined to being RE-specific. Two initiatives which have gained popularity in recent years are #TeachMeet and #BrewEd. Both of these are informal teacher-organised events where the aim is to share good practice, and both as the hashtag suggests, are largely organised via Twitter. You might need to explain to the beginning RE teacher that a #TeachMeet is a gathering arranged, sometimes at a school in the early evening or sometimes at a more neutral venue, where participants agree to speak for a usually short amount of time. Do encourage them to join in, and as an expert practitioner, you should look to present at such events (if you don't already do so). The format is usually agreed consensually by the organisers or the attendees of a previous meeting. #BrewEd is very similar, other than the events tend to take place in a pub on a Saturday afternoon! The EEF have a series of podcasts which help teachers understand how to apply lessons learnt from educational research to teaching. Task 17.5 invites you to think about how you might encourage your beginning teacher to engage with social media.

Task 17.5 Encouraging engagement with social media

Set your beginning teacher a challenge of engaging with the RE community on one of the social media platforms or listening to a relevant podcast and then discuss with them what they learnt from the experience.

Debating RE policy

As an experienced practitioner, you will know that RE policy is always being debated. As they set out and in the early years of their career, the beginning RE teacher will engage with these debates and issues and a mentor should be prepared to guide them in this. They will value your understanding of the old debates about, for example, whether RE should be a phenomenological subject or survey and contrast world religions or retain much of its emphasis on Christian nurture. These debates about the purpose of RE continue: Should RE be about religious literacy, critically analysing truth claims, a sociological study of different people's worldviews or developing pupils' theological understanding? Each school, and each teacher, has a different view on these issues and the beginning teacher will develop their opinion over time. A good mentor will help this development of understanding.

Although familiar to you, the beginning RE teacher will be new to the idea that since the advent of the National Curriculum in 1988, RE's anomalous position in the Basic Curriculum, and locally determined, has frequently been debated. Recently, there have been suggestions that there should be a new, more centralised legal settlement for RE in order to reflect the new educational landscape and the change in religious demographics, the Commission on RE (2018) have made similar recommendations, including a 'National Entitlement', national non-statutory programmes of study, reform of SACREs and an end to the requirement for local authorities to convene Agreed Syllabus Conferences. However, other voices in the RE community suggest that the current settlement has its advantages, and the debate continues (see Smalley, 2020).

These issues of RE policy should be becoming as familiar to the beginning teacher as they are to you, but they will value hearing your view on all these topics. Your aim as a knowledgeable other is to encourage the beginning teacher to engage in a process of edification: encountering different opinions and considering their own views in the light of their experiences. Task 17.6 proposes a starting point for such a discussion.

Task 17.6 Discussing local determination

Discuss with the beginning teacher what the advantages and disadvantages of the current system of local determination are.

The wider world of teaching, performativity and the neoliberal system

In 2020 Gavin Williamson, the then Secretary of State for Education, stated that "the purpose of education is to give people the skills they need to get a good and meaningful job"

(DfE, 2020). This is sometimes considered to be a reductive view of education. Task 17.7 allows you to consider the mentoring role in this context.

Task 17.7 Reflecting on the purpose of your mentoring role

Reflect on whether you view your role as a mentor as being intrinsically about helping the beginning RE teacher gain employment, or is there a wider educative purpose to your role?

Is this the same or different to when you are educating your pupils?

Since the 1980s neoliberalism has become pervasive in education. You, as an experienced expert teacher will be all too aware of this, but despite having (in all likelihood) been educated in it, the beginning RE teacher may need help in recognising how the three 'technologies' of market, managerialism and performativity (Ball, 2003) are intrinsic to the current education system. They may not realise that the system is (now) set up in a deliberately competitive way: schools compete for consumers and choices are made by parents based on published league tables of results. Internally, subjects, and teachers, are often made to compete against each other. Results day in August is swiftly followed by the inquest in September into why some teachers' results are below what other teachers achieved.

It will be invaluable for the beginning RE teacher to understand this debate: that for a period, RE was able to avoid many of these pressures, having no nationally prescribed curriculum or assessment tool, but many felt this led to a diminished status of RE as a 'Cinderella' subject. Others valued the space in the curriculum which wasn't driven by results and where teachers were able to be creative, without fear that six weeks of mandala making would impact negatively on the term's progress scores. But RE as a subject community jumped at the chance of neoliberal equality, offering the chance to be successful with GCSE short courses and then full courses on an hour a week, with incredible 'results'. These results were incredible in that RE departments on limited time and resources would often be the best in the school, despite Ofsted (2013) pointing out that knowledge was superficial, and teaching was done in order to pass the exam.

That is the most instrumental rationale for doing RE – to pass the exam. It is often allied to the sentiment that pupils need to do well, to get good qualifications in order to get the best college places, and eventually jobs. We, of course, as educators as well as mentors need to first recognise our own positionality in this debate: Are we helping these beginning RE teachers because we want them to be better educated or to help them get a job?

Summary and key points

This chapter has used Takahashi's model of the 'knowledgeable other' to suggest three ways in which mentors can develop the beginning RE teacher. It has then shown some ways that a mentor can induct the beginning RE teacher into the networks and debates of the RE community.

- The mentor needs to become the 'knowledgeable other' when mentoring RE beginning RE teachers.
- Teacher knowledge can be thought of as consisting of subject knowledge, pedagogical knowledge and curriculum knowledge.
- Part of the mentor's role is encouraging the beginning RE teacher to develop expertise in all three of these dimensions.
- Since knowledge is constantly being created, through research, the mentor should be abreast of the latest developments in the field, to enable the beginning RE teacher to be challenged and directed appropriately.
- In the first half of the chapter, we concentrated on knowledge that would directly improve classroom delivery before suggesting some support structures, outside of the school, which are available to the beginning teacher of RE.
- In the latter half, we have considered some of the debates which surround policy and practice in RE and education more generally. These are valuable topics to discuss with beginning RE teachers, in order to help them develop as reflective educational professionals.

Further resources

National Association of Standing Advisory Councils on Religious Education (NASACRE) – www.nasacre.org.uk
    This website is intended to be a resource space for local SACREs. It does contain guidance and material useful for schoolteachers, and importantly has a database containing contact details for individual SACREs: www.nasacre.org.uk/database

The NATRE website –www.natre.org.uk/
This is the 'go-to' site for RE teachers' support. It has links to news stories, courses and local networks and support. It is a good use of the school budget to purchase a membership which enables you to receive a termly magazine and share these resources with your beginning RE teacher.

The RE:ONLINE website– www.reonline.org.uk/
The website of Culham St Gabriel's Trust, one of the largest funders of RE support. A huge site, which you can direct the beginning teacher to in order to develop their subject knowledge, read the latest research summaries and gather high-quality teaching resources. There are interesting blogs to read and the 'Research of the Month' feature is a really good way to keep your own knowledge up to date.

The Educational Endowment Foundation website –https://educationendowmentfoundation. org.uk/
The EEF is a charity funded by the Department for Education whose remit is to use research to discover 'what works' in terms of improving pupils' education. On the site there is the EEF toolkit, which tries to suggest what are the most cost-effective interventions. There are also frequent guidance reports into various educational interventions, case studies and practical advice on acting in line with evidence as well as opportunities to get involved with research.

Farmington Institute – Harris Manchester College, Oxford: www.farmington.ac.uk/
The Farmington Institute offers scholarships to teachers of RE so that they can develop their expertise by completing a relevant research project over a term. They are able to pay for

supply cover for the teacher and cover expenses (which can include accommodation). The reports produced by scholars are available via the Farmington website and are themselves a valuable resource.

Podcasts

The following includes the details of a number of podcasts mentioned in this chapter which you may find helpful.

British Broadcasting Corporation. (1998-present). *In Our Time*. [Audio podcast]. https://www.bbc.co.uk/programmes/b006qykl

Education Endowment Foundation (2018-present). *Trialled & Tested/Evidence into Action*. [Audio podcast]. https://educationendowmentfoundation.org.uk/news/podcast

Smith, L. (Host). (2020-present) *The RE Podcast*. [Audio podcast] https://www.therepodcast.co.uk/

Symes, J (producer) (2016-present) *The Panpsycast* [Audio podcast]. https://thepanpsycast.com/home

References

Allan, D., Boorman, D., O'Doherty, E., & Smalley, P. (2019). Lesson study. In Cain, T. (ed.), *Becoming a research-informed school* (pp. 159-176). Routledge.

Ball, S. J. (2003). The teacher's soul and the terrors of performativity. *Journal of Education Policy*, 18(2), 215-228. https://doi.org/10.1080/0268093022000043065

Commission on Religious Education. (2018). *Religion and worldviews: The way forward. A national plan for RE*. London: Religious Education Council of England and Wales.

Department for Education (DfE). (2020). *The forgotten 50%: Why further education is vital to economic recovery* [online video]. https://www.youtube.com/watch?v=-eZnr5tqRkl

Easton, C., Goodman, A., Wright, A., and Wright, A. (2019). *A Practical Guide to Critical Religious Education Resources for the Secondary Classroom*. Routledge.

Education Endowment Foundation. (2018-present). *Trialled & Tested/Evidence into Action*. [Audio podcast]. https://educationendowmentfoundation.org.uk/news/podcast

Fordham, M. (2020, February 8). What did I mean by 'the curriculum is the progression model'? *Clio et cetera*. https://clioetcetera.com/2020/02/08/what-did-i-mean-by-the-curriculum-is-the-progression-model/

Grimmitt, M., (2000). *Pedagogies of religious education: case studies in the research and development of good pedagogic practice in RE*. McCrimmon.

Kueh, R. (2018). Religious Education and the 'Knowledge Problem. In Castelli, M. and Chater, M. (Eds). *We need to talk about religious education: manifestos for the future of RE* (pp. 53-69). Jessica Kingsley Publishers.

Myatt, M. (2016). *High challenge, low threat: finding the balance*. John Catt Educational Ltd.

Myatt, M., (2018). *Curriculum: gallimaufry to coherence*. John Catt Educational Ltd.

Ofsted. (2013). *Religious education: realising the potential*. https://assets.publishing.service.gov.uk/government/uploads/system/uploads/attachment_data/file/413157/Religious_education_-_realising_the_potential.pdf

Ofsted. (2019.) *School inspection handbook*. https://www.gov.uk/government/publications/school-inspection-handbook-eif/school-inspection-handbook

Ofsted. (2021), *Research review series: religious education*. https://www.gov.uk/government/publications/research-review-series-religious-education

O'Grady, K., (2018). *Religious education as a dialogue with difference: fostering democratic citizenship through the study of religions in schools*. Routledge.

Shulman, L. S. (1986). Those who understand: knowledge growth in teaching. *Educational Researcher*, *15*(2), 4-14. https://doi.org/10.3102/0013189X015002004

Shulman, L. S., (2008). "Send Me in, Coach!" Ruminations on the Ethics of Mentoring in Teaching and Research. *The New Educator*, 4(3), 224-236.

Smalley, P. (2020). A critical policy analysis of local religious education in England. *British Journal of Religious Education*, 42(3), 263-274. https://doi.org/10.1080/01416200.2019.1566114

Stern, J. (2018). *Teaching religious education: researchers in the classroom* (2nd ed.). Bloomsbury Academic.

Takahashi, A. (2014). The role of the knowledgeable other in lesson study: examining the final comments of experienced lesson study practitioners. *Mathematics Teacher Education and Development*. 16(1), 4-21.

Winch, C., Oancea, A. and Orchard, J., (2015). The contribution of educational research to teachers' professional learning: philosophical understandings. *Oxford Review of Education*. 41 (2), 202-216. https://doi.org/10.1080/03054985.2015.1017406

Wintersgill, B. (2017). *Big Ideas for Religious Education*. University of Exeter.

Wintersgill, B., Cush, D. and Francis, D. (2019). *Putting big ideas into practice in religious education*, RE:ONLINE.

INDEX